JOHN WEBSTER

T&T Clark Studies in English Theology

Series editors
Karen Kilby
Michael Higton
Stephen R. Holmes

JOHN WEBSTER

The Shape and Development of His Theology

Jordan Senner

LONDON • NEW YORK • OXFORD • NEW DELHI • SYDNEY

T&T CLARK
Bloomsbury Publishing Plc
50 Bedford Square, London, WC1B 3DP, UK
1385 Broadway, New York, NY 10018, USA
29 Earlsfort Terrace, Dublin 2, Ireland

BLOOMSBURY, T&T CLARK and the T&T Clark logo are trademarks of Bloomsbury Publishing Plc

First published in Great Britain 2022
Paperback edition published 2023

Copyright © Jordan Senner, 2022

Jordan Senner has asserted his right under the Copyright,
Designs and Patents Act, 1988, to be identified as Author of this work.

For legal purposes the Acknowledgements on pp. vii-viii constitute
an extension of this copyright page.

Cover image: clairevis/iStock

All rights reserved. No part of this publication may be reproduced or transmitted in any form or by any means, electronic or mechanical, including photocopying, recording, or any information storage or retrieval system, without prior permission in writing from the publishers.

Bloomsbury Publishing Plc does not have any control over, or responsibility for, any third-party websites referred to or in this book. All internet addresses given in this book were correct at the time of going to press. The author and publisher regret any inconvenience caused if addresses have changed or sites have ceased to exist, but can accept no responsibility for any such changes.

A catalogue record for this book is available from the British Library.

Library of Congress Cataloging-in-Publication Data
Names: Senner, Jordan, author.
Title: John Webster : the shape and development of his theology / Jordan Senner.
Description: London ; New York : T&T Clark, 2022. | Series: T&T Clark studies in English theology | Includes bibliographical references and index. |
Identifiers: LCCN 2021015823 (print) | LCCN 2021015824 (ebook) | ISBN 9780567698834 (hardback) | ISBN 9780567698872 (paperback) | ISBN 9780567698841 (pdf) | ISBN 9780567698865 (epub)
Subjects: LCSH: Webster, John, 1955-2016. | Theology. | Theology, Doctrinal.
Classification: LCC BX4827.W35 S46 2022 (print) | LCC BX4827.W35 (ebook) | DDC 201/.7–dc23
LC record available at https://lccn.loc.gov/2021015823
LC ebook record available at https://lccn.loc.gov/2021015824

ISBN:	HB:	978-0-5676-9883-4
	PB:	978-0-5676-9887-2
	ePDF:	978-0-5676-9884-1
	eBook:	978-0-5676-9886-5

Series: T&T Clark Studies in English Theology

Typeset by Integra Software Services Pvt. Ltd.

To find out more about our authors and books visit www.bloomsbury.com
and sign up for our newsletters.

CONTENTS

Acknowledgements	vii
Abbreviations	ix
Introduction	1
Research parameters	4
Secondary literature	5

Chapter 1
ORDERING AND GROUNDING THE GOD-CREATURE RELATION   9

1.1 Introduction	9
1.2 Christocentric approach to the God-creature relation	10
1.3 Trinitarian approach to the God-creature relation	13
1.4 Theocentric approach to the God-creature relation	19
1.5 Key aspects of Webster's mature theology of the God-creature relation	25
1.5.1 Doctrine of divine perfection	26
1.5.2 Theory of mixed relations	30
1.5.3 Concept of dual causality	36
1.6 Conclusion	42

Chapter 2
CHRISTOLOGY   45

2.1 Introduction	45
2.2 Early Christology: Divine identity and narrative description	46
2.3 Christology in transition: The priority of God *in se*	53
2.4 Mature Christology: Divine perfection and metaphysical distinction	60
2.5 Excursus: Narrative description and metaphysical ambition	76
2.6 Conclusion	81

Chapter 3
ECCLESIOLOGY   83

3.1 Introduction	83
3.2 Early ecclesiology: Coinherence and continuity	84
3.3 Ecclesiology in transition: Trinitarian deduction	87
3.4 Ecclesiology in transition: Divine perfection	96
3.5 Mature ecclesiology: Distinction and mediation	104
3.6 Conclusion	113

Chapter 4
BIBLIOLOGY 115
   4.1 Introduction 115
   4.2 *Holy Scripture* (2003) 116
      4.2.1 Dogmatic location of Scripture and its readers 116
      4.2.2 Theological ontology of Scripture 118
      4.2.3 Ecclesiology and anthropology of reading 126
      4.2.4 Summary 133
   4.3 *Domain of the Word* (2012) 134
      4.3.1 Dogmatic location of Scripture and its readers 134
      4.3.2 Theological ontology of Scripture 137
      4.3.3 Ecclesiology and anthropology of reading 142
   4.4 Conclusion 146

Chapter 5
THEOLOGICAL THEOLOGY 149
   5.1 Introduction 149
   5.2 *Thomas Burns Lectures* (1998) 150
      5.2.1 Dogmatic location of reason 151
      5.2.2 Theological anthropology of the theologian 155
      5.2.3 Operations of reason 158
   5.3 Summary 161
   5.4 *God without Measure* (2016) 164
      5.4.1 Cognitive principles of reason 165
      5.4.2 Dogmatic location and anthropology of the theologian 166
      5.4.3 Operations of reason 174
   5.5 Conclusion 177

Conclusion 179

Bibliography 186
Index of names 198
Index of subjects 200

ACKNOWLEDGEMENTS

The writing of this book was made possible by the support and encouragement of friends, family and mentors. First, I would like to thank the Institute of Religion and Culture (Canada) for awarding me a research grant in 2016. I hope this book embodies some of the virtues of the institute's founder, Jim Houston, whose passion for the 'personal' has left its mark on a whole generation of students like me.

I wish to thank those professors, past and present, who have made significant contributions to my theological formation: Mickey Klink, for first introducing me to the ancient vision of a 'pastor theologian'; Hans Boersma and Bruce Hindmarsh, for showing me that reason and piety are coinherent realities; Tim Baylor, Steve Holmes and Judith Wolfe, for guiding me through the PhD process with patience and wisdom.

The community at St Andrews was a hospitable and vibrant place to engage in the theological reflection that culminated in this book. A handful of friends and conversation partners were particularly important companions on the journey: Rebekah Earnshaw, Jared Michelson, David Westfall, Kim Kroll, Simon Dürr, Christa McKirland, Dennis Bray, and last but not least, my golf-partner Matt McKirland. It has been a privilege to know these people not only as academics but also as brothers and sisters in Christ.

Theology is an ecclesial science, done in and for the church. So I would like to thank the clergy of the Anglican Network in Canada for believing that stepping away from full-time pastoral responsibilities for the sake of study could be a gift to the church in the long run. And I would like to thank Saint Andrews Episcopal Church and Holy Trinity Anglican Church for giving me the privilege of preaching the gospel and praying with them, and for reminding me that the church (in all her diversity and permutations) belongs to God.

I owe a debt of gratitude to my parents, whose prayer and financial support have made all of my education possible, regardless of whether they understood why I would possibly want to study that long. Their ability to bless their children and grandchildren amidst significant geographical distance has been a wonder and joy. My in-laws have been a source of practical support and encouragement, knowing well the demands that academic work places on both scholar and family.

Finally, I would like to thank my family. My children, Annabelle and Jeremy, have been a source of many sacred interruptions – just what a theologian needs to be reminded that life is about much more than grand ideas. They have been persistent in their requests that I pay attention to the ladybirds, watch their dance shows, read a few books and play at the park. They have borne with an occasionally absent-minded father, expressed excitement over the prospect of 'reading' my book and reminded me that the kingdom of God belongs to those who are like these 'little ones'.

My wife, Susie, deserves more gratitude and credit than I can give. She sacrificed the comfort of home in order to go on this intellectual and ministerial journey and has managed not only to survive but also to bless the community around her. She has listened to many theological ramblings, corrected far too many typos and allowed me to spend many evenings in the office. More than all this, she has been a faithful friend, loving companion and image of God's goodness.

Someone once said, 'To whom much has been given, much will be required.' By God's grace, I have been given much.

ABBREVIATIONS

ATR	Anglican Theological Review
Barth	John Webster. *Barth*. London: Continuum, 2000.
BER	John Webster. *Barth's Ethics of Reconciliation*. Cambridge: Cambridge University Press, 1995.
BMT	John Webster. *Barth's Moral Theology: Human Action in Barth's Thought*. Edinburgh: T&T Clark, 1998.
CD	Karl Barth. *Church Dogmatics*. 14 Volumes. Translated by G. W. Bromiley. Edinburgh: T&T Clark, 1936ff.
CG	John Webster. *Confessing God: Essays in Christian Dogmatics II*. London: Bloomsbury T&T Clark, 2005.
DW	John Webster. *The Domain of the Word: Scripture and Theological Reason*. London: Bloomsbury T&T Clark, 2012.
GIH	John Webster. *God Is Here: Believing in the Incarnation Today*. Hampshire: Marshall Morgan & Scott, 1983.
GWM	John Webster. *God without Measure: Working Papers in Christian Theology*. 2 Volumes. London: Bloomsbury T&T Clark, 2016.
EJ	John Webster. *Eberhard Jüngel: An Introduction to His Theology*. Cambridge: Cambridge University Press, 1986.
Holiness	John Webster. *Holiness*. London: SCM Press, 2003.
HS	John Webster. *Holy Scripture: A Dogmatic Sketch*. Cambridge: Cambridge University Press, 2003.
IJST	International Journal of Systematic Theology
MoTh	Modern Theology
NB	New Blackfriars
SJT	Scottish Journal of Theology
ST	Thomas Aquinas. *Summa Theologiae*. Latin/English Edition of the Works of St. Thomas Aquinas. Volumes 13–20. Translated by Fr. Laurence Shapcote, O.P. Edited by John Mortensen and Enrique Alarcón. Lander, WY: The Aquinas Institute for the Study of Sacred Doctrine, 2012.
WC	John Webster. *Word and Church: Essays in Christian Dogmatics*. London: Bloomsbury T&T Clark, 2001.

INTRODUCTION

In the wake of Professor John Webster's (1955–2016) unexpected and untimely death, the time has come for evaluation of his theological work and legacy.[1] Penetrating evaluation requires detailed interpretation as well as synchronic and synthetic understanding, and so there is a need for a large-scale introduction to his theology. While scholarly work on Webster's thought has already begun, a full-length monograph has yet to be produced. This book will attempt to fill this lacuna by offering a *grandes lignes* interpretation of Webster's theology.

I will seek to accomplish this purpose through an analysis of Webster's account of the God-creature relation. A central and unifying theme running throughout Webster's published corpus is his desire to articulate a *theologically grounded and ordered construal of the relations between God and creatures*.[2] What Webster once

---

1. For an (auto)biographical account of Webster's life and theological development, see John Webster, 'Discovering Dogmatics', in *Shaping a Theological Mind: Theological Context and Methodology*, ed. Darren C. Marks (Aldershot: Ashgate, 2002), 129–36; Ivor J. Davidson, 'John', in *Theological Theology: Essays in Honour of John Webster*, eds. R. David Nelson, Darren Sarisky, and Justin Stratis (London: T&T Clark, 2015), 17–36; idem., 'In Memoriam: John Webster (1955–2016)', *IJST* 18:4 (2016): 360–75.

2. A cursory glance at his corpus is enough to make the point. Webster's doctoral thesis traced the theme of 'distinguishing between God and man' in Jüngel's thought, showing how Jüngel attempts to develop a non-reductive and complementary account of the God-creature relation (*EJ*, 4). Much of his writing on Barth revolved around topics in moral theology, arguing that Barth's doctrine of God does not overwhelm human creatures but establishes them within a covenantal relation that creates space for genuine human action which corresponds to God's action (see *BER*; *BMT*). Webster's writings on bibliology sought to locate the canon within the economy of God's gracious and communicative presence, thereby clarifying the relation between God's self-revealing activity and creaturely texts (see *HS*). Even as Webster started to develop 'a reordered conception of the substance of Christian doctrine', one which revolved around a doctrine of divine perfection, his focus remained on the consequences of this 'reordering' for his 'understanding of the relation between God and creatures' (*CG*, ix, 2). Finally, his mature collections of essays are devoted to unpacking the implications of teaching about 'God's infinitely deep, fully realized life in giving an account of Christian faith, particularly as it touches upon the relations of God and creatures' (*DW*, ix–x).

observed about Barth's early theology holds true for his own theology: the topics that drew his attention 'were those in which the character of God's relation to creatures assumes great importance'.³ For Webster, this included Christology, ecclesiology, bibliology, moral theology, the nature of theology and much more. Thus, the God-creature relation will provide a helpful vantage point from which to view the systematic shape and logic of his theology. It will also provide an opportunity to trace the development of his thought over time, for changes in Webster's understanding of the God-creature relation are often indicative of larger shifts in his thought concerning the order and interrelation of doctrines, especially judgements about what constitutes the 'material epicentre' of Christian doctrine.

Therefore, Chapter 1 will be devoted to mapping the material and architectural developments in Webster's theology that shape his understanding of the God-creature relation. In particular, I will seek to convey the ways in which his evolving conception of the 'material centre' and 'heuristic key' of Christian theology shapes the way he grounds, contextualizes and depicts the relation-in-distinction between God and creatures. The first half of the chapter will map the development of Webster's thought in terms of three phases – Christocentric, Trinitarian and Theocentric – whereby the 'material centre' that governs his theology shifts from Christology to the economic Trinity, and finally, to the immanent perfection of God. The second half of the chapter will offer a conceptual analysis of three aspects of Webster's mature theology – his doctrine of divine perfection, theory of mixed relations and concept of dual causality – that are pivotal to his mature way of framing and characterizing the relation-in-distinction between God and creatures. In this way, Chapter 1 will propose a heuristic framework for interpreting Webster's theology, the defence of which will be the purview of Chapters 2–5.

Chapters 2–5 will explore different aspects of Webster's account of the God-creature relation: Christology (hypostatic relation), ecclesiology (redemptive relation), bibliology (communicative relation) and theological theology (rational relation). Chapter 2 will offer an analysis of Webster's Christology with a particular focus on the hypostatic union. I will argue that his understanding of the relation between the divine and human natures of Christ evolves from an emphasis on indivisibility and identity to an emphasis on distinction and asymmetry. This occurs as the theological ground of Jesus' unsubstitutable identity shifts from his human history to the immanent life of God. Moreover, I will argue that these developments reflect a larger movement in his thought regarding the relation between theology and economy, which is also mirrored in his understanding of the relation between narrative description and metaphysical ambition. The result is a Christology that seeks to register the divine depth and salvific efficacy of Jesus' human history.

Chapter 3 will offer an analysis of Webster's ecclesiology. I will argue that his understanding of the relation between God and the church evolves from

3. John Webster, *Barth's Earlier Theology: Four Studies* (London: T&T Clark, 2005), 12.

an emphasis on coinherence and continuity to an emphasis on distinction and asymmetry. This occurs as the theological ground of the church's being and action shifts from Jesus' human history to God's immanent perfection. I will also argue that the way in which Webster articulates the distinction and asymmetry between God and the church develops along with his account of divine perfection, which is reflected in the fact that the doctrine of creation replaces the doctrine of election as the primary hinge between theology and economy. The result is a reordered account of ecclesial action as a 'moved movement' and therefore a gift and mediation of grace.

In this way, Chapters 2 and 3 will seek to demonstrate the explanatory power of narrating Webster's development in terms of two primary shifts: from Christocentric to Trinitarian, and from Trinitarian to Theocentric. And they will demonstrate how the doctrines of divine perfection and creation (especially teaching about mixed relations and moved movement) have a governing function in Webster's mature theology. But these chapters will also raise a key question related to Webster's account of divine perfection that will introduce some complexity into our understanding of Webster's movement from Barth to Thomas: Is God's perfection 'inclusive' or 'exclusive' of his economic action and relation to the world?[4]

Chapters 4 and 5 will narrow the scope of our discussion to the last twenty years of Webster's career, allowing us to develop a more detailed picture of his 'constructive' phase. Chapter 4 will offer an analysis of Webster's bibliology. I will argue that his bibliology is driven by a consistent concern to resist the secularization of Scripture and interpretive activity without thereby diminishing the creaturely integrity of text and reader. In other words, he seeks to articulate a non-competitive account of the relation between God's self-revealing activity and creaturely activities and products. Yet the way in which Webster articulates this non-competitive relation evolves as he grounds the economy of grace (including God's revelatory missions) in the immanent life of God, and as he coordinates the Spirit's work of inspiration and illumination with teaching about God's providential ordering of history. His intent is to develop a more robust account of the creaturely (textual and anthropological) coordinates of divine revelation.

Chapter 5 will offer an analysis of Webster's account of theological reason. I will argue that his account of 'theological theology' is driven by a consistent concern to register the ontological and epistemological priority of God in relation to the activities of the knowing subject. In other words, he seeks to articulate how the theologian's reasoning is conditioned and defined by God's presence and action. Yet the way in which he articulates this divine 'priority' and 'conditioning' evolves as the ultimate ground of the activities of theological reason shifts from God's eschatological presence in Christ to God's perfect knowledge, and as the Spirit's

---

4. At the most basic level, God's perfection is 'inclusive' if his relation to or activity in the world is somehow intrinsic or integral to his fullness and 'exclusive' if no aspect of his beatitude or fullness would be lost were the world not to exist.

work of regeneration and sanctification is coordinated with teaching about the nature and ends of reason, which are derived from God's original ordering of creation. His intent is to develop a more robust account of the creaturely integrity and dynamics of reason.

In this way, Chapters 4 and 5 will seek to demonstrate the explanatory power of narrating Webster's development in terms of two primary shifts: Chapter 4 will focus on the shift from Trinitarian to Theocentric, and Chapter 5 will give a broader sense of the overarching shift from Christocentric to Theocentric. And they will demonstrate how the works of nature (especially teaching about God's teleological ordering of human nature and providential ordering of history) provide the context for understanding the works of grace in Webster's mature theology. But these chapters will also draw attention to a few salient features of Webster's theology from around the turn of the twenty-first century that only receive a passing mention in Chapter 1: his personalist doctrine of God as self-revealing Subject, his emphasis on the interruptive nature of God's eschatological presence and his adventitious theology of grace. This will allow us to trace how these features of his thought, which are significant for his account of the God-creature relation and display a Barthian cast of mind, develop in his mature theology. In some cases (such as his theology of grace) Webster leaves Barth for Thomas altogether, and in other cases (such as his personalist account of God as self-revealing Subject) Webster uses conceptual resources from Thomas to articulate an insight he originally learned from Barth. Thus, Chapters 4 and 5 will also introduce complexity into our understanding of the development of Webster's mature theology and thereby suggest some of the ways in which the heuristic framework of Chapter 1 requires nuance.

This *in nuce* is the argument of my book, but before embarking upon the extended journey, I want to make a few comments about the research parameters of the book and its relation to the growing field of secondary literature on Webster's theology.

Research parameters

First, the primary subject matter of this book is the internal logic and development of Webster's theological ideas, not his biographical narrative or social and historical setting, although I hope my work reflects an appropriate awareness of these. This means, for example, that I will not devote much space to explaining the socio-political dynamics of intellectual life at Cambridge during Webster's years as a student or to discussing the influence of his friendship with George Schner while teaching at Wycliffe College in Canada. My discussion of his context will be limited to the realm of intellectual ideas, drawing attention to particular theologians or movements insofar as they influenced or provide an illuminating contrast to his thought.

Second, this book will focus on Webster's constructive theology and on his historical theology (e.g. his many books on Jüngel and Barth) only insofar as it sheds light on Webster's own theological development.⁵ On the one hand, this means I will not engage in many questions related to the accuracy of Webster's interpretation of these German theologians, leaving that task to experts in Jüngelian and Barthian theology. On the other hand, this means I will have space to engage constructive works from the 1980 to 90s – for example, Webster's first published monograph (*God Is Here: Believing in the Incarnation Today* (1983)) and his first lecture series (Thomas Burns Lectures (1998)) – that have remained hidden in the shadow of Webster's historical scholarship during this period.

Third, this book intends to build an argument regarding the explanatory power of the heuristic framework developed in Chapter 1. But I hope my work displays an appropriate sense of the limitations and provisionality of the framework as well as a sensitivity to the complexities of Webster's theological development. Evaluative judgements of Webster's dogmatic theology will be kept to a minimum in an effort to foreground its inner logic. This book intends to make a synthetic and synchronic proposal about how to read Webster's theology as whole, since no such proposal exists to date, but it does so in the hopes that others will confirm its strengths, reveal its weaknesses and push the field of Webster scholarship forward in the years to come.

Secondary literature

Substantive engagement with Webster's theology is relatively sparse for a figure whose prominence and importance in English-speaking theology in the twenty-first century were matched only by a select few – e.g. Rowan Williams, Robert Jenson, Kathryn Tanner. The most significant body of secondary literature revolves around Webster's bibliology, where some believe his work 'offers the most insight'.⁶ Other loci in Webster's theology that have received attention in recent years include ecclesiology and the nature of theology.⁷ Of those who have published on Webster's theology, four authors stand out as offering the most insightful and interesting readings: Brad East, Martin Westerholm, Katherine Sonderegger and Tyler Wittman.

---

5. Webster professed that his historical engagement with the theology of Karl Barth was driven by constructive theological questions: '[M]y chief interest in reading and commenting on Barth has been and remains theological: What moved this person to speak of God in these astonishing ways? What instruction may we take from his astonishment in the matter of our own theological witness?' (*Barth's Earlier Theology*, viii). Webster was a sympathetic, yet by no means uncritical, reader of Barth.

6. Darren Sarisky, 'The Ontology of Scripture and the Ethics of Interpretation in the Theology of John Webster', *IJST* 21:1 (2019): 59. For secondary literature on Webster's bibliology, see Chapter 4.

7. For secondary literature on Webster's ecclesiology, see Chapter 3; on the nature of theology, see Chapter 5.

East and Westerholm have written articles that are pertinent to the topic of this book because they have sought to identify defining shifts in Webster's theological evolution.[8] East argued that the primary shift occurs when the doctrine of the Trinity replaces Christology as that which governs Webster's theology. I agree with East and seek to build upon his work in Chapter 1 by suggesting that we need to think of a second defining shift for Webster, namely a shift within his Trinitarian theology from a focus on the economy to a focus on God's immanent life. Westerholm, on the other hand, has identified a shift of a different sort. He argues that Webster's thought never abandons the 'typically modern notion that human being and activity are decisively illumined by the history in which they stand'.[9] Thus, the defining shift in Webster's thought (regarding the nature of theological inquiry in particular) has to do with his conception of the kind of history in which humans are located: from the 'history of ideas' to the 'history of salvation'.[10] Westerholm interprets other shifts in Webster's thought – i.e. the increased prominence of the doctrine of creation – as a secondary move by which Webster seeks to secure the history of salvation from collapsing into mere contingency. I think Westerholm has correctly brought issues related to Webster's conception of history to the fore, so I seek to build upon his work in Chapters 4 and 5 by showing how the concept of 'location' plays a significant role in shaping Webster's bibliology and theological theology. Yet I will also suggest that Westerholm is not quite accurate when he identifies a focus on the 'history of ideas' with Webster's thought in the 'Theological Theology' lecture (1997) and a focus on the 'history of salvation' with his thought in *God without Measure* (2016). Instead, I will argue that it is better to think of Webster as already locating human beings (and their reasoning activities) primarily within the 'history of salvation' in the late 1990s, but that his understanding of salvation history itself changes in subsequent years

---

8. Brad East, 'John Webster, Theologian Proper', *ATR* 99:2 (2017): 333–51; Martin Westerholm, 'On Webster's *God without Measure* and the Practice of Theological Theology', *IJST* 19:4 (2017): 444–61. Michael Allen's articles also offer helpful descriptions of aspects of Webster's development, yet their analysis runs rather close to the details of Webster's texts and thus do not offer much in terms of a heuristic by which to synthesize the underlying currents of his thought (see 'Toward Theological Theology: Tracing the Methodological Principles of John Webster', *Themelios* 41:2 (2016): 217–37; 'Toward Theological Anthropology: Tracing the Anthropological Principles of John Webster', *IJST* 19:1 (2017): 6–29; 'Reading John Webster: An Introduction', in *T&T Clark Reader in John Webster*, ed. Michael Allen (London: T&T Clark, 2020), 1–19).

9. Westerholm, 'Practice of Theological Theology', 447.

10. According to Westerholm, the former focuses on 'some penultimate aspect of human history' (e.g. the rise of nominalism, German idealism or postmodernism), and the latter on the moral and spiritual history of God's relation with humanity. It is not a question of either-or, but which one 'provides the orienting context for theological work' (Westerholm, 'Practice of Theological Theology', 451).

as teaching about divine perfection, creation, providence and the Spirit takes on more prominence in his thought.

This brings us, finally, to the excellent essays on Webster's doctrine of God penned by Katherine Sonderegger and Tyler Wittman.[11] Sonderegger deftly draws attention to the personalist elements in Webster's doctrine of God, which I note in Chapters 4 and 5. She also suggests that Webster's desire to develop a non-competitive account of the relation between theology and economy led him to speak of the economy as somehow 'included' in God's inner life. Sonderegger has raised a central issue for understanding Webster's account of the God-creature relation. Yet, unlike Sonderegger, I am convinced that Webster's mature account of divine perfection (seen most clearly in his essays on the doctrine of creation) does not conceive of the economy as 'included' in God's inner life, although his earlier accounts did. Like Wittman, I argue that Webster's mature theology articulates an 'exclusive' account of God's perfection, motivated in part by a desire to register the qualitative distinction between theology and economy, which in turn funds a gracious and non-competitive characterization of their relation. This reading of Webster's mature doctrine of God is laid out *in nuce* at the end of Chapter 1, to which we now turn, and expanded upon in Chapters 2 and 3.

11. Katherine Sonderegger, 'The God-Intoxicated Theology of a Modern Theologian', *IJST* 21:1 (2019): 24–43; Tyler Wittman, 'John Webster on the Task of a Properly Theological *Theologia*', *SJT* 73:2 (2020): 97–111.

Chapter 1

ORDERING AND GROUNDING THE GOD-CREATURE RELATION

1.1 Introduction

This chapter is intended to function as an overture for the subsequent four chapters, sketching the significant points of development in Webster's thought that shape his understanding of the relation between God and creatures. In particular, I will seek to convey the ways in which Webster's evolving conception of the 'material centre' and 'heuristic key' of Christian theology shapes the way he grounds, contextualizes and depicts the relation-in-distinction between God and creatures. The narrative I lay out here will be broad, attempting to give a sense of the whole. It will be left to the subsequent four chapters to demonstrate the explanatory power of this developmental narrative as well as offer a more detailed and nuanced analysis of various aspects of Webster's understanding of the God-creature relation. Hence, I will not attempt to defend the framework in Chapter 1 (beyond offering a few illustrative quotations); its defence will be the demonstration of its usefulness in Chapters 2–5.

The argument of this chapter will unfold in two parts. The first half (Sections 1.2–1.4) will briefly map the development of Webster's thought in terms of three phases – Christocentric, Trinitarian and Theocentric – each of which is marked by a distinctive account of which doctrine(s) constitutes the 'material centre' and provides the 'heuristic key' for Christian theology as a whole and thereby orders thought about the God-creature relation. This threefold schema identifies two primary shifts in Webster's thought that impact his understanding of the God-creature relation: (1) a shift from Christology to the doctrine of the Trinity as the cardinal Christian doctrine, and (2) a shift from the economic action of the Trinity to the immanent perfection of the Trinity as the material epicentre of Christian doctrine. There are other very significant developments – e.g. from an eschatological doctrine of grace to a Thomist doctrine of creation as that which provides the most basic context within which to talk about the God-creature relation – but they are corollaries of these primary shifts. The second half of the chapter (Section 1.5) will offer a conceptual analysis of three aspects of Webster's mature theology – his doctrine of divine perfection, theory of mixed relations and concept of dual causality – that are pivotal to his mature way of framing and characterizing the relation-in-distinction between God and creatures. In this way, this chapter will lay out the developmental narrative and conceptual analysis that will function as a heuristic framework for interpreting Webster's theology, particularly as it relates to the God-creature relation. We turn now to the first phase of his theological development.

1.2 Christocentric approach to the God-creature relation

From the early 1980s to roughly the mid-1990s, Webster's thought can be described as broadly 'Christocentric' and 'Christomorphic'.[1] Christology, especially the doctrine of the incarnation, is the *articulus stantis et cadentis ecclesiae*.[2] Christ is the centre around which all thought about God, humanity and their relation is constructed; he is the origin and terminus of Christian theology.[3]

This material claim is indebted largely to the influence of Eberhard Jüngel and Karl Barth upon the young Webster. While taking aspects of Barth's thought in a more Lutheran and existential direction, Jüngel did share Barth's fundamental desire to ground all theological speech in the self-revelation of God in the human history of Jesus Christ, thereby emphasizing the identity and correspondence between God *in se* and *pro nobis* and resisting any notion of an abstract *Deus absconditus* behind Jesus of Nazareth.[4] The way to achieve this goal was to construct

---

1. My use of this language is indebted to Katherine Sonderegger (see *Systematic Theology*, Volume 1: The Doctrine of God (Minneapolis, MN: Fortress Press, 2015), xvii). Christocentrism refers to the way in which the material content of theology focuses 'principally on Christology', while Christomorphism refers to the way in which the form of theology is shaped by Christology: 'Jesus Christ orders and molds dogmatic teaching, even areas devoted to other *loci*' (xxiii).

2. John Webster, 'Jesus – God for Us', in *Anglican Essentials: Reclaiming Faith within the Anglican Church of Canada*, ed. George Egerton (Toronto: Anglican Book Centre, 1995), 96.

3. Webster, 'Jesus – God for Us', 91–3.

4. *God's Being Is in Becoming*, a creative paraphrase of Barth's doctrine of God in the *Church Dogmatics*, seems to have captured the young Webster's theological imagination more than any of Jüngel's other writings. In this book, Jüngel turns to Barth to fill in some of the gaps that he identifies in Helmut Gollwitzer's *Existence of God as Confessed by Faith*. According to Jüngel, Gollwitzer offers a problematic understanding of how God's being in and for Himself (*pro se*) is related to his being a subject within history (*pro nobis*). By making a distinction between God's essence and his will, and grounding God's self-revelation in his will rather than his essence, Gollwitzer has left open the possibility of 'a metaphysical background to the being of God which is indifferent to God's historical acts of revelation' (Eberhard Jüngel, *God's Being Is in Becoming: The Trinitarian Being of God in the Theology of Karl Barth – A Paraphrase*, trans. John Webster (Grand Rapids, MI: Eerdmans, 2001), 6). The problematic possibility of an abstract *Deus absconditus* is, according to Jüngel, the result of an understanding of the being of God that is insufficiently determined by Trinitarian dogma and the historical revelation of God in Christ.

a theological ontology from the ground up, beginning with the particularity of Jesus' human history, especially, for Jüngel, his suffering and death. The result was a radical rethinking of the classical doctrine of God: God's being is in 'becoming' or, as he states elsewhere, in 'coming', both *in se* and *pro nobis*.[5] Hence, God cannot be known or spoken of abstractly apart from his relation to creatures in Christ, and creatures cannot be known or spoken of abstractly apart from their relation to God in Christ. With all of this, the early Webster is in whole-hearted agreement.

It is this claim about the material object of Christian theology that guides Webster's formal organization of theology, especially his account of the God-creature relationship. A prime example of this can be seen in his first full-length book *God Is Here: Believing in the Incarnation Today* (1983). The book is structured in three parts, each of which answers a key theological question: Who is Jesus, who is God and who am I? Crucially, questions two and three (theology proper and anthropology) derive their material content from question one: 'We can, that is, only answer the questions "who is God?" and "who am I?" by listening to the story of Jesus.'[6] Thus, Christian theology is concerned with 'thinking about God and man in the light of Jesus Christ'.[7] One result of this Christomorphic ordering of theology is that God and creatures can never be spoken of in abstraction from one another. Even the distinction between God and the world is something revealed in and by their Christologically grounded and mediated relation. Rather than the radical distinction between God and creatures being the context within which to understand their relation (Webster's mature thought), it is the Christological relation between God and creatures that serves as the theological context within which to understand their distinction (Webster's early thought). In the words of Jüngel, 'God differentiates himself from humanity precisely at the point at which he reveals himself to humanity.'[8] Once again, this way of articulating the God-creature distinction is intended to mitigate against the thought that God *in se* is anything other than who he has revealed himself to be in the human history of Jesus Christ, namely God *pro nobis*. It is for this reason that Webster's thought in the 1980s tends to avoid investing heavily in the use of metaphysical categories, preferring instead to operate within narratival and historical categories.[9]

---

5. Jüngel, *God's Being Is in Becoming*, 75–122; idem., *God as the Mystery of the World: On the Foundation of the Theology of the Crucified One in the Dispute between Theism and Atheism*, trans. Darrell L. Guder (Edinburgh: T&T Clark, 1983), 380–9.

6. *GIH*, ix.

7. *GIH*, 2.

8. Jüngel, *God's Being Is in Becoming*, 60. See also Eberhard Jüngel, *Theological Essays*, trans. J. B. Webster (Edinburgh: T&T Clark, 1989), 58–9. This line of thought can be traced back to Barth, who states, 'Revelation and it alone really and finally separates God and man by bringing them together' (*CD* I/2, 29). This quote comes from Barth's discussion of Jesus Christ as the objective possibility of revelation.

9. As will be seen in our discussion of Webster's Christology in Chapter 2, this emphasis on narrative is due in part to the influence of the postliberal school, especially Hans Frei.

As a result of this Christocentrism and Christomorphism, Webster's early theology is marked by the way in which he employs the material resources and conceptual categories of Christology across a broad range of doctrinal loci: the doctrine of God, ecclesiology, anthropology, moral theology and the theology of grace. Christology functions as the 'heuristic key' to all other doctrines.[10] While it will be left to later chapters to demonstrate the validity of this claim, here it is worth drawing attention to a broad shift in emphasis within Webster's early Christology that has an impact on the way in which it grounds and governs his theology as a whole and especially his understanding of the God-creature relation.[11] The shift can be stated as follows: a movement from a focus on the human history of Jesus Christ as the eschatological event that grounds and evokes other human histories to a focus on the eschatological presence of the risen Christ as the ontological and moral field within which human thought and action occur.[12] This shift in emphasis seems to have been precipitated in part by the influence of Barth's exposition of the *munus propheticum Christi* in *CD* IV/3. Webster expressed concern with the way Jüngel employed the existential and hermeneutical thought of Bultmann in an effort to bridge Lessing's gap between the *illic et tunc* of Jesus Christ's human history and the *hic et nunc* of our human histories, believing that Barth's use of doctrinal material from within Christology to bridge the gap does a better job of registering the priority and gratuity of God's action within the realms of soteriology, anthropology and ethics.[13] Dovetailed with this emphasis on Christ's self-mediating and self-revealing presence is an openness, beginning in the 1990s, to the project of developing a theological ontology, epistemology and anthropology out of the resources of Christology and eschatology – i.e. the resurrection of Jesus Christ.

10. *WC*, 151. Webster shows an early awareness of the impact that Trinitarian theology and pneumatology have upon one's understanding of the God-world relation (cf. 'The Identity of the Holy Spirit: A Problem in Trinitarian Theology', *Themelios* 9:1 [1983]: 4–7), and yet the overwhelming majority of his writings during this period remained resolutely Christomorphic.

11. I mention this Christological shift here because my analysis of Webster's Christology (Chapter 2) will focus on his understanding of the hypostatic union and therefore will not address this development. And yet this shift is of some significance for what we will say in Chapters 4–5 regarding Webster's bibliology and theological theology.

12. Although not the focus of our current discussion, this shift could be demonstrated by a comparison of three articles on moral theology from this period: John Webster, 'Christology, Imitability and Ethics', *SJT* 39 (1986): 309–26; idem., 'The Imitation of Christ', *Tyndale Bulletin* 37 (1986): 95–120; idem., 'Eschatology, Ontology and Human Action', *Toronto Journal of Theology* 7:1 (1991): 4–18.

13. Cf. John Webster, 'Introduction', in *God's Being Is in Becoming: The Trinitarian Being of God in the Theology of Karl Barth – A Paraphrase*, trans. John Webster (Grand Rapids, MI: Eerdmans, 2001), xxi. Elsewhere, Jüngel describes this hermeneutical problem as something posed by Hegel and finds the solution in Gadamer's notion of 'effective history' (*Theological Essays*, 214–31).

In so doing, Webster believes he can articulate the theological grounds for the necessity and indispensability of talk about divine agency and creativity for understanding human nature, agency and history.[14]

At this point, clarity is paramount for our reading of Webster's early theology: although the differences between the aforementioned emphases are genuine, Webster's approach remains thoroughly Christocentric and Christomorphic in both cases. It is a matter of which aspects of Christology bear more weight within Webster's thought and for what theological purposes. In either case, it is still Christology (often cast in an eschatological register) that provides the material and conceptual resources through which to articulate the relation-in-distinction between God and creatures. It is only in the late 1990s and early 2000s that we see a discernible shift from Christology to the doctrine of the Trinity as the cardinal Christian doctrine, to which we now turn.[15]

1.3 Trinitarian approach to the God-creature relation

Around the turn of the twenty-first century, there is a discernible shift in the dogmatic order and proportion of Webster's thought. The doctrine of the Trinity replaces Christology as the cardinal Christian doctrine from which all other doctrines derive and by which they are governed. And so, for example, Webster states, 'Christian theology has a singular preoccupation: God, and everything else *sub specie divinitatis*. All other Christian doctrines are applications or corollaries of the one doctrine, the doctrine of the Trinity, in which the doctrine of the church, no less than the doctrine of revelation, has its proper home.'[16] Quotes of a similar nature, highlighting the material and formal function of the doctrine of the

---

14. Webster, 'Eschatology, Ontology and Human Action', 5. Webster states, 'The life, death and resurrection of Jesus constitute *the* context in which all other human living and dying are to be set; his history is a judgment which renders relative all other frames of reference …. [A]s the risen Lord, he renders relative, and is not himself relativized …. If this is the case, then it commits us to saying that Jesus' history has ontological and epistemological priority. As the risen one, sharing in the limitlessness of God, he is that than which nothing greater can be conceived' (6)

15. Brad East has already drawn attention to this shift in Webster's thought ('John Webster', 340-2), but he did not offer a thorough explanation of the reasons for the shift, which we will attempt in the next section. Moreover, East did not draw attention to a second shift in Webster thought – namely from the economic acts of the Trinity to the immanent perfection of the Trinity – overlooking the fact that Webster's early Trinitarian theology has very little to say about God's life *in se*. This shift from God *ad extra* to God *in se* as the material epicentre of Christian dogmatics is, according to the interpretation of Webster offered in this book, equally important for understanding the complexity of his theological development.

16. *HS*, 43.

Trinity, are made in relation to a host of other doctrinal topics: not only the church and revelation, but also Scripture and its readers, anthropology and ethics, as well as the divine attributes.[17] The doctrine of the Trinity orders theological thought and speech about any topic, especially the relation between God and creatures.

Before we give further attention to Webster's doctrine of the Trinity, it is worth asking about the substantive reasons for this shift from Christology to Trinity as the material epicentre and heuristic key of Christian theology. What precipitated this development? First, Webster recognizes the need to ground Christology in the doctrine of God in order to uphold the unsubstitutable identity of Jesus Christ in the face of German idealism and moralism. This will be discussed further in Chapter 2. Second, the doctrine of the Trinity provides Webster with the means by which to articulate the sovereign freedom of God and the gratuity of his action towards humanity. This will be exemplified in Chapter 3. Third, the doctrine of the Trinity enabled Webster to resist abstract theism by giving an account of God's nature that was Christianly specific and biblically derived. Finally, and most importantly for our purposes, the doctrine of the Trinity gave Webster more capacious resources by which to articulate the nature of the God-creature relation and ward off distortions.

A particularly illuminating example of this last point can be found in Webster's discussion of the impact of Trinitarian teaching on an account of the divine attribute of holiness. He states,

> The doctrine of the Trinity tells us who God is on the basis of God's works of creation, salvation and perfection. As such, it is a crucial blockage against a temptation to which all theologies are exposed, namely, that of cramping or truncating the scope of God's relation to the world, and identifying God with only one mode of relation. On a trinitarian account of the matter, talk of the holiness of God indicates the relation of God to the world which we can discern in the full sweep of his works. Above all, the doctrine of the Trinity prevents abstract accounts of God's holiness – 'abstract' in the sense of being developed apart from attention to the identity of God which is enacted in his threefold repetition of himself in the economy of salvation as Father, Son and Spirit.[18]

Elsewhere, Webster makes a similar statement, but this time in the context of developing a theological account of the human person:

> The Trinitarian apprehension of God is thus crucial to an account of the humane character of the Gospel. This is because the personal and differentiated nature of the being of God as Father, Son, and Spirit determines the manner of God's engagement with his creatures. As the triune God, God is neither a remote causal agent nor an ultimate horizon of human history, but one who lives in fellowship

---

17. *HS*, 11–17; *CG*, 2–3; *Holiness*, 31–52.
18. *Holiness*, 47–8.

with humankind, acting on our behalf, with us and, indeed, in and through us, in order that this fellowship should prosper and be brought to its completion.[19]

One more example is worthy of note, this time with respect to the doctrine of Scripture:

> The plunge into dualism [between the transcendent and the historical] is inseparable from the retrenchment of the doctrine of the Trinity in theological talk of God's relation to the world. When God's action towards the world is conceived in a non-trinitarian fashion, and, in particular, when Christian talk of the presence of the risen Christ and the activity of the Holy Spirit does not inform conceptions of divine action in the world, then that action comes to be understood as external, interruptive, and bearing no real relations to creaturely realities. This frankly dualistic framework can only be broken by replacing the monistic and monergistic idea of divine causality with an understanding of God's continuing free presence and relation to the creation through the risen Son in the Spirit's power. In this continuing relation, creaturely activities and products can be made to serve the saving self-presentation of God without forfeiting their creaturely substance, and without compromise to the eschatological freedom of God.[20]

In each of these quotes, Webster upholds the doctrine of the Trinity as the key to avoiding two errors concerning the God-creature relation. First, the error of abstraction: an account of God's being and act is developed apart from God's threefold personal identity as revealed in his threefold personal action in the economy of salvation. As a result, God's relation to creatures is conceived primarily in terms of extrinsic causal will and power. For Webster, the doctrine of the Trinity causes one to envisage the God-creature relation very differently, in terms of a personal and moral relation. Second, the error of immanentism: God is identified with a feature of human history such that his sovereign freedom and gracious initiative in relation to creatures is muted. For Webster, the doctrine of the Trinity also allows one to affirm that God's relation to creatures is free, original, creative and gratuitous. In Barthian terms, God always remains Subject in his relation to the world. (The personalist elements of Webster's doctrine of God shine through most clearly in his bibliology and account of theological reason, which will be discussed in Chapters 4 and 5.) God cannot be abstracted from his relation to creatures, but neither can he be identified with that relation or creaturely reality (e.g. biblical text) *tout court*. God's relation to creatures is an act of free self-determination and self-revelation.[21] But this does not imply that it is arbitrary or

---

19. John Webster, 'The Human Person', in *The Cambridge Companion to Postmodern Theology*, ed. Kevin J. Vanhoozer (Cambridge: Cambridge University Press, 2003), 224.
20. *HS*, 21.
21. Cf. *CD* I/1, 375–83; I/2, 1–44; II/2, 94–145.

accidental. As Webster is fond of saying at this juncture in his career, 'to be for the creature is who God *is*', but this 'for the creature' is depicted as an ever-fresh act of giving rather than a givenness.²²

To summarize what I have been arguing thus far: Webster's shift from Christology to the doctrine of the Trinity is motivated, in part, by a desire to give a theological account of the relation-in-distinction between God and creatures. According to Webster, the doctrine of the Trinity provides a more expansive context – God's works of origination, reconciliation and perfection – within which to situate and depict the God-creature relation, one which is much less prone to the errors of abstraction and immanentism. At this point, I would like to draw attention to a feature of Webster's Trinitarian thought in the early 2000s that should be apparent by now: its orientation towards the economy of God's works. His doctrine of the Trinity is more like a triune theology of divine agency. He has very little to say about the immanent life of the Trinity, offering almost no discussion of the unity of the divine essence or of the divine processions, relations and persons. This focus on God's economic acts seems to be due largely to the influence of Barth upon Webster, who, at this point in his career, is at the height of his powers as an interpreter of the grand old man from Basil. While Barth by no means neglects questions about the immanent life of the Trinity, the overwhelming emphasis of his theological argument in the *Church Dogmatics* is directed towards the 'identity' and 'correspondence' between God *in se* and *ad extra*, such that his descriptive attention is largely directed towards God in his self-revealing action *ad extra*.²³

We can see the impact of Barth in the way that Webster expounds the doctrines of divine simplicity and aseity in terms of God's concrete acts in the economy. On the one hand, he affirms traditional teaching about divine simplicity: God is 'beyond composition' and all his attributes are identical with his very essence.²⁴ On the other hand, Webster follows Barth in speaking of God's essence as

---

22. Webster, 'The Human Person', 224.

23. This seems to be the case particularly in *CD* IV, where Barth's periodic references to the immanent life of the Trinity appear in order to highlight the freedom and gratuity of Christ's redemptive action; his comments are highly suggestive but not fully elaborated. Hence why his brief and diverse comments have become the subject of heated debate and competing interpretations in recent decades. See, for example, George Hunsinger, 'Election and the Trinity: Twenty-Five Theses on the Theology of Karl Barth', *MoTh* 24:2 (2008): 179–98; Bruce McCormack, 'Grace and Being: The Role of God's Gracious Election in Karl Barth's Theological Ontology', in *The Cambridge Companion to Karl Barth*, ed. John Webster (Cambridge: Cambridge University Press, 2000), 92–110; idem., 'Election and the Trinity: Theses in Response to George Hunsinger', *SJT* 63:2 (2010): 203–24; and Paul D. Molnar, *Divine Freedom and the Doctrine of the Immanent Trinity: In Dialogue with Karl Barth and Contemporary Theology* (London: T&T Clark, 2002).

24. *Holiness*, 37.

1. Ordering and Grounding God-Creature Relation 17

being-in-act, where 'act' is defined concretely and historically.²⁵ God's pure actuality, and therefore the doctrine of divine simplicity, does not denote God's being *in se* apart from his works, but rather the correspondence between his being *in se* and his works *ad extra*. Hence, Webster can say that theological talk about divine simplicity 'is an indication of the pure and singular act of God's being, his being for himself by his being for us in his merciful work as Father, Son and Spirit. God's simplicity is his irreducible "thisness", executed in the drama of his works'.²⁶ We see a similar move in his account of divine aseity: 'God is essentially, to the depths of his triune being, God for us and God with us, the one whose mercy evokes the miracle of human fellowship with himself. There is always a double theme in Christian theology, a twofoldness in all its matter which corresponds to the identity of aseity and self-giving in the life of the Holy Trinity.'²⁷ Much more could be said on this topic and will be said throughout this book, but my point here is simply that Webster's Trinitarian theology in the late 1990s and early 2000s is resolutely focused on the acts of the divine persons in the economy of salvation and that this is of no little significance for his depiction of the God-creature relation.

We can expand on this point by giving further attention to the character of the divine economy as described by Webster at this point in his thought. First, the economy is triune. This is normally articulated in terms of a threefold schema that maps the economic actions appropriated to each of the divine persons: creation/election (Father) – reconciliation (Son) – perfection (Holy Spirit).²⁸ Second, the economy is focused on the works of grace. While there are some notable exceptions which foreshadow later shifts in Webster's thought,²⁹ generally speaking his account of divine agency and creativity is still tied primarily to God's acts of new creation rather than original creation. Third, the economy is cast in an eschatological register. Webster persistently draws attention to the 'transcendent', 'intrusive' and 'interceptive' nature of God's gracious acts in history, especially when talking about the nature of the church, revelation or theological reason.³⁰

---

25. Cf. *CD* II/1, 257–321. For an excellent discussion of Barth's doctrine of divine simplicity, see Tyler R. Wittman, 'Facticity and Faithfulness: Divine Simplicity in Barth's Christology', *Pro Ecclesia* 26:2 (2017): 415–34. Wittman argues that Barth repositions the traditional doctrine of divine simplicity and the scholastic notion of *actus purus* around a Christocentric concept of God's faithfulness. The result is that 'simplicity applies not so much to God's being or act per se, but rather to their indissoluble identity as an "actuality" in God's self-revelation' (419).
26. *Holiness*, 38.
27. *Holiness*, 53–4.
28. Webster, 'The Human Person', 224–5; *Holiness*, 48, 51–2, 98; *HS*, 86–106.
29. See, for example, Webster, 'The Human Person', 224–5.
30. *CG*, 5.

Fourth, the economy is a moral space.³¹ It is about 'the history of covenantal fellowship between God and his creatures'.³² In sum, the economy of salvation is triune, gracious, eschatological and moral.

How exactly does this account of the economy of grace relate to Webster's account of the relation-in-distinction between God and creatures? The answer to this question lies in the role that the notion of 'dogmatic location' begins to play in Webster's thought during this period. Behind this concept seems to be a rather simple question: In which theological context (in relation to which doctrines and in which order and proportion) should the theologian talk about a given topic? So, for example, should one talk about the nature of the church primarily in relation to the perichoretic relations of the Trinity, the incarnate history of the Son or the Pentecostal gift of the Spirit? Should one talk about the nature of revelation primarily in relation to the doctrine of the Trinity and derivatively in relation to human subjectivity and the epistemic conditions of knowing, or the reverse order? For Webster, the formal concept of 'dogmatic location' helps orient theological reason towards its subject matter in its proper order (of being) and systematic interrelation. It also proves to be a serviceable means by which to critically evaluate modern theological proposals and offer alternative constructive proposals. Hence, Webster often speaks of the dogmatic 'mislocation' of particular doctrines in modern theology – the doctrines of the resurrection and Scripture being chief among them – and argues for the dogmatic 'relocation' of those doctrines.³³ This conceptuality will be a significant part of our discussion of Webster's bibliology and account of theological reason (Chapters 4–5), so we will refrain from discussing it in greater detail here. What is important to note at this point is the way in which this notion of 'dogmatic location' is related to Webster's desire to ground and contextualize the God-creature relation within a triune account of divine agency, which he accomplishes by locating his discussion of creatures and their acts within a Trinitarian theology of the economy of grace. Creaturely being and acts are what they are only in relation to God's originating, reconciling and perfecting acts as Father, Son and Holy Spirit. For Webster, formal questions about 'dogmatic location' become an important way of contextualizing

---

31. Webster delineates four essential elements of a theological account of this 'moral space': 'It is an account of the identity of God (the triune creator, reconciler, and perfecter); an account of the identity of the human agent as both a divine gift and a human task; an account of the encounter between this God and his creature; and an account of the differentiated teleology of their actions. All Christian language is, directly or indirectly, a depiction of moral space, for what it does is express one or other aspect of God or of God's creatures as agents in relation' (*WC*, 283).

32. Webster, 'The Human Person', 225.

33. Cf. *CG*, 19–20; *HS*, 5–9. Similar language – 'de-regionalisation' and 're-regionalisation' – appears in Webster's account of theological reason during this period (see discussion in Chapter 5).

speech about creaturely realities within an overall account of the relation between God and creatures and a way of grounding that relation in the freedom and gratuity of divine action.

This last point about the freedom and gratuity of divine action is particularly important for Webster's evolving thought. It is what motivates him to develop a robust account of the distinction and asymmetry between God and creatures, at this point through a doctrine of election and an eschatological theology of grace. But, as we will argue in the following chapters, it is precisely these elements of his thought that at times betray his desire to give a non-competitive account of the God-creature relation, occasionally leading to an overly passive account of human agency and negative account of creaturely mediation. Webster himself becomes aware of these tensions in his thought and eventually turns to classical teaching about divine perfection and, consequently, the doctrine of creation in an effort to rectify them. This leads us to the third and final phase of Webster's theology.

1.4 Theocentric approach to the God-creature relation

The final phase of Webster's theological development begins in the mid-2000s, around the time that he starts employing the language and logic of divine 'perfection'. For the purposes of this book, I will refer to this phase as Webster's 'mature theology'. It is important to note from the outset that this phase of his thought remains thoroughly Trinitarian. So, for example, he states in no uncertain terms,

> The ruler and judge over all other Christian doctrines is the doctrine of the Holy Trinity. The doctrine of the Trinity is not one doctrine among others; it is foundational and pervasive. To expound any Christian doctrine is to expound with varying degrees of directness the doctrine of the Trinity; to expound the doctrine of the Trinity in its full scope is to expound the entirety of Christian dogmatics.[34]

It is no mistake that this quote functions as the opening statement of an essay (originally published in 2009) on the doctrine of justification, as if to say as clearly as possible that the doctrine of the Trinity, not justification or Christology, is the *articulus stantis et cadentis ecclesiae*.[35] Hence, when I use the term 'theocentric' in reference to Webster's mature theology, I do so to denote, not a turn away from the primacy of Trinitarian theology, but rather a development within Webster's doctrine of the Trinity itself: namely the increased prominence and material

---

34. *GWM* I:159.
35. Similar statements can be found in essays on Christology, providence and soteriology (*GWM* I:43, 128, 145).

prioritization of theological-metaphysical teaching about God *in se*. In other words, the immanent life of the triune God becomes the material epicentre and heuristic key of Christian theology.

It is a well-known commonplace of Webster's mature essays to define theology as talk about 'God and all things in relation to God' – 'God' being the first and principle object, and 'all things' being the secondary and derivative object. Moreover, 'God' is described under the twofold aspect of his immanent (*ad intra*) activities and his transitive or transeunt (*ad extra*) acts; that is, God is considered absolutely and only then relatively. Thus, the material content of theology follows a very definite sequence: God *in se*, God *ad extra* and all things in relation to God. The distinctive mark of the third and final phases of Webster's thought is the way in which the first part of this sequence (teaching about God *in se*) precedes, governs and grounds all that he says about the second and third parts.

As I noted above, the development of a theology of divine perfection coincides with this shift in Webster's Trinitarian theology. In one of his earliest statements on the matter, he offered a succinct definition which tied the two closely together: 'God's perfection is the fully realized singularity and unity of the Holy Trinity.'[36] More will be said in the following section about the content of Webster's account of divine perfection and its consequences for his understanding of the God-creature relation, but for now it is simply worth noting that the language of perfection has a rather broad referent in his writings. It does not merely indicate the attributes of the one divine essence; rather, perfection language usually occurs as a reference to God's wholly realized life and self-sufficient being, which is in no way dependent or contingent upon creation. In his earliest writings on the matter, divine perfection was expounded in terms of God's immanent activities (divine processions) *and* his transitive acts (divine missions).[37] The distinction and ordered relation between immanent and transitive remained central to Webster's mature theology to the very end, and yet over time the language of perfection became increasingly concentrated on the former, acting as a sort of placeholder for the immanent life of the triune God – including teaching about the divine essence and the divine persons.

One implication of this concentration upon God's immanent perfection is that Webster's mature theology accentuates the non-necessary nature of God's acts *ad extra* and specifies that those acts are not constitutive of God's essential integrity. Yes, God's creative and communicative activity is 'fitting' to his perfection (especially his goodness), yet no aspect of his perfection is realized in these acts, meaning his relation to creation is not constitutive of his perfection. Added to this concentration on God *in se* as the referent of the language of perfection is a growing conviction that classical teaching about the unity of the divine essence is of great significance for Trinitarian theology (*pace* social Trinitarianism) and

---

36. *CG*, 2.
37. See, for example, John Webster, 'God's Perfect Life', in *God's Life in Trinity*, eds. Miroslav Volf and Michael Welker (Minneapolis, MN: Fortress, 2006), 143–52.

for perceiving the nature of the relation between God and creatures.[38] But before giving more detailed attention to Webster's account of divine perfection and its consequences for his account of the God-creature relation, I would like to draw attention to the reasons for this shift in material focus as well as the effect it has on Webster's ordering of theology and construal of the economy.

What precipitated this shift in material emphasis from the economic action of the Trinity to the immanent life of the Trinity, from God's works *ad extra* to God's being *in se*? First, Webster recognized the need to ground God's temporal works (creation, salvation, perfection) in God's inner life in order to uphold the gratuity and saving efficacy of those works. Second, Webster wanted to offer an account of God's identity that resisted contemporary theologies which historicize the being of God. He attempted to do so by giving a material account of the self-sufficiency and wholly realized life of God *in se* apart from creatures. Third, Webster came to the conclusion that Kant's restriction of human knowledge to the noumenal, which finds its theological correlate in the restriction of theological knowledge to God's acts in the economy, was mistaken. Divine revelation really does beckon human reason to know something of its cause (God *in se*),[39] even though this knowledge always remains ectypal; and crucially, the form and content of revelation are not strictly identical (*pace* some readings of Barth). Hence, creaturely knowledge of God *in se* is a real possibility, and the object of that knowledge 'cannot be resolved into or exhausted by historical manifestation'.[40] These reasons – regarding the ground of God's acts *ad extra*, the sufficiency of God's being *in se* and human knowledge of both – are what eventually led Webster to his mature material ordering of theology: '[T]heology proper precedes and governs economy.'[41]

This ordering of theology (God *in se*) and economy (God *ad extra*) became the dominant theme of Webster's mature thought, which explains why he displayed a keen sensitivity to formal questions about the 'proportion', 'relation' and 'sequence' of doctrines. A distortion in these formal matters may be symptomatic of a distortion in one's grasp of the material order of theology and economy, which in turn leads to problems in one's understanding of the God-creature relation and of

---

38. Thus, in his essay 'Trinity and Creation', Webster describes the material order of the doctrine of the Trinity in a threefold sequence: 'first the divine essence, then the distinction of persons, and (only) then the procession of creatures from God' (*GWM* I:85). He is following the order of the *prima pars* of Aquinas' *Summa theologiae*, which he also saw reflected in the many writings of the Protestant Scholastics (cf. *GWM* I:4-6).

39. The topic of causal relations will be discussed in Chapter 5. Here it is worth noting that unlike Kant, who argued that causal relations are provided by the structural categories of the human mind, Webster believed causal relations to be part of the objective structure of reality that can be discerned by the human mind. Thereby God's revelatory acts (effects) can lead the human mind to a knowledge of the agent of those acts (cause), his inner being and processions (*GWM* I:7-8, 57-8).

40. *GWM* I:6.

41. *GWM* I:3.

the nature of the economy in which that relation is situated. This last point needs some explanation.

First, the proper ordering of theology and economy is crucial for a proper understanding of the relation between God and creatures. Webster states, 'Theologies which accord primacy to economy may come to treat God and created things as paired, parts which together make a whole and which are constituted by their mutual relations.'[42] His concern here has to do with those theologians who attempt to avoid an abstract doctrine of God by focusing on God's historical acts in time (something to which Webster's earlier thought was deeply committed), thereby rendering the divine identity in terms of *dramatis personae* or, even worse, 'dramatic coherence' (Jenson). In either case, Webster fears that God is conceived as a 'magnified historical agent acting on the same plane as other such agents'.[43] The results are not only deleterious for the doctrine of God but also for one's account of the God-creature relation, which cannot be characterized as benign and non-competitive if God and creatures exist and act on the same ontic plane. For the mature Webster, however, it is teaching about divine perfection and, as we will discuss in a moment, the doctrine of creation *ex nihilo* that leads theological reason in the opposite direction: 'God and creatures are incommensurable, and God's presence and action in time does not entail that his relation to creatures is a real relation.'[44] Far from threatening God's genuine relation to creatures, this affirmation is the ground of the loving and non-threatening character of their relation.[45]

Second, the proper ordering of theology and economy is crucial for a proper understanding of the nature of the economy within which creatures live and move and have their being. According to Webster, the intelligibility of God's outer works and of creaturely being is predicated upon a grasp of the perfection of God's inner life. Why give so much attention to the dynamics of God in himself before analysing his temporal works?

> In order to characterize the agent of these acts, and so to come to understand and give due weight to both the acts themselves and their objects. God's outer works are most fully understood as loving and purposive when set against the background of his utter sufficiency – against the fact that no external operation or relation can constitute or augment his life, which is already infinitely replete. Once this is grasped, the nature of creaturely being begins to disclose itself as pure benefit, intelligible only as God is known and loved in his inherent completeness.[46]

In other words, it is an understanding of the unique nature and identity of the divine agent that enables theological reason to grasp the unique character of the

---

42. *GWM* I:8.
43. *GWM* I:8.
44. *GWM* I:8.
45. This point is discussed below in Sections 1.5.2 and 1.5.3.
46. *GWM* I:6.

divine acts and the creaturely effects of those acts.[47] Theology illuminates economy precisely because *agere sequitur esse*.[48]

The influence of Aquinas' *Summa theologiae*, especially the *prima pars*, is not difficult to discern in what we have said about the ordering of Webster's mature theology as well as its material content.[49] In the next section, we will discuss three aspects of his mature theology that reflect this indebtedness to Aquinas and have a unique bearing on his conception of the God-creature relation: doctrine of divine perfection, theory of mixed relations and concept of dual causality. But before doing so, it is worth drawing attention to a key development that was precipitated by this orientation towards the metaphysical and epistemological priority of God *in se*: namely the placement of the doctrine of creation as a 'cardinal' and 'distributed' doctrine alongside the doctrine of the Trinity.[50] As such, the doctrine

---

47. A similar logic undergirds Webster's frequent reference to the close connection between processions and missions. Knowledge of the character of the divine missions requires knowledge of the nature of the divine processions. He states, 'The economy is the domain of the divine missions. But those missions remain opaque unless immediately referred to the divine being and the divine processions. Knowledge of the character and ends of God's temporal works follows from knowledge of their origin in the eternal nature and personal properties of their agent' (*GWM* I:9).

48. *GWM* I:53.

49. In terms of the ordering of theology, Webster is strongly influenced by Aquinas' understanding of the function of teaching about the immanent Trinity for the doctrines of creation and salvation. Aquinas argues, 'There are two reasons why the knowledge of the divine persons was necessary for us. It was necessary for the right idea of creation. The fact of saying that God made all things by His Word excludes the error of those who say that God produced things by necessity. When we say that in Him there is a procession of love, we show that God produced creatures not because he needed them, nor because of any other extrinsic reason, but on account of the love of His own goodness …. In another way, and chiefly, that we may think rightly concerning the salvation of the human race, accomplished by the Incarnate Son, and by the gift of the Holy Spirit' (*ST* Ia.32.1 ad 3). In terms of the material content of his doctrine of the Trinity, Webster gains from Aquinas a greater appreciation for the function of teaching about the undivided divine essence in relation to teaching about the personal distinctions. His reading of Aquinas on these matters is particularly influenced by the work of Gilles Emery. See, for example, Gilles Emery, *The Trinitarian Theology of Saint Thomas Aquinas*, trans. Francesca Aran Murphy (Oxford: Oxford University Press, 2007).

50. Some of Webster's essays on divine aseity make the connection between God's inner life and the doctrine of creation explicit: God is life in and from himself, and from himself God gives life to creatures (*GWM* I:19). Hence, the relation-in-distinction between God and creatures can be articulated as a distinction between God who is a plenitude of life in himself and creatures who receive life *ab extra*. By articulating divine aseity in terms of divine life and life-giving, it was only a short step for Webster to begin reflecting upon the doctrine of creation as God's original gift of life.

of creation functions as the 'hinge' or 'bridge' between theology and economy.[51] There are many reasons for the unique placement and prominence of the doctrine of creation in Webster's mature thought: it is uniquely situated to draw attention to the perfection of God apart from creatures, the priority and gratuity of divine action, the dependence and integrity of creaturely being, the distinction between uncreated and created being, as well as the asymmetric and non-reciprocal (and therefore non-competitive) nature of the relation between them. But the function of the doctrine of creation in Webster's thought is not only material; it is pedagogical as well: 'Most of all it requires the ordering of theological intelligence and spiritual appetite away from a conception of the Christian faith in which the phenomenon of God's engagement with creatures in time is considered *id quo maius cogitari nequit*.'[52] In other words, reflection on the key elements of the doctrine of creation, especially the identity of God the Creator and his act of creation *ex nihilo*, is a means of intellectual and spiritual conversion and sanctification, whereby one becomes attuned to the metaphysical and epistemological priority of God in himself, to his radical perfection and goodness.[53]

As a 'cardinal' and 'distributed' doctrine, the doctrine of creation plays a foundational role in relation to all other doctrines. Webster is fond of quoting Robert Sokolowski's dictum that creation 'opens the logical and theological space for other Christian beliefs and mysteries'.[54] This is so, explains Webster, because 'contemplation of that teaching enables discernment of essential properties of the relation between God and created things which will be further displayed when considering the history of their interaction as it unfolds in the economy'.[55] What we see here is not a displacement of the economy of grace by the doctrine of creation, but rather a situating of that economy within the context of the relation between God and creatures established at creation. The works of nature (creation and providence) become the presupposition for understanding the works of grace (election, reconciliation, perfection); the history of creation is the context in which the divine missions take place.[56] This setting of the works of grace within the works of nature has a significant effect on Webster's theology of grace and creaturely action. There is a retreating and resolving of the eschatological tension between

---

51. *GWM* I:99, 117.
52. *GWM* I:116.
53. Cf. *GWM* I:101–2. Webster also claims that the distinction between God's immanent and transitive operations has a similar pedagogical purpose: '[B]y so ordering God's works, it sets before the mind the principle that because God the creator is perfect in himself, he has no need of creation, acquiring no augmentation from its existence, and being deprived of no good by its absence' (*GWM* I:102–3).
54. *GWM* I:99, 118 (quote from Robert Sokolowski, 'Creation and Christian Understanding', in *God and Creation: An Ecumenical Symposium* (Notre Dame, IN: Notre Dame University Press, 1990), 179).
55. *GWM* I:118.
56. Cf. *GWM* I:9.

divine and human action that was an occasional feature of his thought in the 1990s and even in the early 2000s. He becomes committed to the principle that grace preserves and perfects nature as well as to a doctrine of infused and sacramentally mediated grace. In addition to this he adopts a scholastic account of creaturely action as a 'caused cause' or 'moved movement' as well as the Aristotelian-Thomist idiom of nature, ends and virtues.

The key takeaway is this: Webster's mature theology reflects much of the architectonic structure and employs many of the conceptual resources found in Aquinas' thought, especially as it came to expression in the *Summa theologiae*. In particular, he found the doctrine of divine perfection and teaching about creation *ex nihilo* to be particularly companionable for articulating the radical distinction between God and creation while simultaneously clarifying the benevolent and non-competitive character of their relation, thereby creating space for a more robust account of creaturely being and action. In order to expand on this point, I will now offer a conceptual analysis of three key aspects of Webster's mature theology.

1.5 Key aspects of Webster's mature theology of the God-creature relation

Thus far I have mapped Webster's theological development in terms of three phases – Christocentric, Trinitarian, Theocentric – drawing attention to the way he orders theology as a whole and the implications this has for the way he frames the God-creature relation. In particular, I have sought to convey the ways in which Webster's evolving conception of the 'material centre' and 'heuristic key' of Christian theology shapes the way he grounds, contextualizes and depicts the relation-in-distinction between God and creatures. The remaining chapters of this book will seek to demonstrate the explanatory power of the developmental narrative I have sketched by looking at individual loci within Webster's dogmatic corpus: Christology, ecclesiology, bibliology and theological theology. The chapters will begin at various points in Webster's theological developmental, but each will work towards an analysis of his mature thought on a specific topic. Thus, his mature theology will receive more overall attention than the other phases of his development.[57] So I think it pertinent at this point to offer a brief conceptual analysis of three key aspects of Webster's mature theology that will reoccur at various points in the remaining chapters as being particularly formative for his account of the God-creature relation. They are as follows: the doctrine of divine perfection, the theory of mixed relations and the concept of dual causality, all of which reflect a rather Thomist cast of mind.

---

57. This is due partly to the focus of my book (Webster's constructive thought) and partly to the evolution of Webster as a scholar (the first half of his career was devoted primarily to historical theology, the second half to preparing for his own systematic theology). Moreover, Webster's fascination with particular doctrinal loci ebbs and flows throughout his career.

1.5.1 Doctrine of divine perfection

On a number of occasions, Webster gestures towards the importance of a theology of divine perfection for contemporary Christian theology, arguing that a 'good many debates of the moment turn on how God's perfection is to be conceived'.[58] This is especially true when explicating the nature of the relation between God and creatures, a point to which Webster constantly draws attention.[59] Not only does a theology of divine perfection illuminate the nature of the God-creature relation, but it also functions as a critical lever by which Webster judges the adequacy of contemporary theological proposals about that relation.[60] And so, for example, he makes this concluding remark in an essay on the eternal generation of the Son: 'Amongst the more important tasks of Christian dogmatics in the present is the articulation of an evangelically-determined theology of God's perfection. There are more options available than either materially-unspecific perfect being theology, or neo-Hegelian presentations of God's career in time.'[61] To get a sharper sense of where Webster's theology of divine perfection is situated within the contemporary theological landscape, it is worth unpacking this suggestive statement before drawing attention to some key elements of Webster's material account of the doctrine.

The aforementioned quote hints at the fact that Webster wants to develop a theology of divine perfection in contradistinction to two contemporary options. The first option seems to be a version of perfect being theology that can be found in some stands of the analytic philosophical tradition. Take, for example, Katherin A. Rogers's description of the two principles by which to describe a perfect being: 'A perfect being ... must have all the great-making properties and he must have them to an unlimited extent.'[62] While not necessarily objecting to the many 'great-making properties' that Rogers goes on to exposit, Webster would take issue with such terminology and its use to describe 'a' (note the indefinite article) perfect being. For Webster, the problem with this type of perfect being theology is twofold: first, it fails to take into account the means by which a theology of divine perfection should proceed – not by reflection upon 'great-making' properties, but by exposition of God's self-revealed name ('I AM WHO I AM');[63] second, it fails to register the *particular mode* of perfection which theology must confess of God in the wake of his salvific missions, namely his triune perfection. Hence, for Webster, 'materially-unspecific perfect being theology' is that which underestimates

---

58. John Webster, 'Review Article: Webster's Response to Alyssa Lyra Pitstick, *Light in Darkness*', *SJT* 62:2 (2009): 202.

59. *CG*, 2; *DW*, ix–x; *GWM* I:123.

60. John Webster, 'Perfection and Participation', in *The Analogy of Being: Invention of the Antichrist or the Wisdom of God*, ed. Thomas Joseph White (Grand Rapids, MI: Eerdmans, 2011), 379.

61. *GWM* I:41.

62. Katherin A. Rogers, *Perfect Being Theology* (Edinburgh: Edinburgh University Press, 2000), 13.

63. It is somewhat regrettable that Webster does not, so far as I am aware, discuss how the pre-modern Christian tradition developed a theology of the divine names in terms of the perfections of the divine essence.

'the corrections to the concept of perfection introduced by trinitarian and Christological teaching about the Father's begetting of the Son' and, we might add, by pneumatological teaching about the spiration of the Spirit from the Father and the Son.[64] The divine processions are the particular mode of God's perfection.[65]

The second option Webster resists – 'neo-Hegelian presentations of God's career in time' – is undoubtedly a reference to Robert W. Jenson. For Jenson, commitment to a history is constitutive of God's perfection: 'Since the biblical God can truly be identified by narrative, his hypostatic being, his self-identity, is constituted in *dramatic coherence* .... Why should commitment in a history not be instead an ontological *perfection*? We are free to say that even – or, rather, especially – God is one with himself just by the dramatic coherence of his eventful actuality.'[66] This implies that God's relations to creatures are intrinsic to his self-identity and, even more, that God has no identity outside of his commitment to creatures.[67] For Webster, the problem with this account of divine perfection is threefold: First, it fails to account for the doctrines of divine simplicity and aseity; second, it fails to adequately articulate the distinction between processions and missions, the former being constitutive of God's eternal identity and the latter being a repetition and revelation in time of that identity but not its constitution; third, it mischaracterizes the economy of salvation as a sort of theogony rather than an act of pure generosity. In contrast, Webster emphasizes the perfection of God *in se* apart from creatures, not in order to absorb the temporal economy into eternity, but rather to specify the ontological ground and condition of possibility for the economy, that which gives the history of salvation its saving efficacy. Moreover, by stressing the non-necessity of God's act of and relation to creation, Webster does not intend to devalue or denigrate the reality of that act and relation, but rather to draw attention to their utter gratuity and benevolence.[68]

---

64. *GWM* I:38.
65. *GWM* I:21, 27, 34, 36–7, 152.
66. Robert W. Jenson, *Systematic Theology*, Volume 1: The Triune God (Oxford: Oxford University Press, 1997), 64.
67. Jenson, *Systematic Theology* 1:65, 75.
68. This is a point that Webster first learnt from Barth. He states, 'Barth is deeply committed to God's triune self-sufficiency. Certainly, he insists upon the correspondence between God's *opera externa* and God *in se*, and believes that some notions of divine independence are ruinous. But Barth retains a sense of the infinite recess of God's life in himself, without which grace would not be grace' (Webster, 'Review Article', 208). And yet Webster came to believe that Barth was at times rather light in his treatment of the immanent life of God: 'Barth was at some points so committed to the identity of God's being and God's outer works that he risked saying too little about the *opera Dei ad intra* .... Barth concentrated with such loving attention on the temporal mission of the Son that he passed too swiftly over the "whence" of the transitive divine act in the eternal plenitude of God's triune processions' (John B. Webster, 'Foreword', in *Trinitarian Theology after Barth*, eds. Myk Habets and Phillip W. Tolliday [Eugene, OR: Pickwick, 2011], xi–xii). This seems to be one reason why Webster made recourse to the pre-modern tradition, especially Augustine and Aquinas, believing that they gave him metaphysical and conceptual resources by which to fill out the lacuna in Barth.

By briefly positioning Webster's account of divine perfection in relation to Rogers and Jenson, we have come to see some of its key elements. It is a positive, material concept, which offers an analytic (rather than synthetic) description of God's plenitude and fullness, developed on the basis of God's self-declaration and salvific missions. And crucially, the particular mode of God's perfection is unpacked in terms of the eternal divine processions. Divine perfection is 'God's triune self-sufficiency',[69] 'God's wholly realized triune life in himself.'[70]

To this painting I would like to add one more brush stroke: the increased prominence of teaching about the undivided divine essence,[71] especially the classical doctrine of divine simplicity.[72] It is this element of Webster's mature doctrine of God that Sonderegger's otherwise judicious discussion of the matter seems to overlook.[73] His publications in the 2010s, particularly on the doctrine of creation, employ theological-metaphysical teaching about divine unity and indivisibility in an effort to develop a non-comparative and non-contrastive account of divine perfection. God's perfection is absolute, not relative, and therefore incomparable. On the one hand, Webster's account of divine simplicity follows the contours of

---

69. *GWM* I:92.

70. Webster, 'Perfection and Participation', 379.

71. One can trace a shift in Webster's account of divine perfection from a focus on the question *Qui est Deus?* to *Qui et Quid sit Deus?* It is appropriate to speak not only of God's triune identity, but also of his nature or essence. For the mature Webster, to speak about the divine quiddity is not to go behind the back of the divine triunity as if the essence is more basic than the persons. Nor does he think Aquinas is guilty of the many charges levelled against him in this regard. Rather, he follows the reading of Aquinas offered by Gilles Emery, who interprets Aquinas' discussion of the divine essence and the divine relations/persons (in the *prima pars*) as an act of 'redoublement' – signifying one and the same reality (*res significata*) according to two aspects or modes of signification (*modus significadi*) (Cf. Gilles Emery, 'Essentialism or Personalism in the Treatise on God in St. Thomas Aquinas', in *Trinity in Aquinas*, 2nd ed. [Washington, DC: Catholic University of America Press, 2008], 165–208). Hence, Aquinas is interpreted as employing a rather patristic mode of Trinitarian logic, whereby one makes a distinction but not a separation between what is said of God substance-wise (what is common to the persons) and what is said relation-wise (what is proper to the persons). For Webster, the Christian doctrine of God must think of 'essentialism' and 'personalism' as directly, rather than indirectly, proportional; and a classically Thomist way of doing this is to conceive of the divine persons as subsistent relations or modes of the one divine essence (*GWM* I:86–8, 123–4).

72. There has been a flourish of literature in recent years on the doctrine of divine simplicity, including both spirited defences as well as new critiques. For recent retrievals of the traditional doctrine, see James E. Dolezal, *God without Parts: Divine Simplicity and the Metaphysics of God's Absoluteness* (Eugene, OR: Pickwick Publications, 2011); Steven J. Duby, *Divine Simplicity: A Dogmatic Account* (London: T&T Clark, 2016); D. Stephen Long, *The Perfectly Simple Triune God: Aquinas and His Legacy* (Minneapolis, MN: Fortress Press, 2016). For recent critiques of the doctrine from within the analytic philosophy tradition, see R. T. Mullins, 'Simply Impossible: A Case against Divine Simplicity', *JRT* 7 (2013): 181–203; Alvin Plantinga, *Does God Have a Nature?* (Milwaukee, WI: Marquette University Press, 1980).

73. Cf. Sonderegger, 'God-Intoxicated Theology', 41–3.

Aquinas' *via negativa* approach to knowledge of the divine essence. It consists of a series of negations: a primary negation (God is 'non-composite') followed by multiple derivative negations – God is not composed of potency and act (he is *actus purus*), of essence and existence (they are identical in him), of genus and species (God is not contained in any genus but is the principle of all genera), or of subject and accident.[74] On the other hand, it is important to see that for Webster the negation of creaturely limits and composition is predicated upon a positive conception of God's fullness and plenitude. He states, 'It is important to be clear that divine simplicity is not mere absence of composition but singular, infinite fullness, perfect integrity, and abundance of life.'[75] If his account of divine simplicity were a matter of pure negation, then Webster would be falling into the very error he is seeking to avoid: a comparative or contrastive account of divine perfection. And yet the positive moment in theological speech must have as its correlate a negative moment in order to register the transcendence and uniqueness of God.

We can see this dynamic interrelation between affirmation (kataphatic claims) and negation (apophatic claims) also at play in Webster's interpretation of the traditional metaphysical attributes of immutability and impassibility: 'God is immutable – already infinitely sufficient and complete and therefore beyond alteration or acquisition – and impassible – inexhaustibly alive, stable and entire in himself and so beyond the reach of any agent or act of contestation or depredation.'[76] Notice how Webster grounds his negative claims in a positive, material concept of God's perfection. Notice also the use of the word 'beyond', a word which is repeated often in Webster's discussions of the divine essence in order to express the negation. It is used to denote the transcendence of God's perfection: his positive plenitude and self-sufficiency are such that he transcends all creaturely limitations and compositions. The negations communicate something of God's positive transcendence, because they are predicated upon his inner fullness and super-eminent perfection.[77]

---

74. Cf. *ST* Ia.3.

75. John Webster, 'Attributes, Divine', in *The Cambridge Dictionary of Christian Theology*, eds. Ian A. McFarland, David A. S. Fergusson, Karen Kilby, and Iain R. Torrance (Cambridge: Cambridge University Press, 2011), 47.

76. *GWM* I:120.

77. Another way of stating the logic at work in Webster's theology of the divine essence is to talk about the interplay between the *via negativa* and *via eminentiae*. In a perceptive discussion of the doctrine of analogy, Charles J. Rennie notes that the fundamental presupposition of the *via negativa* is the principle of dissimilarity: '[W]hile the creature is in some way like God, God is in no way like the creature' ('Analogy and the Doctrine of Divine Impassibility', in *Confessing the Impassible God: The Biblical, Classical, & Confessional Doctrine of Divine Impassibility*, eds. Ronald S Baines, Richard C. Barcellos, James P. Butler, Stefan T. Lindbald, and James M. Renihan [Palmdale, CA: RBAP, 2015], 73). The *via eminentiae* does not qualify the principle of dissimilarity so much as clarify the ultimate reason or ground for the dissimilarity, namely God's transcendent perfection. Rennie argues, '[T]he *via eminentiae* reminds us that God *is* infinitely beyond all that we can conceive, so that it stresses the limitations, not the achievements, of our knowledge …. The *via eminentiae* does not merely imply that God is the most perfect being, but that he is perfection and being itself of an altogether different order' (Rennie, 'Analogy and the Doctrine of Divine Impassibility', 77–8).

And so, we see that one of the primary functions of the doctrine of divine simplicity in Webster's mature thought is to register the absolute otherness of God in relation to creation.[78] Thus, he argues, 'Because God is simple, he is absolutely and not merely contingently other than the world …. God is *non aliud*, beyond relations of similarity or contrast.'[79] Or again: 'God is entirely beyond the totality of things. There is in God no *esse-ad*, no constitutive relation to that which is not himself.'[80] As we will explain in the following section, it is these claims, which derive from convictions about God's simple perfection, that undergird Webster's characterization of the God-creature relation as a mixed relation. For Webster, a robust theology of God's perfection apart from creation is foundational not only for one's doctrine of God but also for a proper understanding of God's acts *ad extra* and his relation to creatures. Far from implying God's abstract removal or deistic distance from creation, this account of divine perfection, precisely because it focuses on his non-comparative and absolute otherness, specifies God's capacity for intimate relations with creation. God does not depend upon or compete with creatures but is the free and generous cause of their being and act. His relation to creatures is 'non-constitutive', 'non-necessary', 'non-reciprocal' and 'non-real', and therefore it is gratuitous and non-competitive.[81] This leads us to a discussion of the theory of mixed relations.

1.5.2 Theory of mixed relations

The theory of relations was a topic of heated debate in the high middle ages, and its conceptual unpacking was by no means monolithic.[82] Hence, it is important to note that the tradition of thought from which Webster draws is, unsurprisingly,

---

78. This is not the only function. First and foremost, the doctrine of divine simplicity is employed to articulate the essential unity of the divine persons (cf. *GWM* I:86–92); only then does it function to characterize God's relation to creatures. For a helpful discussion of the different functions that the doctrine of divine simplicity performs based upon the theological contexts within which it is employed, see Long, *The Perfectly Simple Triune God*, xix-xxiii, 143–70.

79. *GWM* I:120. For a defence of the scholastic claim that God is *non aliud*, see Ian A. McFarland, 'The Gift of the *Non aliud*: Creation from Nothing as a Metaphysics of Abundance', *IJST* 21:1 (2019): 44–58.

80. *GWM* I:121.

81. This is what Webster refers to as the 'evangelical import' of the 'metaphysics of God *a se* and *in se*' (*GWM* I:41).

82. For a brief discussion of the diverse theories of relations in the thirteenth and fourteenth centuries, with an excellent exposition of Aquinas' thought in particular, see Mark Gerald Henninger, 'Aquinas on the Ontological Status of Relations', *Journal of the History of Philosophy* 25:4 (1987): 491–515.

that associated with Aquinas.⁸³ For Webster, teaching about 'mixed' relations is a consequence of the doctrines of divine perfection and creation *ex nihilo*. It is a way of characterizing the God-creature relation: the creature's relation to God is 'real' while God's relation to the creature is 'non-real', 'logical', 'conceptual' or 'rational'. As I will show at other points in this book, the theory of mixed relations bears significance not only for Webster's conception of the Creator-creature relation, but also for his characterization of the relation between the divine and human natures of Christ in the hypostatic union (Chapter 2) as well as the redemptive relation between God and the church (Chapter 3). The wide applicability of this Thomist conceptuality is a consequence of the prominent role the doctrine of creation assumes in Webster's mature thought as the 'hinge' between theology and economy. Here we see a reversal of Barth's assertion that the covenant is the internal basis of creation. For Webster, the history of fellowship between God and creatures presupposes the act of creation *ex nihilo* as its foundation and condition of possibility. Therefore, the theory of mixed relations becomes the context within which to understand all other aspects of the God-creature relation, whether it is hypostatic or redemptive.

In order to gain some clarity on what exactly Webster means when he uses the language of 'real' and 'non-real' relations, first we need to understand a significant point of divergence between Aristotelian and modern conceptions of relationality. For Aristotle, relations inhere in things or substances, whereas modern thought has tended to criticize the substance metaphysics implied in that claim. Modern thought challenged and reversed what F. LeRon Shults has called the 'privileging of substance over relationality' that was germane to much of the Western philosophical tradition.⁸⁴ Shults builds upon the insights of Wolfhart Pannenberg in claiming that Kant and Hegel are the key figures responsible for this philosophical shift whereby relationality became the overarching category within which to understand substance.⁸⁵ For Aristotle, a relation is an accident of

---

83. Aquinas' fullest exposition of the matter can be found in *De potentia* III.3 and VII.8–11, but he also touches upon the issue in *Summa Contra Gentiles* II.11–4 and *ST* Ia.28.1 and 45.3. For helpful analyses of Aquinas' account of God's relation to creation, see Emery, *The Trinitarian Theology of Saint Thomas Aquinas*, 84–9, 340–2; Norman Kretzmann, *The Metaphysics of Creation: Aquinas' Natural Theology in Summa Contra Gentiles II* (Oxford: Clarendon, 1999), 47–53; Matthew R. McWhorter, 'Aquinas on God's Relation to the World', *NB* 94 (2013): 3–18; Tyler R. Wittman, *God and Creation in the Theology of Thomas Aquinas and Karl Barth* (Cambridge: Cambridge University Press, 2019), 113–26.

84. F. LeRon Shults, *Reforming Theological Anthropology: After the Philosophical Turn to Relationality* (Grand Rapids, MI: Eerdmans, 2003), 13.

85. Cf. Wolfhart Pannenberg, *Systematic Theology*, vol. 1, trans. Geoffrey W. Bromiley (Grand Rapids, MI: Eerdmans, 1991), 364–7; Shults, *Reforming Theological Anthropology*, 11–36.

a substance, whereas for Kant and Hegel substance itself comes to be redefined in terms of constitutive relationality.[86]

The effect of this philosophical shift upon twentieth-century theology is wide-ranging. Examples include the way many theologians began to conceive of God's relation to the world as constitutive of his essence as well as the way relations were viewed as constitutive of human personhood and identity. Thus Pannenberg, along with a formidable group of modern theologians (e.g. Moltmann, Jenson), has drawn attention to a key implication of this claim for the doctrine of God: theology cannot talk about God apart from his relation to the world. Shults, among others (e.g. Schwöbel, Gunton) have drawn attention to the implications for theological anthropology: theology must take into account the psychological, social, physical and cultural relations in which human lives are embedded and which are constitutive of personhood.[87] Webster knew this theological culture well, and while he had no problem recognizing the way in which relations (especially to God) are constitutive of human persons,[88] he became increasingly troubled by the way some theologians were drawing similar implications regarding God's being and his relation to the world. It is in this context that Webster's recourse to the theory of mixed relations is to be understood. Teaching about divine perfection, argued Webster, not only 'orders thought' about creatures but also 'unsettles conventions about relations'.[89] He reaches for scholastic teaching about mixed relations in order to give metaphysical and conceptual expression to this unsettling: the creature's relation to God is 'real' while God's relation to the creation is 'non-real', meaning not constitutive of his essence or identity. In other words, Webster wants to uncouple God and humans as being in the same category of relations, and he feels that the scholastics, especially Aquinas, provide him with the theological-metaphysical tools to do so.[90]

At this point, it is worth offering a brief exposition of the Thomist distinction between 'real' and 'non-real' (or 'rational') relations, to which Webster's articulation

---

86. For an exhaustive analysis of the relation between substance and accident in Aquinas' metaphysics, see John F. Wippel, *The Metaphysical Thought of Thomas Aquinas: From Finite Being to Uncreated Being* (Washington, DC: The Catholic University of America Press, 2000), 197–294.

87. Modern philosophical developments in the theory of relations are closely connected with theological developments in notions of personhood. See, for example, the suggestive collection of essays in *Persons, Divine and Human: King's College Essays in Theological Anthropology*, eds. Christoph Schwöbel and Colin E. Gunton (Edinburgh: T&T Clark, 1991).

88. For claims that social relations are constitutive of human creaturehood, see *GWM* II:126, 163, 185–6.

89. *GWM* I:123, 124.

90. Webster is resisting what Kevin J. Vanhoozer has dubbed the 'new orthodoxy', which 'holds that the same kinds of relation that characterize God's Trinitarian life apply to the God-world relation as well' (*Remythologizing Theology: Divine Action, Passion, and Authorship* (Cambridge: Cambridge University Press, 2010), 241).

of the matter is indebted, before offering further comments regarding the function of this distinction in Webster's thought, not only for articulating the 'Christian distinction' between God and the world but also for understanding their loving and non-competitive relationship.

According to Aquinas, the creature's relation to God is a 'real' relation. A real relation has two aspects: its *esse-in* (inherence in a substance or subject) and its *esse-ad* (orientation or ordering towards another). And, as Tyler R. Wittman notes, a real relation must fulfil four conditions: '(1) both terms of the relation must be real, (2) distinct from one another, (3) members of the same ontological order, and (4) there must be a foundation for the relation in each term.'[91] Examples of real relations to which Thomas (and Webster) draw attention are the relations of creatures to God and the relations between the persons of the Holy Trinity, though the latter are categorically different from the former in that they are subsistent relations – i.e. relations whose term lies within and are identical with the one divine essence. When describing the creature's relation to God, however, it is appropriate to speak of a relation of causal dependence, of an *esse-ad* relation to something outside of the creature which inheres in the creature's being. Creatures have being *per participationem*.[92] Therefore, the relation of the creature to God is real in the creature, meaning an ordering towards God is constitutive of creaturely nature and identity.[93]

God's relation to creatures, on the other hand, is 'non-real' or 'rational', which is to say that such a relation is not constitutive of God's being.[94] It is not a claim that God has no relation to creatures or that such a relation is a mental fiction,

---

91. Wittman, *God and Creation*, 114.
92. *GWM* I:106.
93. In this way, teaching about mixed relations not only registers the fact that God's relation to creatures is non-constitutive and therefore non-necessary and non-reciprocal (see below), but also highlights the nature of creaturely dependence on God. It funds a thoroughly relational view of the creature, who cannot be conceived or known apart from relation to God, though God can be conceived apart from the creature. Along these lines, Martin J. De Nys argues, 'Since God is the principle of the very being of creatures, any creature is that which it is only in the context of its relation to God. God, according to the classical view, is not simply the principle on account of which something begins to exist, but more essentially the principle on account of which something does exist …. A creature does not occur at all outside of its relation to God. Relation in this case does not follow upon subsistence or identity. This relation encompasses subsistence and identity. Subsistence and identity emerge within this relation' ('God, Creatures, and Relations: Revisiting Classical Theism', *The Journal of Religion* 81:4 [2001]: 600–1).
94. A note about etymology: in the scholastic context in which the theory of mixed relations was developed, the word 'real' (*realis*) often meant 'of the thing', assuming an Aristotelian framework in which relations inhere in things (as noted above). Hence, to characterize God's relation to the world as 'non-real' is not to deny that God relates to the world, but to deny that such a relation is a necessity of his nature.

but rather a characterization of 'the *kind* of relation which he has to creatures'.[95] We must remember that this unique depiction of God's relation to creatures is a consequence of teaching about God's transcendent perfection *in se*, namely 'that God the creator is not ordered to another, and that God is wholly outside the genus of that which is ordered to him'.[96] In other words, divine perfection is such that there is in God no *esse-ad* relation to that which is not himself (the second aspect of a real relation does not apply), and he transcends the ontological order of created things, thereby sharing no common foundation with them (the third and fourth conditions of a real relation are not met).[97] The implication is that God's relations to creation are expressive of his wisdom and will, not his essence.[98] God's being is and can be conceived as fully realized apart from creatures. It is important not to misunderstand Webster here. He often notes how it is fitting for God to act as he has in relation to creatures because of the nature of his goodness and love.[99] And yet he is adamant that such acts *ad extra* are not necessary and in no way extend, modify, supplement or constitute the divine life.[100] God does not need to

---

95. *GWM* I:107.
96. *GWM* I:124.
97. Henninger lays particular stress on Aquinas' denial of condition three, arguing that divine transcendence, not immutability, is the primary reason Aquinas rejects the notion that God's relation to creation is 'real'. Hence, the God-creature relation is non-mutual because God is outside of any genus: 'Thomas claims that if *a* and *b* are real and mutual, then *a* and *b* have the same reason for the relation (*eadem ratio ordinis*). Thomas explains "the same reason for the relation" in terms of the foundations being of the same type …. The intuition is that two things cannot be mutually related if the two foundations are incommensurable, i.e., radically different' (Henninger, 'Aquinas on the Ontological Status of Relations', 510). Because *a* and *b* are of different orders of being, and therefore incommensurable, they have no common basis for comparison or relation.
98. *GWM* I:125.
99. On this topic, see Wittman, 'John Webster on the Task of a Properly Theological *Theologia*', 106–8.
100. The distinction between antecedent necessity and consequent necessity may be of some help in understanding Webster on this point. He is not saying that the nature of God's acts in the economy is arbitrary and could have taken many possible forms; rather he is saying that, though creation exists, it might not have. In other words, the contingency of creation as a whole, and therefore the non-necessary nature of God's creative act, is in view, not the manner of God's action in the economy, which, he argues elsewhere, has a certain sort of necessity based on the nature and life of God once God has determined to create. For an opposing view, see Norman Kretzmann, *The Metaphysics of Theism: Aquinas' Natural Theology in Summa Contra Gentiles I* (Oxford: Clarendon, 1997). He critiques Aquinas' non-necessitarian view of creation, which Webster shares, claiming that Aquinas goes against the Dionysian principle (i.e. God's self-diffusive goodness) that he often cites. Instead, Kretzmann reverses Aquinas' judgement: 'God's will is necessitated as regards *whether* to create, but fully free as regards *what* to create' (225).

create and is not changed by doing so. The creature depends on God who does not so depend on it, and thus their relation is 'non-mutual' or 'non-reciprocal'.

It must be admitted that this way of characterizing God's relation to creatures is primarily negative or apophatic, stipulating what it is not. God's relation to creatures is non-constitutive and non-necessary, meaning the integrity and sufficiency of God's being is in no way affected by that relation.[101] It is this aspect of the theory of mixed relations that has received heavy criticism in recent years, of both a philosophical and existential nature. Does this not lead to the privation and denigration of the creature? Does this not conceive of the metaphysics of reality in terms of stable essences instead of historical processes and interpersonal relations? Does this not call into question the personal love and compassion of God for his creation? It is this last criticism that seems to be the underlying motivation behind many of the philosophical objections. W. Norris Clarke summarizes well the modern intuition that a personal relation of love requires some form of reciprocity:

> [O]ne of the central tenets of man's religious belief (at least in Judaeo-Christian religion) is that God is one who enters into deep personal relations of love with his creatures. And an authentic interpersonal relation of love necessarily involves not merely purely creative or one-way love, but genuine mutuality and reciprocity of love, including not only the giving of love but the joyful acceptance of it and response to it.[102]

A similar intuition undergirds Nicholas Wolterstorff's critique of the classical tradition (with Augustine identified as its fountainhead) for conceiving of God's love exclusively as benevolence. In contrast, Wolterstorff proposes that a modern vision of God's love as suffering love is in fact closer to the picture one gets from the biblical materials.[103] How does Webster respond to critiques of this nature? He argues that the characterization of God's relation to creation as 'non-real', while admittedly a negative characterization, ultimately has a positive theological purpose. Far from threatening or diminishing the loving nature of God's relation to creation, it is the very foundation of that loving and intimate relation.[104]

---

101. *GWM* I:116.

102. W. Norris Clarke, S. J., *Explorations in Metaphysics: Being-God-Person* (Notre Dame, IN: University of Notre Dame Press, 1994), 183. Clarke argues that theology must take the existential challenges to the concept of non-reciprocal relations seriously (183), suggesting that the way forward is to allow modern notions of the 'personal' to control a theological account of divine perfection and immutability (207–8). God is really related to creatures by 'an intentional relation of personal consciousness' (194–7).

103. Nicholas Wolterstorff, 'Suffering Love', in *Philosophy and the Christian Faith*, ed. Thomas V. Morris (Notre Dame, IN: University of Notre Dame Press, 1988), 196–237.

104. For a discussion of Webster's commitment to mixed relation and its relation to the differing conceptions of divine love, see Kevin J. Vanhoozer, 'Love without Measure? John Webster's Unfinished Dogmatic Account of the Love of God, in Dialogue with Thomas Jay Oord's Interdisciplinary Theological Account', *IJST* 19:4 (2017): 505–26.

It is worth explaining Webster's logic here, because it goes against the grain of much contemporary theological intuition. First, God's relation to creation is non-real, meaning no aspect of his essential integrity is contingent or dependent upon creation. This means that the existence of creation is of no personal benefit or self-interest to God (i.e. he gains nothing from creation), and therefore the act of creation and his relation to creation are utterly gratuitous and generous and loving, purely for the benefit of the creature. It also means that God does not compete with the creature, as if he could gain or lose anything in relation to the creature, and thus he is not 'reluctant to bestow upon the creature its own intrinsic substance and powers'.[105] Second, it is precisely because God is beyond any genus, and therefore shares no common foundation with creatures by which his relation to them could be characterized as 'real', that he can be present in every genus as the principle of all being. Webster states, 'In God, absence of reciprocity is not absence of relation but the ground of limitless relation. God does not stand in relation to the creature as some commensurable particular agent in the same order of being, but more intimately and comprehensively as the principle of all being.'[106] In other words, God's transcendent perfection, which is the ultimate reason for characterizing his relation to creation as 'non-real', is the foundation for his immanence. The theory of mixed relations, far from jeopardizing God's relation to creation, actually serves to characterize that relation as loving and non-competitive and thereby opens space for a compatibilist account of divine and human agency.

1.5.3 Concept of dual causality

The concept of dual (primary and secondary) causality comes to the fore in Webster's mature essays in contexts where he is developing a theological-metaphysical account of human actions (intellectual, volitional and social) or products (textual and institutional) as 'caused causes' or 'moved movements'. As will become clear in Chapters 3–5, this conceptuality plays a key role in a wide range of loci within Webster's dogmatic corpus: ecclesiology, bibliology, theology of reason and moral theology.[107] He seems to employ this conceptuality for three reasons: First, it specifies divine action as the ground and motive power of creaturely acts; second, it highlights the integrity and efficacy of creaturely acts; third, it gives expression to a non-dualist and non-competitive account of divine and human agency.

The background to this line of thinking in Webster's mature theology is Aquinas' articulation of primary and secondary causality. Its foundational

---

105. *GWM* I:126.
106. *GWM* I:125.
107. A sample of the relevant references is as follows: bibliology (*DW*, 15–7), ecclesiology (*GWM* I:188–9, 193), theological reason (*DW*, 54–6, 172–3, 180–2, 187–8; *GWM* I:218; *GWM* II:145), and moral theology (*GWM* II:136, 152, 179).
108. The relevant references in Webster's corpus are as follows: creation (*GWM* I:108–13; *GWM* II:34) and providence (*GWM* I:135–40).

principles are established in the doctrine of creation and fleshed out in the doctrine of providence.[108] But before we venture into that territory, it is important to note that Webster latched onto this scholastic conceptuality late in his career because he thought it could effectively articulate a theological insight regarding the relation between God and creatures that he originally learned from Barth. In his first full-length engagement with Barth's theological ethics, Webster expressed appreciation for the covenantal structure of Barth's articulation of the relation between divine and human action, precisely because it depicted that relation as asymmetrical, gracious and non-competitive. While he had some misgivings about Barth's late theology of baptism and mediation – namely that they suffer from a deficient doctrine of creation – he learned from Barth how to make a fundamental distinction 'between divine omnicausality and divine sole causality'.[109] To affirm the latter would imply that divine action overwhelms or hampers human agency, whereas to affirm the former implies that divine action grounds and evokes human agency. According to Webster, many of Barth's interpreters align him with the latter option (sole causality), when, in fact, one of the fundamental insights of the *Church Dogmatics* is that former (omnicausality) does not imply the latter. Hence, a distinctive theological account of human agency emerges as being 'neither identical with, nor in competition with, the activity of God, but in correspondence with God's activity, subordinate to that activity and in that very subordination enjoying its genuine substance'.[110] Barth's anti-modern moral anthropology, which specifies divine action as the ground and context of (rather than a threat to) human freedom, was tremendously appealing to Webster in the 1980s and 1990s, although he eventually came to the judgement that Barth's theological development of the point was somewhat deficient. Thus, when Webster began to employ the conceptuality of primary and secondary causality in his later years, he was not leaving Barth's fundamental insight behind, but rather seeking to articulate that insight through different conceptual resources – those afforded by the doctrines of divine perfection, creation and providence (as developed in the scholastic tradition, both Catholic and Protestant) rather than Christology and covenant. This, Webster believes, does a better job of achieving what Barth was attempting to achieve – a depiction of the theological space in which a robust account of creaturely being and action can take shape without in any way forfeiting the originality and gratuity of divine action.

Thus, Webster writes in 'Love Is Also a Lover of Life', an essay originally published in 2013:

> [T]o attribute all created effects to God as omni-causal is not to rob creatures of their proper action, because what God in his perfect wisdom, power, and goodness causes is creatures who are themselves causes. The idea whose spell

---

109. *BER*, 167. See also *BMT*, 8; *Barth*, 157. For Barth's use of this particular language, see *CD* IV/4, 22.

110. *BER*, 167.

must be broken is that God is a supremely forceful agent in the same order of being as creatures, acting upon them and so depriving them of movement. What Aquinas commends here – something which Barth also reached towards in his theology of covenant and of God's evocation of active human partners – is that the plenitude of God apart from creatures does not entail the thought of God's segregation as sole cause, but rather the opposite: God's perfection is seen also in bringing into being other agents. God bestows being and activity: this is part of the special sense of creation out of nothing in the Christian confession.[111]

Another paradigmatic statement can be found in Webster's essay 'On the Theology of Providence' (2009):

Here the conceptuality of secondary causality proves immensely resourceful. God's providential activity is omni-causal but not solely-causal. His ordering of the history of creation includes the employment of creaturely ministers. Their ministerial operations do not threaten but draw life from divine sovereignty; divine sovereignty does not eliminate but generates creaturely operation.[112]

Two comments are in order. First, notice how a theology of divine perfection and sovereignty functions in giving an account of the integrity of creaturely being and action: the former is the generative source of the latter. For Webster, much rides on a non-contrastive and non-comparative understanding of divine perfection and sovereignty – they bestow and perfect creaturely being and activity rather than compete with or stunt it.[113] Whereas Webster's thought in the late 1990s and early 2000s sought to avoid depicting God as a 'supremely forceful agent' by developing a doctrine of God whose focus was on his economic missions (Christology and pneumatology), now he seeks to do so through teaching about God *in se* and the doctrines of creation and providence. Second, the doctrine of creation *ex nihilo* is particularly important for the mature Webster because it registers the fact that God is not an agent 'in the same order of being as creatures' but rather 'the principle and cause of being to other things'.[114] Thus, God is not in a comparative or competitive relation with creatures, vying for or acting in the same ontic 'space'.

---

111. *GWM* I:112.
112. *GWM* I:140.
113. There is a subtle shift in the way Webster articulates this point in his later years, yet the impulse to do so through a doctrine of divine perfection remains the same. Compare, for example, the following quotes: 'God's perfection includes his perfecting of creatures' (*CG*, 2); 'anxieties about [the] debasement of creatures may stem from insufficient consideration of what might be called the perfecting effect of God's perfection' (*GWM* I:111). As I will discuss in Chapters 2–3, the difference between the language of 'includes' and 'effect' is of no little significance.
114. *GWM* I:103 (quoting Aquinas, *Summa Contra Gentiles* II.6.1).

Therefore, Brian J. Shanley is correct when he interprets the language of primary and secondary causation as describing a metaphysical relationship: 'The primary-secondary couplet helps make it clear that the causalities operate at different metaphysical levels. A secondary cause is a real cause acting through its own intrinsic power to produce a commensurate effect, but only insofar as it acts in dependence upon the primary cause (*in virtute primi agentis*).'[115] Shanley also argues that, for Aquinas, the nature of this metaphysical relationship between God and creatures is predicated upon an understanding of God as Creator. He explains,

> As Creator, God utterly and uniquely transcends the categorical order of mundane causes (for example, necessary and contingent) so as to be no threat to created causes but rather their enabling origin. The same God who transcends the created order is also intimately and immanently present within that order as upholding all causes in their causing, including the human will. The Creator God is not a rival in danger of overpowering human agency, but rather the one who generously creates us to be genuinely free in imitation of God's own freedom.[116]

This is what Robert Sokolowski calls the 'Christian distinction'[117] – that God transcends and is not part of the created order – and it is this distinction, established by the doctrine of creation *ex nihilo*, that secures the non-competitive nature of the Creator-creature relation and undergirds the logic of primary and secondary causation.

In order to parse this out in a bit more detail, it is worth taking a brief glance at two fundamental principles of dual causality developed in Aquinas' discussion of divine government in *Summa theologiae* Ia.105, from which Webster draws in his articulation of the matter. The first principle states that two agents can be the cause of a single act if those agents are not of the same order of being. 'One action does not proceed from two agents of the same order. But nothing hinders the same action from proceeding from a primary and secondary agent.'[118] Aquinas articulates this principle in response to an objection which states that the same act cannot proceed simultaneously from two agents, and therefore divine determinism is the unavoidable conclusion of the fact that God works in the creature – i.e. God is solely causal. Aquinas objects to the premise and thereby the conclusion. Crucial to his argument is his conviction that God (primary agent) does not act upon creatures (secondary agents) as an efficient cause alone, but

---

115. Brian J. Shanley, 'Divine Causation and Human Freedom in Aquinas', *American Catholic Philosophical Quarterly* 72:1 (1998): 108.
116. Shanley, 'Divine Causation and Human Freedom in Aquinas', 100.
117. Cf. Robert Sokolowski, *The God of Faith and Reason: Foundations of Christian Theology* (Washington, DC: The Catholic University of America Press, 1982, 1994), 1–52.
118. *ST* Ia.105.5 ad 2.

rather as a final and formal cause as well.[119] The latter is particularly important: as formal cause, God gives creaturely agents their forms, including 'active powers', and preserves those forms that creatures might move towards their end (God who is the *summum bonum*).[120] Aquinas makes recourse to the Aristotelian schema of a fourfold causality in order to give conceptual expression to the theological-metaphysical point that 'God works in things in such a manner that things have their proper operation.'[121]

The second principle Aquinas develops in his discussion of divine government expresses the same fundamental logic as the first principle but does so in terms of 'interior' and 'exterior' principles of action. Creatures are moved by both an interior and exterior principle of action, the latter being the cause of the former. 'To be moved voluntarily, is to be moved from within, that is, by an interior principle: yet this interior principle may be caused by an exterior principle; and so to be moved from within is not repugnant to being moved by another.'[122] Aquinas articulates this principle in response to an objection which states that for an action to be voluntary it must arise from the interior inclination of the will, and therefore the will cannot be moved by another (i.e. God). A similar logic seems to be at work in the prior objection which states that God cannot move the creature's will because 'whatever is moved from without, is forced'.[123] Aquinas responds by questioning the assumption that God as an external principle of action is somehow in competition with the creature's will as an interior principle of action. Crucial to his argument is the conviction that God is the creator and sustainer of the creature's 'power of willing' and of the will's interior inclination towards the good.[124] As Creator, God is able to move the will 'efficiently by inclining it interiorly' and therefore non-coercively.[125] Or, as Simon Oliver has argued, creation *ex nihilo* is not an ordinary

---

119. Webster notes that the advent of modernity involved a reduction of divine causality to efficient causality, with deleterious effects on theological conceptions of the God-creature relation (*GWM* I:109, 188). Kenneth L. Schmitz narrates the transformation of Aristotle's fourfold causal structure in the seventeenth century in a slightly different manner. According to Schmitz, the formal cause ceases to be a cause at all, the final cause is reduced to subjective anthropology, the efficient cause is transformed to mean something like 'active force' rather than 'productive' being, and the material cause is analysed in terms of qualities rather than potencies (Kenneth L. Schmitz, *The Texture of Being: Essays in First Philosophy*, ed. Paul O'Herron (Washington, DC: The Catholic University of America Press, 2007), 32–5).

120. Aquinas also talks about *esse* as the formal principle of all things (cf. *ST* Ia.4.1 obj. 3, 7.1 resp., 8.1 resp.), which gives rise to the interpretive question as to whether this 'being' is God himself or created being, but this is not what I am talking about here.

121. *ST* Ia.105.5 resp. Cf. Simon Oliver, 'Aquinas and Aristotle's Teleology', *Nova et Vetera* 11:3 (2013): 849–70.

122. *ST* Ia.105.4 ad 2.

123. *ST* Ia.105.4 obj. 1.

124. *ST* Ia.105.4 resp.

125. Shanley, 'Divine Causation and Human Freedom in Aquinas', 112.

causal act 'so much as the intrinsic basis of all causality'.[126] God's creative causality does not compete with or stifle the creature's free causality, but is its original and enabling source.

Both of these principles – that two agents can be the cause of a single act if they are not of the same order of being, and that a human action can arise from both an exterior and interior principle because God moves the creature to act by giving and sustaining an interior principle of action – are key aspects of Webster's mature account of the God-creature relation. As we have argued, these principles are established by fundamental tenets of the doctrine of creation and fleshed out in the doctrine of providence. At several points in this book, I will demonstrate how these principles have a widespread effect on Webster's theology of grace and of creaturely action and mediation. Webster's forays into the doctrines of creation and providence coincide with a reconfiguring of the architectonic shape of his theological system whereby the works of nature become the context in which the works of grace are situated and interpreted. The consequences for his theology of grace and pneumatology are significant. In particular, grace comes to be understood as those divine actions and gifts (infused habits or virtues) which perfect created nature. The operations of the Spirit do not override but preserve the operations of nature, moving the creature interiorly by bestowing, conserving and governing creaturely powers. The significance of this retooled theology of grace will be seen in a number of areas – not only the doctrines of regeneration and sanctification, but also inspiration and illumination, revelation and anthropology, as well as ecclesial action and sacramental mediation.

These developments also cause Webster to reconsider his earlier polemic (from the late 1990s and early 2000s) against the doctrine of infused grace and the idiom of virtue and practice.[127] For now, it is sufficient for us to draw attention to this development and to state that it involves no relaxation of Webster's prior concerns to register the radical distinction between God and creatures and to emphasize the priority of divine creativity in relation to human action. The difference lies in the doctrines which Webster employs to make these theological points. In his mature theology, the doctrine of creation carries much of the weight once laid upon the doctrine of election, Christology and an eschatological theology of grace. And so, for example, instead of resisting the theological problems of naturalism and rationalism via the works of grace alone, Webster's mature theology does so by also developing an account of created nature in which there is no 'pure nature' and an account of created reason in which there is no 'pure reason'.[128] Instead of resisting the idiom of virtue and practice because it runs the risk of theological immanentism, Webster's mature theology simply contextualizes that language

---

126. Simon Oliver, 'Trinity, Motion and Creation *Ex Nihilo*', in *Creation and the God of Abraham*, eds. David B. Burrell, Carlo Cogliati, Janet M. Soskice, and William R. Stoeger (Cambridge: Cambridge University Press, 2010), 141.
127. This topic will be discussed in Chapters 3 and 5.
128. See, for example, *DW*, 180–2.

within an account of divine creativity via a theology of creation, regeneration and the Spirit. The mature Webster believes that the doctrine of creation provides the resources by which to register the Creator-creature distinction as well as the priority of divine action, yet in a way that is less contrastive and competitive,[129] and therefore which opens 'logical and theological space' for a more robust account of creaturely being and action.[130]

1.6 Conclusion

In conclusion, I would like to summarize what this chapter has sought to accomplish and then gesture towards the function of the remaining chapters of this book in relation to what has been laid out here. In the first half of this chapter, I mapped Webster's theological development in terms of three phases – Christocentric, Trinitarian and Theocentric – drawing attention to the way in which he orders theology as a whole and the implications this has for his conception of the God-creature relation. In particular, I sought to convey the ways in which Webster's evolving conception of the 'material centre' and 'heuristic key' of Christian theology shapes the way he grounds, contextualizes and depicts the relation-in-distinction between God and creatures. In the second half of this chapter, I offered a conceptual analysis of three aspects of Webster's mature theology that guide his characterization of the God-creature relation: doctrine of divine perfection, theory of mixed relations and concept of dual causality. I sought to show how Webster's 'non-contrastive' and 'non-comparative' account of divine perfection funded a characterization of God's relation to creatures as 'non-real' and 'non-reciprocal', which in turn opened the logical and theological space for a 'non-competitive' account of divine and human agency.

I have laid out this developmental narrative and conceptual analysis in order to provide a heuristic framework for understanding Webster's theology, particularly as it relates to his evolving account of the relation-in-distinction between God and creatures. The remaining chapters of the book will have a twofold function: (1) to demonstrate the explanatory power of my heuristic framework, and (2) to provide a more detailed and nuanced exposition of key elements of Webster's understanding of the God-creature relation.[131] I will achieve this by analysing four doctrinal loci in Webster's thought – Christology (hypostatic relation), ecclesiology (redemptive relation), bibliology (communicative relation) and theological theology (rational relation) – each of which will be the focus of a single chapter. These loci have been chosen because they were topics to which Webster devoted much attention,

---

129. *CG*, x.
130. Cf. Sokolowski, 'Creation and Christian Understanding', 179–92.
131. It is worth reminding the reader that I have not attempted to defend the heuristic framework in Chapter 1 (beyond offering a few illustrative quotations); its defence will be the demonstration of its usefulness in Chapters 2–5.

they are helpful vantage points from which to demonstrate the broad contours of the developmental narrative laid out in this chapter, and they draw attention to different aspects of Webster's understanding of the relation between God and creatures, thereby giving us a holistic picture of his thought.

The chapters on Christology and ecclesiology (Chapters 2–3) should be read together as demonstrating similar elements of the aforementioned narrative. This is due both to the material interconnectedness of the topics as well as to the fact that Webster engaged these topics to some degree in the early 1980s, meaning we are able to trace his thought on the matter from the beginning to the end of his career and thereby display the broadest level of development from Christocentric to Trinitarian to Theocentric. The chapters on bibliology and theological theology (Chapters 4–5) should also be read together as demonstrating similar elements of the aforementioned narrative. This is due both to the material interconnectedness of the topics (the creature's rational relation to God is grounded in God's communicative relation to the creature) as well as to the fact that Webster begins to publish constructive accounts of these matters around the same time – near the end of his tenure in Wycliffe and his transition to Oxford (the mid- to late 1990s). Thus, the analysis of these chapters begins in the middle of Webster's theological development and works its way towards his mature thoughts on Scripture and reason. This will allow us to provide a more detailed exposition of the second half of Webster's theology, where he formed an identity as a 'theologian's theologian'[132] – not only as one of the foremost systematic theologians in the contemporary English-speaking world, but also as one who saw the task of prophetically reminding fellow theologians of the theological and spiritual nature of their common vocation as a significant part of his personal vocation.

---

132. The phrase comes from East, 'John Webster', 334.

Chapter 2

CHRISTOLOGY

2.1 Introduction

This chapter will explore John Webster's dogmatic Christology.[1] It will seek to expound the way in which Webster construes the relation between the divine and human natures of Christ and how this influences his characterization of Jesus' human history. This doctrinal locus will provide a helpful window into the development of Webster's thought regarding the relation between theology and economy as well as raise a constructive question about the relation between narrative description and metaphysical ambition in the Christological task. The main argument will be laid out in three sections followed by an excursus. The first and third sections will analyse Webster's early and mature Christology respectively, and the second section will map the crucial theological moves that precipitated the development from the former to the latter.[2] My thesis is a fairly simple one: Webster's understanding of the relation between the divine and human natures of Christ shifts from an emphasis on indivisibility and identity to an emphasis on distinction and asymmetry. There is a corresponding shift in Webster's characterization of Jesus' human history: from grounding the unsubstitutability of Jesus' identity in the narrative of his human history to grounding his human history in the immanent life of God. These shifts reflect a larger movement in his thought regarding the relation between theology and economy and are reflected in his developing understanding of the relation between narrative description and metaphysical ambition.

In this way, the argument of this chapter will seek to demonstrate the explanatory power of two elements of the heuristic framework given in Chapter 1. First, it

---

1. Although dogmatic and moral Christology are closely related in Webster's work, for the sake of clarity and argument I will prescind from discussion of his moral Christology, which focuses of the relation between Christ's work and Christian moral action, in this chapter.

2. A note about sources and periodization: my discussion of Webster's early Christology will draw primarily from his writings in the 1980s, and for his mature theology I will focus primarily on volume 1 of *GWM*. My identification of the key transitions in his Christology will draw from a series of articles and essays from the 1990s and 2000s.

will draw attention to the significance of the two primary developmental shifts in Webster's thought – from Christocentric to Trinitarian, and from Trinitarian to Theocentric – for his understanding of the hypostatic union. Second, it will demonstrate how the doctrines of divine perfection and of creation (especially teaching about mixed relations) exercise a governing function in Webster's mature theology, even in Christology. But this chapter will also raise a question that will introduce some complexity into the understanding of Webster's movement from Barth to Thomas laid out in Chapter 1: How are we to understand his use of the language of 'inclusion' when describing the relation between the divine processions and missions? It is a question of some significance for our analysis of Webster's mature thought on the relation between theology and economy and therefore between God and creatures.

2.2 Early Christology: Divine identity and narrative description

Webster's early theology is characterized by a thoroughgoing Christocentrism learned from Eberhard Jüngel. Christology is the 'material centre' and 'heuristic key' of all Christian doctrine.[3] In his early years, Webster was convinced that the many ills of modern theology find their root in the steady 'displacement' of the figure of Jesus as the material epicentre of theology, a point to which we will return in due course. Therefore, his early Christology is concerned with depicting the person of Jesus as the sum and substance of the Christian gospel and with finding conceptual resources by which to keep the uniqueness and unsubstitutability of his identity front and centre. This leads us to one of the unique and defining characteristics of Webster's Christology at this point, namely the way in which he dovetails Jüngel's emphasis on the divine identity of Jesus with Hans Frei's emphasis on the narrative identity of Jesus.

We begin with Webster's Christology of *divine identity*, which, following Jüngel, is defined in close connection with the human history of Jesus. Beginning with the union of the divine and human natures in the one person of Christ, and thereby avoiding any definition of the divine and human natures *in abstracto*, Webster offers a short yet suggestive description of their relation:

> We don't mean that he is composed of two different elements. We mean something more precious. We mean that the *whole* of Jesus is human and the *whole* of Jesus is divine. His humanity and his divinity aren't in competition: they are identical. The human is the divine and the divine is the human. What is true of God is true of this man. What is true of this man is true of God.[4]

While the precise meaning of the word 'identical' is somewhat difficult to pin down, it is not difficult, given his dependence on Jüngel and Jüngel's dependence

---

3. *CG*, 151.
4. *GIH*, 11.

on Barth, to catch the theological force of Webster's claim. Like Jüngel and Barth, the early Webster sees Christology as the doctrinal locus where one discerns and depicts the relation between theology and economy. The theological claim that Jesus' humanity and divinity are not in competition but 'identical' is motivated by a concern to emphasize the inseparability of God's immanent being and economic activity. If divinity and humanity are 'identical' in Jesus Christ, then there is no other God than the one revealed in his particular human history. This is a point that Webster reiterates throughout his book *God Is Here* (1983), stating, for example:

> [T]he miracle at the heart of the Christian faith in God is this: in Jesus, God has shown us who he really is. Jesus' life – his teaching, death, resurrection and exaltation – don't merely point us to some incomprehensible mystery. They don't even simply illustrate or express a God who is too wrapped about with clouds of glory to show himself to us. Jesus *embodies* God.[5]

In other words, God's self-revelation is identical with the human history of Jesus (the incarnation), meaning there is no separation or interval between revelation's human form and its divine content. Webster seems to think Jüngel's strongly Lutheran interpretation of the *communicatio idiomatum* allows one to articulate this fundamental point. This interpretation has significant theological consequences for Webster's doctrine of God, which will become clear when we discuss his account of Christ's passion, but first we must explore further the understanding of the incarnation that undergirds his construal of the relation between Christ's divinity and humanity in terms of 'identity'.

For the early Webster, the incarnation is an event of divine 'becoming'. He states, '[H]e is a God who *becomes*. Of course, God cannot become *better* than he is, for God is perfect and his perfection cannot be added to. But he can *become himself*. And the way in which God becomes himself is in becoming a man: "The Word *became* flesh" (Jn. 1.14).'[6] By defining divine perfection so as to include divine self-becoming, Webster can construe God's act of becoming incarnate as the unique form, not change, of his divine perfection. As with Jüngel so also with Webster: there is an incarnational motivation behind this metaphysically and theologically freighted concept of 'becoming'. By affirming that 'becoming' is not accidental to God's 'being' but rather the self-determined form of his being, then one can affirm in the strongest possible way that there is no competition or separation between God and Jesus' human history. As Webster explains in his discussion of this theme in Jüngel's thought, 'it seeks to take the history of Jesus with full seriousness, using the language of "being" to state the identity between that history and the life of God'.[7]

---

5. *GIH*, 48.
6. *GIH*, 55–6.
7. *EJ*, 69. The concept of 'being' used here has distinctly Hegelian hues. Like Barth and Jüngel, Webster does not abandon metaphysical or Trinitarian language altogether but seeks to rework them around his central Christological affirmations, which are undoubtedly influenced by Hegel's metaphysics of becoming.

As a corollary of God's self-determination to be himself in the flesh of Jesus Christ, Webster argues that Jesus' humanity is the humanity of God, and therefore the story of his human life is the story of God's life. The incarnation 'means that God has a life-story. God's life is so bound up with Jesus' life that the story of Jesus is the story of God'.[8] He makes the same point elsewhere using a slightly different idiom: 'God *identifies himself* in the man Jesus.'[9] The concept of God's self-identification is drawn, once again, from Jüngel's Christology. It is designed to affirm God's presence in the world *as* a human being in such a way that highlights not only the divine identity of Jesus but also the human identity of God. In fact, the aforementioned quotes make clear that the former is grounded in the latter.[10] For Webster, this language does not imply any compromise of Jesus' life as a human history but rather specifies that this particular human history is part of the divine identity: 'The history of Jesus [is] to be understood as the *essentia dei* and not as a simulacrum of the divine, an image not in the end possessed of the substantial properties of that which it signifies.'[11] Webster's focus is on the indivisibility and inseparability of the divine and human natures in Christ, with very little being said about the asymmetry or distinction between them, because incarnational 'becoming' is interpreted not so much as the assumption of that which is not God but rather as the identification of what it means for God to be God. The Jüngelian concept of 'identification' reinforces the point that the humanity of Jesus is 'the actuality of God in the world',[12] and therefore that God's being and presence in the world can be discerned only by tracing the human story of this particular man from Nazareth.

This last point leads us into Webster's Christology of *narrative identity*. There is a certain difficulty in assessing the place of narrative categories in

8. *GIH*, 55.

9. *GIH*, 114. Cf. *EJ*, 36; John Webster, 'Eberhard Jüngel', in *The Modern Theologians: An Introduction to Christian Theology in the Twentieth Century*, vol. 1, ed. David F. Ford (Oxford: Blackwell, 1989), 96.

10. Elsewhere, Webster draws out the implications of God's self-identification in the man Jesus: 'All this means, then, that Jesus' flesh is the way in which God is God. And so Jesus is God among us. To think of Jesus properly is to think of him *as God*. And, no less important, to think of God is to think of him *as Jesus*' ('Jesus – God for Us', 90).

11. John Webster, 'Atonement, History and Narrative', *Theologische Zeitschrift* 42 (1986): 119. This quote manifests the influence of Jüngel's interpretation of Barth's Trinitarian theology in *Gottes Sein ist im Werden*, which won the young Webster's admiration (*EJ*, 16–7). Jüngel suggests that the promise of Barth's theology lays in his identification of God's being *pro se* with his being *pro nobis*, thereby affirming that God's essence is identical with his revealed being (cf. John Webster, 'Jesus' Speech, God's Word: An Introduction to Eberhard Jüngel', *Christian Century* 112 [1995]: 1177). The distinction between God's immanent and economic life, or between his essence and will, is a false one, because 'God's way of being himself is by being God for us' (*EJ*, 18).

12. *EJ*, 36.

Webster's early Christology because there is a level of circularity in the way he construes the relationship between theological-metaphysical propositions and narrative description. Formally, he often states that the priority is on the latter, but materially, they seem to be mutually interpretive. In some places his focus on narrative description leads to an affirmation of the divine identity of the man Jesus, and in other places his metaphysical claims about the humanity of God lead to the necessity of narrative description. But all in all, the primary function of the concept of 'narrative' or 'story' in Webster's early Christology is to draw attention to the unique and unsubstitutable identity of the man Jesus Christ.

The first way narrative accomplishes this task is by offering 'an identity-description of a particular historical agent'.[13] Webster's comments on this topic are highly instructive for our present discussion, so it is worth quoting him at length:

> [Narrative] identifies personal agents in a manner that cannot without irreparable damage be translated into terms other than itself. Thus in a doctrine of the atonement, the personal identity of the atoner is to be rendered in narrative terms, by rehearsing his biography, tracing the movements of his history. And in describing Jesus in this way, we are implicitly refusing any suggestion that his history is less than primordial, and so are asserting that his identity can only be grasped in and with the actualities of his life-story. The more we shift towards propositional, the more readily we translate out of the temporal categories of the evangelical narratives, the less secure of our grasp of Jesus' *Istigkeit*, of that which made him into what he was.[14]

Here Webster is indebted to Hans Frei's concept of 'narrative identity'. According to Frei, 'a person is as he acts', and therefore personal identity is best conveyed in the form of narrative, which traces the intentional action of a particular agent over the course of time.[15] Like Frei, Webster's anthropology concentrates on the concrete and particular, believing that the attempt to offer a metaphysical or essentialist definition of 'human nature' is an abstraction that distracts theology from that which truly constitutes personal identity. Webster states, 'Man with a capital M doesn't exist: there is no such creature as Man in general. There are only particular men and women, with their own individual life-stories, fears and hopes, griefs and delights.'[16] It is one's actions in history, not a nature or state of being, that constitute personal identity. The same logic is applied to Christology, leading Webster to

---

13. Webster, 'Atonement, History and Narrative', 120.
14. Webster, 'Atonement, History and Narrative', 120.
15. Hans W. Frei, *The Identity of Jesus Christ: The Hermeneutical Bases of Dogmatic Theology* (Philadelphia, PA: Fortress Press, 1967), 45.
16. *GIH*, 78.

defy traditional discussions about the relation between the divine and human natures of Jesus Christ in favour of depicting his identity in narrative categories as an integrated whole. 'Story', as opposed to abstract 'theory', is proposed as the key to explaining the Christological claim that 'Jesus Christ is true man and true God'.[17] To shift a description of the identity of Jesus Christ out of the categories of narrative and deed into those of proposition and idea would inevitably involve the loss of some aspect of his uniqueness and unsubstitutability, which are grounded in his historically enacted identity.

Therefore, secondly, Webster makes the closely related claim that narrative description is 'a way of drawing attention to the sheer phenomenality of the man Jesus'.[18] The use of narrative functions to resist metaphysical abstraction and keep Christological reflection rooted in the concrete particularities of Jesus' human history. It calls our attention back to the details of Jesus' life as narrated in the Gospels – the particular intentions, concrete events, personal interactions and dramatic episodes that make up his unique and unsubstitutable identity. The point Webster is seeking to secure is that the Gospel narratives are not an illustration of an ideal or a symbolic representation of some ulterior reality, but rather they 'furnish a primary idiom for the identification and description of Jesus as personal subject and agent'.[19] This conviction leads Webster to share Frei's scepticism towards any attempt to translate Jesus' personal identity into categories other than its narrative form. This does not mean that he excises all forms of propositional analysis from the Christological task, but rather that he clearly designates such analysis as a secondary and derivative level of discourse. Theological propositions seek to 'analyze, abbreviate and condense complexes of events, and ... in so doing they are parasitic upon those events and not ultimately primitive'.[20] And yet, throughout the 1980s we find almost no discussion of the technical vocabulary of classical Christology – nature, substance, hypostasis – in Webster's writings. Narrative categories enjoy prominence in his early Christology. Why?

There is a thoroughly modern presupposition that seems to undergird this emphasis upon the primacy of narrative description, namely that the historical is real and actual. Metaphysical theory, insofar as it seeks to describe or define the natures of created realities that undergird but are not constituted by the particularities of time and space and events, is viewed as an abstraction from reality (or at least reality as it can be known by human beings) and, even worse, an abdication of theological responsibility to the biblical materials. Narrative

---

17. *GIH*, 12.
18. Webster, 'Atonement, History and Narrative', 120.
19. Webster, 'Atonement, History and Narrative', 121. Cf. Frei, *The Identity of Jesus Christ*, 45–6.
20. Webster, 'Atonement, History and Narrative', 122.

categories help Christology remain grounded in historical reality.[21] This emphasis is developed, in part, as a polemic against various strands of nineteenth- and twentieth-century German theology – e.g. Hegelian idealism, Bultmannian demythologization and existentialism, and Jüngelian monism – that Webster found troubling precisely because they devalue the historical particularity of the gospel.[22] According to Webster, much modern Protestant theology has been bedevilled by a 'displacement' of the figure of Jesus, whereby he becomes a symbol or instantiation of something more basic (e.g. God-consciousness in Schleiermacher's theology, religious morality in Ritschl's theology). As a result, Christian theology looks elsewhere for its view of God (e.g. philosophical theism), humanity (e.g. reflective human subjectivity) and the world.[23] Webster utilizes the concept of narrative, in part, to resist various forms of modern idealism and their consequences. By enabling the theologian 'to adhere to the particularity of Jesus' human history', narrative description ensures that 'there does not occur [a] kind of sublation of Jesus' history'[24] and therefore, that the uniqueness Christ's identity as Mediator and the unsubstitutability of his saving deeds are nothing 'less than primordial'.[25]

---

21. A primary reason why Webster's early Christology supplements Jüngel's development of Christ's divine identity with Frei's concept of narrative identity is because he believes the former has a decidedly thin and truncated depiction of Jesus' human history (cf. *CG*, 151–90; John Webster, 'Chalcedonian Christology after Berdyaev in Barth and Jungel', in *Fifty Year Commemoration to the Life of Nicolai Berdyaev (1877–1948)*, ed. George O. Mazur (New York, NY: Semenenko Foundation, 1999), 45–58). According to Webster, Jüngel's writings depict Jesus as an eschatological interruption of the world, not a human embedded within the world. They accentuate Jesus' identity as God's self-revelation (an interceptive speech-event) to such an extent that his identity as a personal agent is muted. The reasons for this eclipse of Jesus' humanity are many: a heavily futurist eschatology, a prioritization of Jesus' words over his deeds, an investment in historical-critical methodologies that do not take the narrative shape of the Gospels seriously, the influence of existentialism (Fuchs; Bultmann) and a preoccupation with ontological questions. And the consequences of this eclipse are many: Jesus lacks location, history and personal agency, and the revelatory aspects of Jesus' work overshadow the soteriological. Therefore, according to Webster, Jüngel's Christology lacks dramatic shape and fails to describe adequately the historical and human form of God's presence in the world: 'Jungel's Christology communicates only imperfectly how Jesus is absolute presence, the embodiment now of the divine "I am"' (*CG*, 189).
22. For Webster's critique of Hegel on this score, see Webster, 'Atonement, History and Narrative', 117–8. For his critique of Bultmann, see John Webster, *Rudolph Bultmann: An Introductory Interpretation* (Leicester: Religious and Theological Studies Fellowship, 1980), 28–9. For his critique of Jüngel, see *EJ*, 5, 60–1, 106, 116–7.
23. *CG*, 151–3.
24. Webster, 'Atonement, History and Narrative', 119–20.
25. Webster, 'Atonement, History and Narrative', 130, n. 67.

This leads us to the third and final function of narrative in Webster's early Christology: it ensures that the doctrine of God (theology proper) is derived from and accountable to the concrete events of Jesus' human history (economy of salvation). An illuminating example of this dynamic can be seen in his exposition of Christ's death in *God Is Here*. As I noted earlier, Webster construes the relation between the divine and human natures of Christ as a relation of 'identity', which opens the door for a strongly Lutheran interpretation of the *communicatio idiomatum* and an understanding of the incarnation as an event in which God 'becomes himself' as a man. This implies that the events of Jesus' human life are an identification and revelation of the nature of God's life. When viewed in this light, the 'events of Good Friday and Easter Sunday' tell us that God's life is 'a life which somehow includes death'.[26] For Webster, this claim is grounded in the fact that God's life is love (he cites 1 John 4:8), the nature of which is defined in reference to the action of the triune God in the economy of salvation rather than the intra-Trinitarian love of the divine persons. As a result, love is defined by the event of Jesus' crucifixion as always involving sacrifice and death: 'Real love always involves death – it involves giving yourself up for the sake of the one whom you love.'[27] Therefore, God's nature as love is inextricably bound to his saving action, so much so that Webster can say, 'God is love, *because* he laid down his life in order to share it with us.'[28] It may have been better if he had used the word 'therefore' instead of 'because', for the latter seems to imply God's nature as love is somehow dependent upon his sacrificial action in the economy as the man Jesus Christ, thereby making the incarnation and cross essential to God's being.[29] That Webster is thinking somewhat along these lines (hence following the path of Jüngel) is demonstrated by the fact that he interprets the doctrine of the Trinity as a sort of gloss on the passion narrative. He states,

> And the God who is love, the God whose life is life and death bound up together, is the Lord who is three-in-one .... [T]o say that God is three-in-one is another way of talking about his death-in-life. As Father, God sends the Son in love to die in the world. As Son, God suffers that death in all its squalor and shame. As Spirit, God brings new life, tearing death apart and pouring himself out upon us. The triune God is the God who is love, the Lord whose life is bound up with death.[30]

26. *GIH*, 56.
27. *GIH*, 57.
28. *GIH*, 57 (emphasis mine).
29. For a critique of such a view on the basis that it makes not only creation but also evil essential to the life of God, see David Bentley Hart, 'No Shadow of Turning: On Divine Impassibility', *Pro Ecclesia* 11:2 (2002): 184–206.
30. *GIH*, 57.

In this way, the passion narrative gives shape and content not only to Jesus' identity (what it means for Jesus to be God) but also to God's identity (what it means for God to be God).

It has been my argument that Webster's early Christology (1980s) is marked by an attempt to weave together Jüngel's Christology of divine identity with Frei's Christology of narrative identity. From Jüngel, he absorbed an understanding of the relation between the divine and human natures of Christ which had heavily Lutheran hues: there is an 'identity' and a radical communication of idioms between the natures. These emphases allowed Webster to affirm a strong correspondence between theology and economy, between God's being *in se* and his action *pro nobis*. The human history of Jesus Christ is God's self-identification. From Frei, Webster borrowed the concept of narrative and used it to draw attention to the unique and unsubstitutable identity of Jesus Christ. This emphasis allowed Webster to resist the influence of modern idealism and metaphysical abstraction on Christology, while also ensuring that the doctrine of God is derived from and accountable to the concrete events of Jesus' human history. Much about Webster's Christology will change by the time we get to his essays in *God without Measure*, but before discussing the Christology found in those works, it is worth drawing attention to two crucial developments from the 1990s to 2000s that act as catalysts for the change.

2.3 Christology in transition: The priority of God in se

The developments are as follows: First, Webster recognized a need to ground Christology in the doctrine of the Trinity; and second, he discovered the importance of classical teaching about God *in se* and its implications for Christology.

The first development found its initial expression in a brief article written in response to George Hunsinger's critical review of Hans Frei's book *The Identity of Jesus Christ*.[31] Hunsinger had argued that Frei's formal proposal about the non-symbolic nature of narratives led to a Christology in which '[a]ll the weight seems to fall on Jesus as a specific and unsubstitutable human being', thereby bringing him dangerously close to the errors of 'Nestorianism and adoptionism'.[32] In response, Webster offers a more sympathetic reading of Frei's book regarding the clarity of its affirmation of Jesus' divinity, yet he does share Hunsinger's overall anxiety about the use of narrative categories in Christology. Webster suggests that 'if it is to achieve its ends it needs anchorage in the doctrine of God, and more specifically in trinitarian and incarnational language'.[33] He goes on to argue that Frei's resistance

---

31. John Webster, 'Response to George Hunsinger', *MoTh* 8:2 (1992): 129–32.
32. George Hunsinger, 'Hans Frei as Theologian: The Quest for a Generous Orthodoxy', *MoTh* 8:2 (1992): 115–6.
33. Webster, 'Response to George Hunsinger', 129.

to moving from narrative description to analytic categories leads him to overlook those aspects of the Gospels which link 'Jesus' humanity to its divine ground'.[34] This new emphasis in Webster's thought does not qualify Frei's insistence that Jesus' identity is 'unsubstitutable', but rather suggests that his unsubstitutability is 'a function of the being and act of God'.[35] The divine life, not simply the irreducible narrative sequence of his historical life, is constitutive of Jesus' particular identity.

This desire to ground Christology in the doctrine of the Trinity stems, in part, from a developing conviction that narrative categories (on their own) are not durable enough to ground the unique and unsubstitutable identity of Jesus Christ, and therefore are not able to sufficiently resist the idealism and moralism of much nineteenth-century modern Christology.[36] This point is important for our understanding of the development of Webster's Christology. He argues,

> Perhaps one of the major reasons for the growth of moralistic and non-incarnational Christologies in the nineteenth century was the dislocation of Christology from the doctrine of the triune being of God: once the Christian doctrine of God has fallen into disrepair and is no longer operative, the doctrine of the incarnation quickly comes to seem a merely arbitrary bit of speculation, leaving theology free to expound the humanity of Jesus as if it could be had in abstraction from his identity as divine agent.[37]

This quote comes from an essay on the incarnation originally published in 2001. At this point, Webster is no longer making recourse to Jesus' 'particular narratable identity' in order to resist speculative idealism and its resultant moralism, but rather to Jesus' identity as 'divine agent'. Nor is Webster narrating the pathology of modern theology in terms of the steady displacement of the figure of Jesus, but rather in terms of the dislocation of Christology from the doctrine of the Trinity. Crucially, both of these shifts are connected: Jesus' identity as 'divine agent' is

---

34. Webster, 'Response to George Hunsinger', 130.
35. Webster, 'Response to George Hunsinger', 131.
36. Darren Sumner suggests that Webster is also motivated by a desire to resist forms of historicism that have found their way into Christology since the nineteenth century ('Christocentrism and the Immanent Trinity: Identifying Theology's Pattern and Norm', in *The Task of Dogmatics: Explorations in Theological Method*, eds. Oliver D. Crisp and Fred Sanders (Grand Rapids, MI: Zondervan, 2017), 152–4).
37. *WC*, 149. According to Webster's logic, there is a direct line of causation from doctrinal atrophy to idealism to moralism. Once Jesus' identity is no longer grounded in the doctrine of the Trinity, his identity is not viewed as irreducible but becomes a 'symbol', 'archetype' or 'expression' of something more basic and general – often a particular moral 'ideal' – and this in turn opens the door for human action to become the real focus of Christology (*WC*, 126–9).

supplied by Trinitarian doctrine, without which the humanity of Jesus becomes theologically unintelligible.[38]

This development in Webster's thought is exhibited in the way he begins to employ the ontological categories of Chalcedon – substance, nature and person – in his theology of the incarnation. So, for example, substance language – stemming from the creedal affirmation that the Son is *homoousios* with the Father – plays a significant role in resisting forms of subjectivism, where the bond between Jesus and God is defined in moral or spiritual terms rather than ontological terms. He writes,

> Ontological concepts, above all, the concept of 'substance', resist the debasement of Christology to spirituality, and so function as an essential element of theological realism. Christology which does not spell out the ontological dimensions of the person of Jesus Christ in relation to God finds it very difficult to resist the pull of subjectivism and moralism, and quickly turns Jesus into a mythological condensation of the religious and ethical commitments of the believing self. The use of ontology is thus a way of ensuring that the identity of Jesus is not subject to the vagaries of religious use, and that what faith confesses is who Jesus indissolubly *is*.[39]

Webster is now convinced that narrative categories are insufficient for ensuring the 'unsubstitutability' of Jesus' identity and that ontological categories are necessary. And yet, it is important to see that Webster's use of these ontological categories is limited and very specific at this point in his thought. He makes a distinction between two types of metaphysics: 'descriptive' and 'analytic'. Descriptive metaphysics focuses on 'the nature of substances', while analytic metaphysics focuses on 'the relation between substances'.[40] This distinction is then employed in a discussion of the hypostatic union, where Webster argues that the Chalcedonian confession primarily employs 'analytic', not 'descriptive', metaphysics. The two natures are not considered in the abstract or in isolation from one another, so as to give a definition of their individual substances, but rather they are considered

---

38. For Webster, the humanity of Jesus is an act of the triune God: 'To be thoroughly incarnational we need a doctrine of the triune God – of God the Father who freely wills this act, of God the Son who is freely obedient and assumes flesh, of God the Spirit through whom God empowers the Son and mediates his incarnate presence' (*WC*, 138). Later in the same essay, Webster argues that this triune act is the basis of the man Jesus and therefore also the basis of our knowledge of his identity: '[T]he secret of the man Jesus is the majestic, saving self-communication of God. In that act of God Jesus Christ has his basis. And in that act, too, is the basis upon which alone Jesus Christ can be known as who he is' (*WC*, 150).

39. *WC*, 122–3. The creedal language of *homoousios* was originally designed to resist forms of subordinationism (especially Arianism). Interestingly, Webster is drawing upon creedal formula to address what he considers to be the most significant modern 'heresies'.

40. *WC*, 122.

in 'the event of their union in the one subject Jesus', so as to give a definition of the relation between their substances.[41]

Webster's preference for the 'analytic' use of ontological categories seems to be motivated by his continuing concern that such categories are employed in a manner that does not overwhelm the human history. The problem with 'descriptive' metaphysics is that it can have the unfortunate effect of committing one 'to a type of abstract theism or to a docetic Christology'.[42] Such abstraction or Docetism misses the primary function of employing ontological categories within Christology, which, according to Webster, is not to 'transpose Christology out of a historical register' but rather to support a 'thoroughly historical ontology'.[43] The 'analytic' use of ontological categories achieves this goal because it focuses on the relation between the natures in the one person of Christ, rather than on the natures in themselves. In so doing, ontology specifies the identity of the historical agent depicted in the Gospel narratives: '[T]he task of ontological language is to point out the identity of the person who is here at work.'[44] Or again: '[It] is not a replacement for Jesus' history, but a means of identifying the unique subject and agent of that history.'[45] That unique agent is God the Son, who is *homoousios* with God the Father.

It is for this reason that the doctrine of the Trinity becomes so central to Webster's Christology: it specifies the divine identity of the man Jesus Christ. Hence, Webster makes reference to the doctrine of the eternal generation of the Son from the Father as that which elucidates the fact that God is the 'acting subject' of the event of the incarnation, 'the one whom we encounter in the history of Jesus'.[46] This is a point that will be expanded to great effect in Webster's mature Christology, which will be discussed in the following section. And yet, for all his newfound emphasis on the doctrine of the Trinity in the early 2000s, Webster says very little about God's life *in se*. Why? Because he is still committed to elements of an actualistic doctrine of God or at least one in which the focus remains on God's acts in the economy. The modern presupposition that the historical is the actual and real still seems to hold considerable weight for Webster at this point. Hence, divine aseity is defined primarily in terms of God's freedom-in-act rather than in terms of God's being in and of himself. This emphasis, indebted to Barth and indicative of his conviction that talk of God apart from his economic works may open the door for Christianly unspecific forms of philosophical theism, can be seen in Webster's discussion of the incarnational 'becoming' in relation to divine aseity.

In his theological exposition of the Johannine phrase 'the Word became flesh' (John 1:14) in his essay 'Incarnation' (2001), Webster seeks to establish the point

---

41. *WC*, 145.
42. *WC*, 144.
43. *WC*, 144.
44. *WC*, 144.
45. *WC*, 145.
46. *WC*, 135, 133.

that the incarnational 'becoming' in no way compromises the aseity of God. He does so by interpreting this 'becoming' as a mode of God's 'sovereign self-possession' and 'inexhaustible plenitude', as an act of God's 'immutable freedom'.[47] The Word's becoming is not a natural procession of the divine being, but rather an act of the Father's free will and the Son's free obedience, both of which imply no change in or augmentation of God. How is this so? First, the incarnation is a free act of assumption. Webster states, '"Becoming flesh" involves no abandonment of deity; the Word does not cease to be entirely himself, but rather takes over, "assumes", that which is not himself, taking it to his own being.'[48] God remains immutable and his aseity uncompromised because his 'becoming' is not the transformation of what or who he is but rather the assumption of what he is not. Second, the incarnation is a free act of self-determination. The notion of divine self-determination is clearly Barthian, and it conceives of God's being in such a way that places priority on the divine will.[49] This means that divine aseity is defined in terms of God's freedom-in-act, and thus its material content is filled out with a particular incarnational and historical density. And so, Webster can go so far as to affirm that divine aseity is not merely the ground of the incarnation but also in some sense fulfilled in the incarnation: 'God's "becoming" is God's determination of himself to be God *in this way*, to take this particular direction which is the fulfilment of his groundless aseity. Self-emptying (*kenosis*) and self-fulfilment (*plerosis*) are not antithetical, but identical.'[50] That divine aseity can be both 'groundless' and find its 'fulfilment' in the incarnation is not a contradiction for Webster, because God's *plerosis* is the freedom of his self-determination for *kenosis*. Hence, the incarnation is not the contradiction or diminution of divine aseity, but rather its historical form. Here we see Webster once again making recourse to the Jüngelian language of 'identity' in an effort to maintain the inseparability of theology and economy (theological reason cannot go behind the back of Jesus Christ and talk of God *in se* apart from his transitive works), and yet that language is supplemented by Barth's emphasis on divine freedom and aseity so as to register a proper sense of the gratuity of the incarnation and of the asymmetrical relation between the divine and human natures of Christ.

This leads us to the second major catalyst of development in Webster's Christology, namely his recognition of a need for a robust doctrine of God *in se* and his exploration of the implications of this material for his understanding of the hypostatic union. He becomes convinced that, without teaching about God's immanent perfection and processions, theology will have an improper grasp of

---

47. *WC*, 136–7.
48. *WC*, 137.
49. For Barth, the affirmation that God's being is God's act gets fleshed out in terms of the doctrine of election (located in the doctrine of God, not God's works) and Christology (God's self-election as the man Jesus Christ). A brief discussion of Webster's doctrine of election and its relation to Barth's can be found in Chapter 3.
50. *WC*, 138.

God and God's works (including the hypostatic union). Theological accounts that eschew some essential elements of speculative divinity have a tendency, according to Webster, to compromise God's freedom and to historicize God's life, either by projecting the events of the temporal economy into the eternal life of God (Moltmann) or by collapsing God's life into the economy altogether (Jenson). But Webster's concern is not just that such modern theologies have an improper grasp of the nature of divine perfection; he also fears that they have misunderstood the nature of God's action in the economy, interpreting the economy as a sort of theogony rather than as an act of free love and pure generosity. Webster's concern is that, in one way or another, God's life becomes dependent on the economy because the latter in some sense contributes to the realization or fulfilment of the former, rather than the economy being dependent on the completeness of God's life *in se*. In other words, the God-creation relation is reciprocal: God and creatures are depicted as a mutually related pair. For much modern theology, this account of the God-creature relation mirrors a conception of the hypostatic union that emphasizes the unity and identity of the divine and human natures in Christ.

And so, in his essay 'Incarnation', we find Webster beginning to grasp for ways of registering the distinction and asymmetry between the divine and human natures in the hypostatic union, so as to preserve a sense of God's immutable perfection as well as the gratuity of the divine act of incarnation. He does so, at first, by drawing upon those characteristically Reformed elements of Barth's Christology, distancing himself to some degree from the Lutheran emphases of Jüngel:

> Unless the dogma of the hypostatic union as a whole is set within the brackets of the *assumptio carnis*, then the union of the natures becomes a *unity*. Over against this, it is vital to retain a firm sense that the hypostatic union is a matter of free grace, and that in an important sense divinity and humanity are asymmetrically related, though without any impugning of the perfection of each nature. Even in union with humanity in Christ, the deity of God remains immutable – directed to the assumption of flesh, by no means a prisoner of its own unchangeableness, but nevertheless unassailably complete in itself.[51]

And yet Webster's description of God's deity as 'unassailably complete in itself' does seem to stand in some tension with his earlier remark that the incarnational 'becoming' is the 'fulfilment of his groundless aseity'. How can there be an external 'fulfilment' of that which is 'complete in itself'? Ultimately, it is not until Webster turns to the classical accounts of divine perfection and triunity, especially as found in the post-Reformed scholastics and Aquinas, that he discovers the theological, metaphysical and conceptual resources by which to speak of God's fully realized life *in se*. 'God's perfection', writes Webster, is 'the utter sufficiency, originality and plenitude of God's life in himself' apart from creatures.[52]

---

51. *WC*, 148.
52. Webster, 'Review Article', 205.

In a review article published in 2009, which discusses Alyssa Lyra Pitstick's book *Light in Darkness*, Webster spells out the implications of this conception of divine perfection for the doctrines of the Trinity and the incarnation.[53] It entails registering a twofold asymmetry: 'an asymmetry between "immanent" and "economic" in teaching about God's triune being and acts, and between the divine and human natures of the incarnate Word'.[54] In terms of the doctrine of the Trinity, this means that God's immanent fullness is the 'ground' and 'premiss' of his acts *ad extra*, including the incarnation.[55] Only when viewed through the lens of God's immanent perfection is the incarnational 'becoming' seen as an act of pure grace.[56] And so, Webster states, '[W]hat is said about the economy of God's acts *ad extra* is "suspended" from a theology of the inner divine life in its entire blessedness, and unbroken peace and fullness.'[57] What is being proposed here is a theological approach that works from teaching about God's immanent perfection towards an understanding of God's acts in the economy; theology illumines economy. This is not intended to deny the fact that God's acts in the economy reveal, and are our means of epistemic access to, God's inner being, but rather to suggest that what is revealed of God's inner life is not strictly identical with the economic form of revelation. Hence, Webster is rather critical of modern doctrines of the Trinity which depict God's inner life in dramatic terms, arguing instead that the 'economic drama does not go all the way down; it reposes on the eternal stillness of the triune being'.[58] So, for example, the concept of kenosis is not to be included in an exposition of God's inner processions (*pace* Balthasar), for such a concept does not cohere with teaching about divine aseity, according to which 'the common aseity of the persons ... is theirs by virtue of the one divine essence in which they all share from eternity'.[59] Here, Webster is no longer defining divine aseity in terms of God's freedom-in-act ('act' referring primarily to his economic works); rather, divine aseity is now defined in relation to the divine essence. This does not mean that teaching about divine aseity is removed from the economy of God's salvific acts, but only that such teaching exercises a different theological function

---

53. In his mature writings, Webster interprets the Reformed tradition as standing 'squarely within the Western Catholic tradition' in the doctrines of God and Christ ('Review Article', 205).

54. Webster, 'Review Article', 204.

55. Webster, 'Review Article', 207, 209.

56. Interestingly, Webster thought Barth could plausibly be interpreted along these lines, though many scholars beg to differ (cf. 'Review Article', 208). Although Webster believed Barth's theological intuitions were right in this regard, he became convinced that the resources found in the patristic and scholastic traditions – e.g. a theological metaphysics of God *in se* and the doctrine of creation – enabled a better articulation of the points Barth was after.

57. Webster, 'Review Article', 205.

58. Webster, 'Review Article', 207.

59. Webster, 'Review Article', 207.

in relation to those acts – namely, it helps register the fundamental distinction between uncreated and created being that grounds those acts and reveals their gracious and loving character.

Webster notes the implications of this 'asymmetry' between God's immanent being and economic acts for his understanding of the incarnation:

> [T]his means retention of a clear distinction between (though not separation or alienation of) the divine and human natures of the incarnate one, a construal of the Word's 'becoming' flesh in such a way that the Word's transcendence of the flesh is uncompromised, and a sense that even in the extremes of fleshly humiliation the Word's sovereign deity is in no way degraded. All of this, of course, is to block any suggestion that God realises his being in the *opera externa* and to steer away from the *crassa mixture* of God and creaturely being of which Calvin rather strongly disapproved.[60]

In this quote, we see *in nuce* the emphases which became characteristic of Webster's mature Christology and which will be the topic of the next section. I will examine the conceptual resources Webster employs to articulate this 'distinction' between the divine and human natures of Christ and seek to explain why making such a 'distinction' was so important to the logic of his mature theology. I will suggest that he was motivated by a concern not only to preserve divine perfection but also to highlight the gratuity and salvific efficacy of the human history of Jesus. His mature articulation of the relation between the divine and human natures of Christ reflects his larger theological project of giving a rightly ordered account of the relation between theology and economy, between God and creatures.

2.4 Mature Christology: Divine perfection and metaphysical distinction

Webster's mature theology is characterized by a theocentrism whose architectural shape is indebted largely to Aquinas. It is the doctrine of the (immanent) Trinity, not Christology, which governs all other Christian doctrines. Webster still insists that '[n]o element in a system of theology is unrelated to Christology',[61] but now he does so based on the premise that Christology 'is an integral element of the doctrine of the Trinity'.[62] This emphasis is notably different from his early theology and displays the fact that the material weight of Webster's theological system has shifted from God's economic acts to God's immanent triune being. Theology proper now precedes and governs economy, including teaching about the incarnation. These developments in the arrangement and proportion of Christian

---

60. Webster, 'Review Article', 205.
61. *GWM* I:57.
62. *GWM* I:43.

doctrine represent the movement of Webster's thought from a broadly Jüngelian and Barthian approach to a Thomist one.[63]

The consequences for Webster's Christology are various and significant. (1) The function of Christology shifts from being primarily heuristic or epistemic (Jesus Christ reveals who God is and who humans are) to soteriological (Jesus Christ reconciles sinful humanity to God). (2) The unique and unsubstitutable identity of Jesus Christ is grounded primarily in the doctrine of eternal generation rather than in the details of his human history. (3) The strict identity between the content of revelation (God *in se*) and the historical form of revelation (the man Jesus Christ) gives way to a type of correspondence that involves significant asymmetry and emphasizes the inexhaustibility of God's life even in the incarnation.[64] (4) The resolute focus on the unity of the one person of Christ gives way to an emphasis on the need to make a clear metaphysical distinction between the divine and human natures of Christ. (5) The employment of narrative description to ensure that the doctrine of God is derived from the concrete events of Jesus' human history gives way to a Christology which allows a theological metaphysics of God *in se* to carry significant weight, clarifying the character of Jesus' human history as narrated in the Gospels.

Any of these topics could provide a fruitful line of inquiry, but I will limit the current discussion to the fourth and fifth items on the list – namely the way in which Webster conceives of the relation between the divine and human natures of Christ and how this in turn shapes his characterization of the human history of Christ. We begin by looking at Webster's mature conception of the relation between the divine and human natures of Christ, approaching this topic through an analysis of two conceptual frameworks, both drawn from Aquinas, that he employs in his theology of the hypostatic union: first, the metaphysical theory of mixed relations; and second, the traditional conceptuality of processions and missions.

---

63. A particularly illuminating example of these shifts can be seen in the way Webster narrates a pathology of modern theology. It is instructive to compare, for example, his essay 'Jesus in Modernity: Reflections on Jüngel's Christology' (1997) with his essay 'Christology, Theology, Economy: The Place of Christology in Systematic Theology' (2015). In the former, he narrates a pathology of modern theology in terms of the slow and steady displacement of the centrality of Christology by philosophical theism. In the latter, he narrates the pathology of modern theology in terms of the atrophy of theology (teaching about God's life *in se*) accompanied by an excessive focus on the economy. In other words, his pathology has changed from the displacement of Christology to the inflation of Christology. '[D]iscrete teaching about the person and work of Christ', writes Webster, 'has often annexed the fundamental role which earlier theologies more naturally recognised in teaching about the Trinity' (*GWM* I:44).

64. Webster's concern to highlight the integrity and transcendence of the divine nature even in the hypostatic union is manifest in his commitment to the so-called *extra Calvinisticum* (cf. 'Perfection and Participation', 385; *GWM* I:184).

Webster applies a Thomist theory of mixed relations to the incarnation, thereby conceiving of the Word-humanity relation in terms that parallel the more general Creator-creature relation. In his essay 'Christology, Theology, Economy', he states, 'In the course of his movement from immanent origin to economic goal, the Word acquires nothing, remains immutable and simple, entirely resolved and composed. Whatever relations the Word bears to creatures are on his side *non-real* (that is, non-constitutive).'[65] Within his doctrine of creation, Webster employs the theory of mixed relations to characterize the Creator-creature relation as 'non-real' for the Creator but 'real' for the creature. Now applied within a Christological context, it characterizes the Word-humanity relation as 'non-real' for the Word but 'real' for Christ's humanity.[66] It is an admittedly brief and underdeveloped claim, yet its implications can be teased out from the literary context of the quote (a discussion of Christology in terms of the relation between theology and economy) and from Webster's explication of the theory of mixed relations in his essays on the doctrine of creation.[67]

First, Webster wants to preserve the Word's simplicity, immutability and impassibility.[68] Here we see how Webster's theology of divine perfection exerts considerable influence upon his Christology. The incarnation is not an event or development or movement in the Word. When the Word assumes human nature in the incarnation, nothing 'happens' to the Word; there is no change or transformation in God, all the change being on the creature's side. Commenting on Aquinas' understanding of Christ as a composite person, Michael Gorman explains the Thomist logic that undergirds Webster's thought:

> In the hypostatic union, the human nature receives, from the relation, the property of being related to the Word, while the Word itself receives nothing from anything; the first of these facts is sufficient for there being a union between them, and the second is sufficient for this union's not violating divine impassibility. As for immutability, parallel reasoning applies. When the

---

65. *GWM* I:47–8 (emphasis mine). See also John Webster, 'Ressourcement Theology and Protestantism', in *Ressourcement: A Movement for Renewal and in Twentieth-century Catholic Theology*, eds. Gabriel Flynn and Paul D. Murray (Oxford: Oxford University Press, 2012), 491.

66. For a discussion of how Aquinas understood the incarnation within the conceptual framework of mixed relations, see Brendan Case, 'Relations in Creation and Christology: A Response to Porter', *NB* 99 (2018): 1–20; Michael Gorman, 'Christ as Composite According to Aquinas', *Traditio* 55 (2000): 143–57; idem., *Aquinas on the Metaphysics of the Hypostatic Union* (Cambridge: Cambridge University Press, 2017), 64–72; Earl Muller, 'Real Relations and the Divine: Issues in Thomas's Understanding of God's Relation to the World', *Theological Studies* 56 (1995): 673–95; Thomas Weinandy, 'Aquinas and the Incarnational Act: "Become" as a Mixed Relation', *Doctor Communis* 32 (1979): 15–31.

67. Cf. *GWM* I:47–50, 83–126.

68. For Webster's definitions of these terms, see *GWM* I:120.

incarnation takes place, change occurs on the side of the assumed nature, not on the side of the Word.[69]

Yet our use of the language of 'change' must be qualified if we are to do justice to the logic of Webster's thought here. The language of 'change', while not inappropriate in every respect, can be somewhat misleading because it assumes something pre-exists that has the potential for change (i.e. human nature has some inner capacity for incarnation).[70] Thus, the language of 'create' is closer to Webster's conception of the hypostatic union since it manifests the fact that Christ's human nature is brought into being in the very act of being united to the Word.[71] The particular human nature of Christ did not exist prior to its union with the Word, and in that sense, it is radically dependent upon the Word for its very existence, though the Word is not dependent on it.

This leads us to the second theological motivation for Webster's conception of the Word-humanity relation as a mixed relation: the need to highlight the dependence of Christ's human nature and salvific work upon the divine person and act of the Word. This means that the human history of Jesus Christ is constituted by its relation to the Word – it is a 'real' relation – and cannot be understood apart from that relation. Hence, borrowing from Aquinas once again, Webster states that the humanity of Jesus Christ is related to his divinity as 'effect' to 'cause'[72] and that his humanity is an 'instrument' of the divine Son (a concept that dates back to Cyril of Alexandria).[73] None of this is intended to minimize or depersonalize the full humanity of the nature assumed by the divine Son in the incarnation, but rather to emphasize the radical ontological dependence of that nature upon the divine Word, a dependence which is the very foundation of the fact that Christ's human facticity and historicity are the revelation of God to us and the means of salvation for us.[74]

---

69. Gorman, 'Christ as Composite According to Aquinas', 148.

70. According to Webster, this is a problem for much evangelical Christology and modern biblical studies, both of which tend to treat Jesus' human history on its own terms as if it can be conceived apart from its relation to the eternal Word (cf. John Webster, 'Jesus Christ', in *The Cambridge Companion to Evangelical Theology*, eds. Timothy Larsen and Daniel J. Treier (Cambridge: Cambridge University Press, 2007), 56–8; *GWM* I:41).

71. Weinandy makes a similar point regarding Aquinas' interpretation of the Word's 'becoming': 'The real effect in the manhood is both that it comes to be, not by way of change, but more dynamically that it comes to be or exist; and also that it is united to the Logos. It is a real and true humanity that comes to be and is related, and thus for Aquinas the real effect in the humanity is created' ('Aquinas and the Incarnational Act', 30).

72. *GWM* I:48, 51, 57–8.

73. *GWM* I:48–9.

74. Along these lines, Case argues, '[A]s creature, Jesus' humanity is entirely determined by its relation to his deity. But Jesus' human actions aren't only (non-competitively) caused by God, but, because of his human nature's assumption by the Son, are themselves God's actions' ('Relations in Creation and Christology', 10).

This approach diverges significantly from a strand of modern Christology that conceives of the man Jesus as in some sense a self-subsistent person rather than an enhypostatic person. According to this modern tradition, the classical characterization of Jesus' humanity as an 'instrument' of the divine Son purchases the union of the person at the cost of the integrity of his human nature.[75] Thus, this tradition rejects the classical grounding of the hypostatic union in the person of the Son, along with the corollary conviction that Christ's human nature does not ground a supposit (*anhypostasis*). For those who argue that, in order to be fully human, Christ's human nature must ground a human person or supposit, the union between the Word and Christ's human nature tends to be located in some aspect of his humanity, whether it be self-consciousness, will or moral activity. In other words, the hypostatic union is cast in operational and moral, rather than substantial, terms.[76] According to this modern tradition, Christ is the highest realization of the potentialities of human nature, not an ontologically unique occurrence with no created analogies. In order to resist this approach, which he believes cannot ultimately resist the collapse of Christology into anthropology and soteriology, Webster highlights the ontological dependence of Christ's humanity

75. Unease with language about the 'instrumentality' of Christ's humanity in some modern Christology is part and parcel of a rejection or revision of the classical distinction between person and nature. Describing Christ's humanity as an 'instrument' of the divine Son makes theological sense if one accepts the fact that a person is an individual existing thing of a rational nature, whereas a nature is that by which a thing exists and acts as a particular thing. A person performs an action, not a nature, yet a nature is the principle of a person's action and that which makes particular actions possible. Jesus Christ is a divine person subsisting as a human nature. Without this person-nature distinction, it is difficult to make sense of the classical affirmation of divine immutability and impassibility even in the incarnation. According to the traditional doctrine of the *communicatio idiomatum*, suffering and passibility can be predicated of the person of Christ by virtue of his human nature, without thereby implicating the divine nature as passible *in se* (see Bruce D. Marshall, 'The Dereliction of Christ and the Impassibility of God', in *Divine Impassibility and the Mystery of Human Suffering*, eds. James F. Keating and Thomas Joseph White (Grand Rapids, MI: Eerdmans, 2009), 281–2). Moreover, it is important to note that this distinction in no way entails separation: 'Nature is only ever the principle *through* which the subject acts, and person is always exclusively the principle *that* or *who* acts. The union-in-distinction of the concepts is inseparable because persons only act naturally and natures are only inherent in concrete subjects' (Thomas Joseph White, 'The Crucified Lord: Thomistic Reflections on the Communication of Idioms and the Theology of the Cross', in *Thomas Aquinas and Karl Barth: An Unofficial Catholic-Protestant Dialogue*, eds. Bruce L. McCormack and Thomas Joseph White, O.P. (Grand Rapids, MI: Eerdmans, 2013), 168).
76. This point was brought to my attention by Thomas Joseph, 'White's Analysis of the Challenges of Modern Christology', in *The Incarnate Lord: A Thomistic Study in Christology* (Washington, DC: The Catholic University of America Press, 2017), 32–53. Yet I do not to endorse every aspect of his reading of Barth.

and salvific work upon the divine person and act of the Son with the support of, *inter alia*, a theory of mixed relations.

Yet we are still left with an important question regarding Webster's application of the conceptual framework of mixed relations to the incarnation: If the Word-humanity relation is like that of the Creator-creature relation generally, then what is unique about the incarnational union? This is a question to which Webster gives no sustained reflection in his later writings, yet one can reasonably imagine him following the lead of Aquinas, who argues that the Word-humanity relation is a mixed relation unlike any other because it is a union in one person.[77] It is a relation that does not give rise to another person, but rather where the person of the Son assumes, and therefore subsists in, a new (human) nature. Commenting on Aquinas' metaphysics of the hypostatic union, Michael Gorman explains how Aquinas construes the difference between the God-creature relation and the Word-humanity relation:

> When the Word becomes incarnate, the number of substances or persons does not increase. By contrast, creation does not bring about a union in person; when God creates things, the number of substances does increase .... When a human nature is joined to the Word, the Word becomes human. But when God creates a cow, God does not become bovine. So it seems that from Aquinas' perspective, the hypostatic union is a mixed relation, but a mixed relation of a special sort, inasmuch as it is a mixed relation that is also a union in person, a union that results in the person's coming to have a new nature.[78]

> In other words, creation and the hypostatic union are both mixed relations, but the latter is a union in person, while the former is an inter-hypostatic relation.[79]

Given his dependence upon Aquinas throughout 'Theology, Economy, Christology', it seems reasonable to believe that, had he given a comprehensive treatment of the hypostatic union in his later years, Webster might have followed Aquinas in this regard. The Word-humanity relation is unique because it is a union in one person, a union that is without creaturely analogy and therefore mysterious because of the depth of its intimacy.[80]

---

77. Cf. *ST* IIIa. 2.9.

78. Gorman, *Aquinas on the Metaphysics of the Hypostatic Union*, 70. Frederick Christian Bauerschmidt offers an excellent treatment of this point in *Thomas Aquinas: Faith, Reason, and Following Christ* (Oxford: Oxford University Press, 2013), 188–206. He argues that the intent of Aquinas' theology of the incarnation is to highlight the mystery that this finite human creature, Jesus, has an infinite subsistence, so that his history is properly the history of God. In other words, the entire point is to ground the unsubstitutability of Christ's identity.

79. Gorman, 'Christ as Composite', 149.

80. Cf. *WC*, 146–7; *HS*, 22–3.

Yet, when the incarnation is a topic of reflection in his later writings, Webster's overwhelming emphasis is on the distinction between and integrity of the divine and human natures in the incarnation, not their union in one person. This leads us to an important question for understanding his Christology: Why the emphasis on distinction? No doubt some modern theologians would be inclined to read this emphasis as evidence of an incipient Nestorianism, which, it may be argued, is inevitable whenever the doctrine of God is beholden to Greek metaphysical categories (e.g. doctrines of simplicity, immutability and impassibility) that have not yet been thoroughly chastened by the historical form of revelation. While this concern (or sharp critique) identifies an important crux in Webster's mature thought – namely the relation between divine perfection and the incarnation – it can easily miss the internal logic of his thought.

The distinction and asymmetry between the Word and the assumed human nature in the hypostatic union is emphasized by Webster for two reasons. First, the radical distinction between uncreated and created being, which holds true even in the incarnation, is what makes the hypostatic union (according to its Chalcedonian interpretation) possible.[81] Because God is outside of any genus, his being is beyond both reciprocity and dialectic, and therefore he is not confined to or constrained by the limits of creaturely relations.[82] This means that God is free to be present to the creature with the utmost intimacy (with a greater intimacy than is possible between two creatures) without thereby overwhelming or stunting creaturely being and action. The infinite qualitative distinction between God and creatures is the very foundation of their relational union.[83] This logic is central, Webster would argue, for understanding not only the Creator-creature relation generally but also the hypostatic union and the theandric action which flows from that union. The asymmetry between the divine and human natures of Christ is what makes their relation non-competitive. This is why the Third Council of Constantinople could argue that there are two wills in Christ (one divine and one human) without there being any clash between them. Where much modern Christology is concerned with taking the unity of the person as the starting point for understanding the integrity of the natures, often assuming that conceptions of divinity and humanity will necessarily be competitive if abstractly or metaphysically conceived, Webster's mature Christology works in the opposite direction, believing that the radical distinction between the divine and human natures is the very condition of possibility for their unparalleled intimacy in the hypostatic union. It is this logic

---

81. Brendan Case argues that, for Aquinas and the classic theological tradition he represents, the logic of non-reciprocal relations expounded in the doctrine of creation undergirds Chalcedon's insistence that the two natures of Christ are both 'unconfused' and 'undivided'. He states, 'The asymmetry between the Lord's acts and ours, that is, underscores the transcendence which keeps the two natures from tripping over and interfering with one another' ('Relations in Creation and Christology', 11).

82. *GWM* I:124–6.

83. Cf. McWhorter, 'Aquinas on God's Relation to the World', 14–19.

that Webster fears has been lost in modern theology, leading to difficulties in articulating the hypostatic union without either uncoupling the human history of Jesus from the divine Son or historicizing God. For Webster, it is important to see that the Chalcedonian 'without confusion' is the theological-metaphysical foundation of the 'without separation'.

Second, Webster's emphasis on the asymmetry between the Word and the assumed human nature in the hypostatic union is partly polemical, in the sense that it is intended to resist and offer a corrective to what he perceives as modern Christology's tendency to view the Word-humanity relation as one of 'identity'. According to Webster, this leads certain strands of modern theology to posit an identity between the content of revelation and its historical form, which, in turn, allows the historical events of Jesus Christ's human story to be projected or traced back into the life of God in such a way that God's immanent life is dramatized (Balthasar) or historicized (McCormack) or made virtually indistinguishable from the economy (Jüngel, Moltmann, Jenson). Against this trend, Webster seeks to rehabilitate a robust theology of God's life *in se* that employs the classical logic of perfection: God is self-sufficient and wholly realized life, lacking no perfection apart from creatures. It is only against the backdrop of a theological metaphysics of God's life *in se* that the mission of the Word, and therefore the historical life of Jesus Christ, can be and be known as the divulgence of divine grace *pro nobis*.[84] The logic of divine perfection, argues Webster, is of great 'evangelical import' because it teaches us how to understand the nature of the economy of salvation, at the centre of which lies the life, death and resurrection of Jesus Christ.[85] The human history of Jesus is not theogony, nor is it the fulfilment or realization of God's being, but rather it is a divine action of pure generosity and therefore of pure benefit for the creature.

Having expounded Webster's application of the theory of mixed relations to the incarnation, we now turn to consider his (notably more frequent) use of the traditional conceptuality of processions and missions. Here we find him following some of the same principles found in the metaphysical conceptuality of mixed relations (radical Creator-creature distinction, immutable perfection of the divine Word, dependence of human nature on the divine Son in the hypostatic union), and yet this theological conceptuality has the added benefit of highlighting the intimate connection between theology and economy, whereby the soteriological efficacy of the latter is grounded in the former. The human history of Jesus Christ is utterly unique ('unsubstitutable', to use Hans Frei's term) and soteriologically effective precisely because it is the repetition in time, under the conditions of Adamic existence, of the eternal procession of the Son from the Father. We will unpack this aspect of Webster's mature Christology through an analysis of (1) his theology of processions and missions and their relation, and (2) the significance of this conceptuality for his characterization of the human history of Jesus Christ.

---

84. *GWM* I:149.
85. *GWM* I:41.

We begin with his theology of processions and missions. For Webster, the formal conceptuality of processions and missions 'characterise God's being as being in relation', first *ad intra* and secondarily *ad extra*.[86] The divine processions are God's immanent activities whose origin and term are within the one divine essence; they have 'no external basis or object'.[87] These processions are the eternal relations of origin which are constitutive of the divine life.[88] Speaking of the procession of the Son in particular, Webster states,

> Eternal generation is the personal and eternal act of God the Father whereby he is the origin of the personal subsistence of God the Son, so communicating to the Son the one undivided essence. Along with the breathing of the Holy Spirit, generation is one of the divine processions by which the triune persons are identified and distinguished, and in which their mutual relations are enacted.[89]

Much could be said about this dense quote, but two items are noteworthy for our particular purposes. First, 'essentialism' and 'personalism' are mutually reinforcing.[90] This implies that the divine persons who are the 'origin' (Father) and 'term' (Son) of the divine procession are consubstantial, 'irreducible modes' of the one divine essence.[91] There is no greater and lesser, before and after, or cause and effect in the relation between the Father and the Son. For Webster, this secures the point that the Son's relation to the Father is 'wholly unique and incommunicable' and therefore of a different ontological order than the relation between Creator and creature.[92] Begetting is not making: the unbegotten-begotten relation is a 'natural relation' (a work within the divine essence) whereas the Creator-creature relation is an 'external relation' (a work of the divine will *ad extra*).[93] This distinction leads us to a second noteworthy aspect of the aforementioned quote, namely that the divine processions are that which identify and distinguish the persons of the Trinity, not merely the missions. While the incarnate mission of the Son reveals his personal divine identity, meaning there is a proper analogy between the Son's mission and his procession, it does not constitute or augment it. Webster's logic follows from his theology of divine perfection:

> The visible reality of the Word in time emerges from his participation in the entire sufficiency and repose of God. In himself the Word lacks nothing, and in his relation to creatures he receives no augmentation, for he is antecedently perfect .... [T]he outward movement of the Word has to be understood as

---

86. *GWM* I:152.
87. *GWM* I:50.
88. *GWM* I:89.
89. *GWM* I:30.
90. Cf. Emery, 'Essentialism or Personalism', 165–208.
91. *GWM* I:87.
92. *GWM* I:33.
93. *GWM* I:35.

arising from his anterior completeness. It is not the accumulation of properties which extend the Word's identity.[94]

The implications of this logic for Webster's characterization of the human history of Jesus Christ will be explored at the end of this section. Here the main point is that not only does this logic seek to preserve the perfection of the Word such that he does not gain or lose his identity in his economic mission, but it also seeks to secure the fact that his incarnate presence really is the presence of the perfect God.

'[A] divine mission', argues Webster, 'includes within itself and refers to an eternal procession by which the identity of its agent is constituted'.[95] The implication is that the temporal mission of the Son 'repeats in outward activity the relation of origin and the oneness of substance proper to the Father and Son as eternal divine persons'.[96] In other words, the divine persons act in their missions according to who they are in their processions (including origin, order and personal properties).[97] The continuity between processions and missions, between God's immanent activities and transitive activities, is grounded in the unity and identity of the acting subject. Processions and missions have the same divine origin or principle, though they have different terms.

This unity and distinction puts us in a position to make sense of a statement in Webster's essay 'It Was the Will of the Lord to Bruise Him' which seems, at face value, to imply that the missions are a constitutive part of the processions, and therefore to contradict (or at least complicate) our earlier statements about Webster's depiction of the hypostatic union as a mixed relation. Webster states, 'The divine missions are already anticipated, included within the life of the relations which is God's being …. The "origin" of each person is not a mere *whence*, but a whence which includes a *whither*. Filiation and sending, spiration and outpouring, are inseparable.'[98] Note the language used here: 'anticipated', 'included' and 'inseparable'. What are we to make of this statement in the light of Webster's insistence elsewhere on the non-reciprocal relation between processions and missions, theology and economy?[99]

Given Webster's long-standing engagement with Barth, it is possible to read the language of 'anticipated', 'included' and 'inseparable' in terms of God's internal readiness for action in time. Katherine Sonderegger interprets and critiques Webster along these lines:

94. *GWM* I:47.
95. *GWM* I:50.
96. *GWM* I:50.
97. On this topic, see the Tyler R. Wittman, 'On the Unity of the Trinity's External Works: Archaeology and Grammar', *IJST* 20:3 (2018): 359–80.
98. *GWM* I:153–4.
99. For a helpful articulation of the subtle yet important difference between the traditional conceptuality of 'processions-missions' and the contemporary conceptuality of 'theology-economy', see Bruce D. Marshall, 'The Unity of the Triune God: Reviving an Ancient Question', *The Thomist* 74 (2010): 1–32.

We may wonder here whether the strong legacy of Barth in Webster's theological formation might lead him to affirm – too readily, I say – an anticipatory or internal relation God is said to have to creation, or to creaturely conditions, such a[s] time or history or finitude …. 'Inclusion', however, or its synonyms, cannot properly mark off the Mystery of God's own Self-presence to the world as it suggests that the world and its kind are in some way *enfolded*, already and always, into the Eternal Reality of God.[100]

Sonderegger goes on to suggest that had Webster worked out the full implications of the doctrine of creation *ex nihilo* for his understanding of the relation between processions and missions, then the language of 'inclusion' would likely have been rescinded. We will circle back to a discussion of this language in the next chapter, but it is worth noting here that it occurs almost exclusively in essays published before Webster's forays into the doctrine of creation. The only exception of which I am aware is the quote offered above from an essay published in 2011. Thus, while this quote may be read as a vestige of Webster's Barthian theological formation, it may also be feasible to read Webster's language in this specific instance as being broadly companionable with the Thomist framework of his mature thought (2010s).[101]

If this is the case, then the language of 'anticipated', 'included' and 'inseparable' could be interpreted in terms of a cause-effect relation. That is to say, the processions do not include the missions as a constitutive part or essential overflow of their being, nor do the processions include the missions based on a primordial act of self-election which is constitutive of the divine processions, but rather the processions include the missions just as a cause or principle includes the goodness of an effect within itself in a preeminent way. We see this sort of logic at work in Webster's essay 'Christology, Theology, Economy' (2015):

> [T]he interior, wholly resolved life of the eternal Son is also fraught with movement beyond itself, willing to direct itself outwards, and in so doing neither completes itself nor is at variance with itself, because *the divine Son is supremely good and therefore creative* …. The procession of the Son from the Father in an 'immanent' act, having no external basis or object, but as such it is the *uncaused cause* of the history of the incarnation.[102]

---

100. Sonderegger, 'The God-Intoxicated Theology of a Modern Theologian', 42–3.

101. Marshall offers the following synopsis of the traditional Thomist view on the relation between processions and missions: 'Mission includes procession, but procession does not include mission; procession is necessary for mission, but mission is not necessary for procession; the divine processions and the persons who are their subjects and terms are constitutive of, but not constituted by, the saving missions they freely undertake' ('The Unity of the Triune God', 20). In other words, there is a non-reciprocal relation between procession and mission such that the latter is revelatory, but not constitutive, of the former.

102. *GWM* I:50 (emphasis mine).

It is because of the creative, causal relation between the processions and the missions that Webster can affirm that the latter are in some sense included within the former or that the former are 'fraught with movement' towards the latter. He does not intend to make God's relation to the world in Jesus Christ a constitutive part of the divine life (McCormack), nor to conceive of the missions as naturally expressive of the divine processions along the lines of an emanation rather than a willed act (LaCugna), nor to conflate the divine processions and missions whereby they become virtually indistinguishable (Jenson).[103] Rather, he is seeking to establish the theological-metaphysical point that the processions are the 'ground' and 'vital principle' of the missions, even though the missions in no way constitute the processions. In other words, the causal priority runs in one direction – from processions to missions.

Yet it is also plausible to interpret the language of 'anticipated', 'included' and 'inseparable' in a less metaphysically specific way – i.e. something like Barth's idea of 'readiness' but with a more Augustinian flavour. So the missions reveal the processions because they are analogous to the processions, and they are analogous to the processions because the order of procession makes the divine persons uniquely suitable for these missions in particular. This links up with the old scholastic question as to whether or not the Father or the Spirit might have become incarnate. Aquinas answers in the affirmative whereas Augustine answers in the negative. For Aquinas, any person of the Trinity could become incarnate because it is an act of divine power, which is common to the persons. For Augustine, however, it is proper for the Son to become flesh because he is begotten (from another), whereas it is not proper for the Father because he is unbegotten (from no one). The principal reason has to do with the way the order of origin among the divine persons structures the mode of their economic actions. 'The begetter sends, what is begotten is sent.'[104] I think it may be best to read Webster in line with the Augustinian tradition on this point. A substantial piece of evidence which supports this claim is the way Webster commonly speaks of the missions as

---

103. Cf. Bruce L. McCormack, 'Processions and Missions: A Point of Convergence between Thomas Aquinas and Karl Barth', in *Thomas Aquinas and Karl Barth: An Unofficial Catholic-Protestant Dialogue*, eds. Bruce L. McCormack and Thomas Joseph White, O.P. (Grand Rapids, MI: Eerdmans, 2013), 99–126; Catherine Mowry LaCugna, *God for Us: The Trinity and Christian Life* (San Francisco, CA: Harper San Francisco, 1991), 319–75; Robert W. Jenson, 'Once More the *Logos asarkos*', *IJST* 13:2 (2011): 130–3.

104. Augustine, *The Trinity*, in *The Works of Saint Augustine*, vol. I/5, trans. Edmund Hill (Hyde Park, NY: New City Press, 1991), IV.28. It is also noteworthy that many of the Reformed Orthodox of whom Webster was particularly fond, such as John Owen and Francis Turretin, followed Augustine in this regard. For a comparative discussion of Aquinas, Barth and the Reformed Orthodox on the relation between the triune processions and economic missions, see Steven J. Duby, 'Trinity and Economy in Thomas Aquinas', *Southern Baptist Journal of Theology* 21:2 (2017): 29–51.

an 'echo' or 'repetition' in time of the eternal processions.[105] The missions mirror and reveal the processions precisely because the unique form of the missions is shaped by the order of the processions and the respective personal properties of the divine persons. Hence, Webster's use of the language of 'anticipated', 'included' and 'inseparable' could reasonably be interpreted as a way of registering the theological principle that missions follow processions: 'The saving roles of the Son and the Spirit are grounded upon their processional roles in the inner life of the Godhead.'[106]

Webster continues to develop this principle in his theology of the divine missions. Like Augustine and Aquinas, Webster specifies that a divine mission involves two types of relations: a relation to the divine sender (*terminus a quo*) and a relation to the creaturely goal (*terminus ad quem*).[107] The effect of a divine mission is a new mode of divine presence to the creature, and yet this entails no change on the part of the divine person sent. How is this so? Because a mission is not a separate divine 'act' from that of a procession – such a conception would seem to compromise God's being as *actus purus* – but rather the addition of a temporal term to an eternal procession.[108] A divine mission does not constitute, change or augment a divine procession, but is the addition of a creaturely term to a divine procession. When considering whether a mission is eternal or temporal, Aquinas states,

> Mission signifies not only procession from the principle, but also determines the temporal term of the procession. Hence mission is only temporal. Or we may say that it includes the eternal procession, with the addition of a temporal effect. For the relation of a divine person to His principle must be eternal. Hence the procession may be called a twin procession, eternal and temporal, not that there is a double relation to the principle, but a double term, temporal and eternal.[109]

Thomas's logic here allows us to make sense of two themes in Webster's mature thought to which we have already drawn attention: first, the *non-reciprocal* nature of the relation between processions and missions; and second, the fact that (to

---

105. *GWM* I:31, 50, 151.
106. *GWM* I:163. Elsewhere, Webster specifically states that the missions are grounded in the processions in such a way that 'God's outer works are not real relations between himself and creatures' (*DW*, 143). The theory of mixed relations applies to his understanding of the procession-mission relation as well. Therefore, *pace* Kenneth Oakes reading of Webster (see 'Theology, Economy and Christology in John Webster's *God without Measure* and Some Earlier Works', *IJST* 19:4 [2017]: 491–504), grounding does not entail reciprocity for the late Webster. For a similar interpretation, see Wittman, 'John Webster on the Task of a Properly Theological *Theologia*', 105–6.
107. *GWM* I:153. For an excellent discussion of Aquinas' theory of mission, see Emery, *The Trinitarian Theology of St Thomas Aquinas*, 363–72.
108. On this point, see Marshall, 'The Unity of the Triune God', 22.
109. *ST* Ia.43.3 ad 3.

borrow Gilles Emery's comment about Aquinas) 'the intra-Trinitarian processions somehow include God's principles of creative and salvific action'.[110] The divine persons act in their missions according to the origin and order of their processions. By construing matters in this way, Webster is seeking to make a distinction between God's immanent and transitive activities that simultaneously highlights the freedom and gratuity of God's relation to the world and clarifies the ground of God's action in the world.

Having analysed Webster's theology of processions and missions and their relation, we are now in a position to inquire into the significance of this conceptuality for his characterization of the human history of Jesus Christ. According to Webster, the processions and missions are the 'first principles' of Jesus' human history: '[B]ecause there are the processions and missions, then a creaturely history unfolds. This history is *of God*; and what is of God really is *this history*, the human history of the Saviour.'[111] In other words, the Gospel narratives depict a human history which rests upon a divine mission, which in turn rests upon the divine procession of the Son from the Father. 'Saving history emerges from and points back to God's entire sufficiency.'[112]

To this theological-metaphysical claim there is a theological-epistemological derivative, namely that 'Christological knowledge is *knowledge by causes*: the visible reality of Jesus Christ becomes an object of understanding only when its underlying invisible principle is kept in mind as that by virtue of which it has phenomenal form.'[113] Knowing the temporal mission of the Son requires knowing the eternal procession by which it is constituted. This means, on the one hand, Christology is a 'historical science' only by derivation, by virtue of the fact that God *is* and has acted *thus* (God's being and will). The human history of Jesus cannot be considered as a 'quantity in itself',[114] but only as 'the one who has his being in union with the Son of God who is eternally begotten of the Father'.[115] On the other hand, this means Christology is a 'historical science' that, while indispensable, has a *telos* beyond itself: 'it must allow this human history to direct us to the triune God', who is the 'first truth' and the 'uncaused cause' of this history.[116]

At this point, some may be inclined to raise a criticism against Webster for allowing his dogmatic-metaphysical emphasis on God's life *in se* to eclipse the importance of narrative description and historical detail in Christology, and that in doing so he allows the divinity of Christ to overwhelm his humanity. I will circle back to this criticism in the next section, but my concern here is to show that this is not at all Webster's intent. For Webster, teaching about the eternal generation of

---

110. Emery, *The Trinitarian Theology of St Thomas Aquinas*, 74.
111. *GWM* I:155.
112. *GWM* I:154.
113. *GWM* I:51.
114. *GWM* I:156.
115. *GWM* I:41.
116. *GWM* I:57.

the Son does not dissolve the human history of Jesus Christ into eternity, nor does it displace his history with metaphysics; rather, it specifies 'what *kind* of human history' we encounter in the life, death and resurrection of Jesus Christ.[117] Far from espousing some sort of withdrawal from human history, he tries to develop a characterization of Jesus' human history which draws attention to its divine cause and uniqueness. This characterization can be summarized in four points.[118]

First, it is a *unique history*. On the one hand, it is a created human existence, full of the familiar stuff of human life (agents, acts, events). On the other hand, it is different from all other human histories because 'it emerges from and returns to that which is other than created time. In its familiarity, it is shot through with the absolute, as in a direct and immediate way its condition of possibility'.[119] This means that Jesus' human history is 'incomparably and irreducibly strange',[120] not imprisoned within the network of human causality that determines all other human histories, but 'transcending all its human circumstances in its dealings with them'.[121] He 'comes to' but is not 'enclosed by' historical circumstances.

Second, it is a *history of signs*. Jesus' history is 'framed by signs or mysteries in which its depth is, in a certain way, made visible and apprehensible'.[122] Its temporal beginning is marked by the virgin birth and its temporal end is marked by the resurrection. These signs register a sense of the 'sheer difference of Jesus' history', which is the 'special visibility of the perfect God'.[123] Incarnate presence cannot be equated *tout court* with historical immanence.

Third, it is a *commissioned history*. The personal history of Jesus Christ is the enactment of the eternal divine will.[124] Here Webster makes recourse, not to Barth's doctrine of election, but to a rather contentious piece of Reformed federal theology to which Barth was vehemently opposed: the covenant of redemption (*pactum salutis*).[125] It denotes the eternal pact between the Father and the Son whereby 'they

---

117. *GWM* I:155.

118. These points are drawn primarily from John Webster, 'Immanuel', Lecture 4, Kantzer Lectures in Revealed Theology from Carl F. H. Henry Center (Deerfield, IL: 17 September 2007); idem., '"It Was the Will of the Lord to Bruise Him": Soteriology and the Doctrine of God', in *God of Salvation: Soteriology in Theological Perspective*, eds. Ivor J. Davidson and Murray A. Rae (Burlington, VT: Ashgate, 2011), 15–34.

119. Webster, 'Immanuel'.

120. *GWM* I:156.

121. Webster, 'Immanuel'.

122. Webster, 'Immanuel'.

123. Webster, 'Immanuel'.

124. *GWM* I:52.

125. For a discussion of the *pactum salutis* that pays attention to its function in Reformed thought as a means of grounding the Son's *status exaninitionis* in the eternal divine will, see T. Robert Baylor, '"He Humbled Himself": Trinity, Covenant, and the Gracious Condescension of the Son in John Owen', in *Trinity without Hierarchy: Reclaiming Nicene Orthodoxy in Evenagelical Theology*, eds. Michael F. Bird and Scott Harrower (Grand Rapids, MI: Kregel Academic, 2019), 165–94.

agree together to enact the covenant of grace' on behalf of lost creatures.[126] Well aware of the many objections to this unique bit of Reformed federal theology,[127] Webster still thinks it is theologically useful because it resists viewing salvation history as temporal surface with no eternal depth. He writes, 'But what kind of creaturely, bodily history is this if it is indeed for our salvation? ... It is history "suspended" from the divine purpose; and that purpose itself extends from the perfection of God's own life.'[128] The seemingly accidental elements of Jesus' human history are in fact the manifestation and enactment of the 'divine necessity'.[129] This is precisely what makes his story an ordered *economy* of salvation.

Fourth, it is *covenantal history*. Jesus' human career takes place within the unfolding drama of God's covenantal relations with creatures. It must be a fully human history precisely because it is the enactment and fulfilment of the divine covenantal purpose from both sides.[130] Webster states, 'The end of the Son's temporal mission is to restore righteous fellowship between God and lost creatures.'[131] This restored fellowship is established by means of a double substitution: Jesus willingly takes the creature's penalty for sin and suffers the Father's judgement upon sin (passive obedience), and Jesus perfectly submits to the Father's will and 'enacts the relation which creatures are to have to God' (active obedience).[132] Jesus' human obedience is intrinsic to his saving mission. And yet, the saving efficacy of his human obedience rests upon 'the being and act of the eternal Word'.[133] Jesus' human history is efficacious by virtue of its divine depth.

It has been my argument that Webster's mature Christology is concerned primarily with making a firm distinction between the divine and human natures of Christ and thereby registering a profound asymmetry between theology and economy, between uncreated and created being. I sought to explain how Webster employs the metaphysical conceptuality of mixed relations and the traditional

---

126. Webster, 'It Was the Will of the Lord to Bruise Him', 28.

127. Webster lists objections from many theological camps: prone to mythological use (Karl Barth), the juridical idiom overwhelms the personal (*la nouvelle theologie*), voluntarist account of the relations between the Father and the Son as well as God and creatures (Radical Orthodoxy), the history of salvation becomes a shadow in which nothing is really at stake which has not already been decided (Robert Jenson). For Webster, these objections can be resolved through careful attention to the way in which the covenant of redemption is rooted in the inner divine life (not Barth's feared *Deus absconditus*, but the personal processions that are the triune life) and is enacted in loving relations to creatures ('It Was the Will of the Lord to Bruise Him', 29-31).

128. Webster, 'It Was the Will of the Lord to Bruise Him', 29-30.

129. *GWM* I:151. We will discuss the nature of this 'divine necessity' in the next chapter (see Section 3.4).

130. Cf. Webster, 'Immanuel'; *GWM* I:157.

131. *GWM* I:172. For Webster, the salvific teleology of the Son's mission is what grounds the inseparability of Christ's person and work (cf. *GWM* I:157).

132. *GWM* I:173.

133. *GWM* I:157.

conceptuality of processions and missions to make this distinction in such a way that does not lead to the separation of the divine and human natures of Christ, but rather to an ordered relation whereby the latter is grounded in the former. For the mature Webster, this way of articulating things had two theological benefits: first, it allowed him to maintain an emphasis on the fully realized nature of divine perfection, to which the incarnation adds nothing and therefore is an act of pure grace; second, it allowed him to stress the divine depth of Jesus' human history as the source of its salvific efficacy.

2.5 Excursus: Narrative description and metaphysical ambition

The foregoing discussion of Webster's dogmatic Christology, especially the way in which his understanding of the relation between the divine and human natures of Christ funds a particular characterization of Jesus' human history, raises an important constructive question about the relation between narrative description and metaphysical ambition in the Christological task. This question has been raised in recent decades by a number of movements and figures, one of which can act as a helpful foil for situating Webster's mature thought on the topic.

Robert Jenson argues that, instead of rejecting metaphysics altogether, Christian theology must engage in a sort of 'revisionary metaphysics' based on the biblical story of Israel and Jesus of Nazareth.[134] To be sure, Jenson recognizes that all Christian metaphysics is in some sense revisionary, but he argues that the classical Christian tradition did not go far enough in its revisions of Greek metaphysics and unfortunately maintained elements of Hellenism (e.g. divine immutability and impassibility; dichotomies between infinite-finite, eternity-time, being-becoming) that are incompatible with the God whose being is revealed in the human history of Israel and Jesus Christ. Jenson's concern with the Augustinian tradition in particular is that it posits a divine eternity behind the historical events of the Gospel narratives and thereby makes the latter a shadow of the former. In order to avoid this fundamental error, he recasts classical metaphysics in narrative categories.[135] As Francesca Aran Murphy deftly observes, metanarrative does 'the strategic work once accorded to monotheism'.[136] The narrated events of Jesus' life

---

134. Robert W. Jenson, *Theology as Revisionary Metaphysics: Essays on God and Creation*, ed. Stephen John Wright (Eugene, OR: Cascade Books, 2014); ibid., Robert W. Jenson, *Systematic Theology*, vol. 1 (Oxford: Oxford University Press, 1997), 207–23.

135. Jenson, *Systematic Theology* 1:63–74.

136. Francesca Aran Murphy, *God Is Not a Story: Realism Revisited* (Oxford: Oxford University Press, 2007), 254. Murphy shares Jenson's conviction that further revision of classical Christian metaphysics (at least of the Augustinian tradition) is needed in order to do justice to the dramatic form of revelation, but she does not believe narrative theologies offer the needed corrective. She argues that one needs a notion of personhood which possesses metaphysical depth and is not reducible to narrative categories in order to

are accorded a metaphysical density beyond which Christian theology need not posit any more ultimate reality. As a result, Christology seems to demand the development of a metaphysics in which the concept of 'substance' is defined by that of 'story', including notions of time, event and process. While Jenson often resists the criticism that his thought is dependent on Hegel, his metaphysical and epistemological prioritization of narrative description often leads him to equate God's being with the biblical story itself – God's being is constituted in 'dramatic coherence' – and therefore to depict the events of Jesus' human history in neo-Hegelian terms as God's becoming or self-actualization.

In comparison to Jenson, Webster's mature theology represents a very different set of theological judgements. He conceives of the relationship between metaphysical ambition and narrative description in non-competitive terms (like Jenson) but does so precisely because the former is the ground of the latter (unlike Jenson), and crucially, he differs from Jenson in his evaluation of the classical Christian metaphysical tradition. Webster's mature understanding of the function of theological metaphysics in the Christological task can be summarized in three points: First, it offers an 'identity-description' of the agent at work in the Gospel narratives; second, it specifies the 'conditions of possibility' for their being this human history and narrative at all; and third, it clarifies 'what *kind* of human history' we encounter in the Gospel narratives. We will briefly discuss each of these functions before offering a concluding remark about the focus of Webster's dogmatic Christology.

First, the doctrine of the immanent Trinity, including teaching about the unity of the divine essence and the processions of the divine persons, 'furnishes an identity-description of the agent of salvation'.[137] This is where the doctrine of eternal generation is of particular importance for Webster's Christology. The identity of Jesus Christ cannot be rendered solely through a narrative account of his action in history, but requires theological-metaphysical ambition because his identity is constituted by his eternal relation of origin.[138] In this regard, Webster follows Aquinas in grounding the identity of Jesus in the Trinitarian being of God and in conceiving of his historical action as following his immanent being (*agere sequitur esse*) rather than constituting it. Therefore, theology is required to go beyond narrative description and develop a theological metaphysics of God *in se* in its attempt to give an account of Jesus' identity.

The second point is closely connected to the first: a theological metaphysics of God *in se* specifies the condition and ground for their being a human history of Jesus and therefore a Gospel narrative.[139] In fact, Webster pushes the point even

---

account for the dramatic nature of the biblical narrative and the irreducible identities of the *dramatis personae*; one must speak of the substantial truth which grounds free personality and thereby makes drama possible (305–6). Following von Balthasar, she fills out the notion of 'metaphysical truth' in terms of God's intra-Trinitarian kenotic love (240, 280–92).

137. *GWM* I:148–9.
138. Cf. *GWM* I:50.
139. *GWM* I:162–3.

further by arguing that the immanent life of the Trinity is the condition and ground of there being a creation at all, which is the condition of their being a history of the covenant. Covenant rests upon creation as its *terminus a quo*, for creation is the 'introduction of being entirely', that gift of existence which is God's first act *ad extra* and which all other divine acts towards the creature presuppose. Thus, both creation and covenant rest upon God's inner perfection as their presupposition. '[T]he founding condition of creation and its history', argues Webster, 'is the Son or Word who as very God shares in the undivided divine essence'.[140] If this is true, then far from overwhelming or absorbing the human history of Jesus into eternity, as Jenson fears, theological metaphysics specifies 'that history's origin, character, and end'.[141]

Even if Jenson were to concede this point, he and Webster would still split paths in their respective evaluations of the ability of classical Christian metaphysics to secure this fundamental point. According to Jenson, much of the classical tradition (following in the wake of Augustine) is beholden to a 'static' notion of being which makes it difficult to see how its conception of God's life *in se* could possibly cohere with the contours of the biblical revelation of that life in terms of a dramatic history. He argues that Christian metaphysics needs to be reconceived as 'story', thereby securing the fact that the history of salvation is not merely grounded in and revelatory of God's immanent triune life, but rather *is* that life. The divine 'name and narrative description not only appear together … but are identical'.[142] Webster, on the other hand, does not share Jenson's critique of the Western tradition of Christian metaphysics, finding in it a concept of divine being that is dynamic and active rather than static. God is 'pure act', and his perfect being is his plenitude of life *in se* as Father, Son and Holy Spirit.[143] In addition, Webster's commitment to the doctrine of divine simplicity and the 'mixed' character of the relations between God and creatures bars him from speaking of God's inner life in dramatic terms or of positing an identity between the biblical drama and the intra-Trinitarian life. Thus, the unity of the divine essence is not conceived in narrative categories, but according to a doctrine of divine aseity. Webster conceives of the perfection of divine being as 'wholly realised life' rather than 'dramatic coherence'. God is life *a*

---

140. *GWM* I:97.
141. *GWM* I:151.
142. Jenson, *Systematic Theology* 1:64. He can even go so far as to say, 'The Father's sending and Jesus' obedience *are* the second hypostasis in God' (Jenson, 'Once More the *Logos asarkos*', 133).
143. *GWM* I:152. Webster's essay 'Eternal Generation' is evidence of the fact that he reads the classical Christian tradition as having taken 'stock of the revisions to the metaphysics of God required by the gospel' (*GWM* I:29) and having registered 'the corrections to the concept of perfection introduced by trinitarian and Christological teaching' (*GWM* I:38). He simply does not buy into the Hellenization thesis, believing that its characterization of the classical doctrine of God is a caricature at best.

se and *in se* (theology), and therefore he gives life to creatures (economy), but his life is not to be identified with the life that he gives to creatures.

What is the upshot of all this? For Webster, the fact that the Son shares in the aseity of the undivided divine essence – has life 'in himself' – both differentiates him from creatures and grounds his saving mission to creatures. He states, '[L]ife *in semetipso* is entirely incommunicable, and so the identity of "Son" and "life" cannot in any way be replicated in the creaturely realm. But if aseity differentiates the divine Son from creatures, it is also at the same time the ground of his saving gift. The Son has, and is, life; and "as he has, so he has given".'[144] In this way, a theological metaphysics of God *in se* specifies the condition and ground for their being the saving history of Jesus Christ.

The third point is closely connected to the second: a theological metaphysics of God *in se* clarifies 'what *kind* of human history' we encounter in the Gospel narratives.[145] This is what Brad East has referred to as the 'hermeneutical' function of the doctrine of divine aseity.[146] The character of the work is illumined by the identity and aseity of the Worker. Without a theological metaphysics of God *in se*, argues Webster, we may misunderstand the character of the economy of salvation: 'If we only look at the saving economy as it were from the angle of its temporal occurrence, we may mischaracterise the kind of temporal occurrence which it is …. [O]nly within the setting of God's own life in its glorious self-sufficiency can the history of salvation be seen as the divulgence of divine grace to us.'[147] From this vantage point, we can see that Webster's critique of Jenson is pointed not only at his tendency to historicize God's life, but also at his characterization of the economy as a sort of theogony rather than an act of free grace. For Webster, theological metaphysics is of great 'evangelical import' because it helps us interpret the Gospel narratives about Jesus' human history in accordance with what they really are, namely the free and saving presence of the perfect God.[148]

It has been my argument that Webster does not pit metaphysical ambition and narrative description against one another, leading either to the absorption of one into the other or the replacement of one by the other; rather, metaphysical ambition attends to that which grounds and illumines the human agent and history that narrative seeks to describe. Once again, it is worth quoting Webster at length:

> The conceptual apparatus is not a speculative replacement for that history, as if the latter were a mere shadow cast by a high metaphysical object: how could incarnation and passion be grasped without reference to their peculiar creaturely-historical intensity? Rather, the theological metaphysics functions a bit like the Johannine Prologue: this is where saving history is *from* … it is from

---

144. *GWM* I:25.
145. *GWM* I:155, 38.
146. East, 'John Webster', 342.
147. *GWM* I:149.
148. *GWM* I:41.

this that saving history is suspended, this is its divine agent, this its inexhaustible inner saving power.[149]

With this view of Webster's understanding of the relation between metaphysical ambition and narrative description in the Christological task, we are now in a position to evaluate a critique wagered against Webster's Christology, namely that it suffers from abstraction and fails to account for the full humanity of Jesus. So, for example, Brad East argues that Webster's Christology lacks 'narrative density, the textured human carnality of the fully human man Jesus of Nazareth, the particularities of whose life – his disputes, teachings, actions, healings, parables, signs, miracles, sufferings – are the flesh and bones of an orthodox doctrine of Christ. Abstraction from these particularities leaves Christ emaciated, ghostly, disembodied'.[150] Others have expressed concern regarding the 'abstract' nature of Webster's theology more broadly: that his focus on teaching about God *in se* leads to a theology that lacks the texture and details of human culture and experience.[151] What are we to make of these criticisms in reference to his Christology?

That there is a descriptive gap in Webster's mature Christology which was not there in his early Christology is true.[152] Yet it is important to note that Webster himself recognizes this gap in his essays, acknowledging that a full-scale systematic theology would require a thorough discussion of all manner of Christological topics.[153] His reasons for focusing on a relatively narrow, but by no means insignificant, range of topics in Christology – namely the theological metaphysics of God *in se* and the hypostatic union – are largely polemical. Though his theological sources and authorities were increasingly pre-modern, Webster never left behind the modern culture of systematic theology altogether. In fact, he understood his vocation as a theologian in reference to it. It was precisely because he believed contemporary theological culture 'instinctively conflates being and time', that Webster's mature Christology focused on 'exhibiting how, correctly made, the distinction and ordered relation of created and uncreated being' is Christologically and soteriologically fundamental.[154] He did not for this reason think narrative

---

149. *GWM* I: 154. Commenting on the 'hermeneutical realism' of Aristotle and Aquinas, White makes a comment about the metaphysical character of history and historical study that bears similarities to Webster's mature approach to these matters: 'They do not oppose the study of being and the study of history. Rather, they see clearly that metaphysical realism regarding existent realities and their essences necessarily forms the basis for any sound hermeneutics of history' (*The Incarnate Lord*, 494).

150. East, 'John Webster', 349.

151. See Willem Maarten Dekker, 'John Webster's Retrieval of Classical Theology', *JRT* 12:1 (2018): 59–63; Tom Greggs, 'The Call to Focus on God: A Review of Webster's *God without Measure*', *MoTh* 34:4 (2018): 657–63.

152. Some of the severity of East's critique may be blunted if he showed awareness of Webster's *GIH* (1983).

153. Cf. *GWM* I: 52–3, 152.

154. *GWM* I:152.

description any less important for a full-scale exposition of the person and work of Christ. Rather, he was trying to raise a theological point which he believed the Christocentrism of much modern theology had forgotten: Christology is necessarily an 'historical science' but is only so derivatively and instrumentally.[155] In other words, his mature Christology is thoroughly theocentric: 'Study of the incarnate Word may not pass too quickly over his phenomenal form; but nor may it terminate there, for it must allow this human history to direct us to the triune God.'[156] For Webster, the ultimate goal of Christology is contemplation of the Holy Trinity.

2.6 Conclusion

My argument in this chapter has revolved around a comparative study of Webster's early and mature Christology, focusing on his understanding of the relation between the divine and human natures of Christ, and how this influenced his characterization of Jesus' human history. In Webster's early Christology, we saw him combine a Jüngelian emphasis on the 'identity' between the two natures of Christ with Frei's emphasis on the category of 'narrative' as central to depicting that identity. I argued that his early Christology was driven by a desire to manifest the correspondence and identity between theology and economy: Jesus' human history is God's self-identification, and so theology is derived from and accountable to the narrated events of the economy. In Webster's mature Christology, we discovered a rather different picture. He used conceptual resources drawn from Thomas to emphasize the radical distinction between the two natures of Christ, thereby distancing himself from previous affirmations of their 'identity'. I argued that his mature Christology was driven by a desire to manifest the asymmetry between theology and economy: Jesus' human history rests upon the perfection of God's life *in se* as its metaphysical and salvific ground, and so economy is suspended from theology.

I also sought to pinpoint two theological shifts from the 1990s and 2000s that acted as catalysts for the development between Webster's early and mature Christology. First, Webster recognized the insufficiency of narrative categories for grounding the unique and unsubstitutable identity of Jesus Christ and the need to ground Christology in the doctrine of the triune God. Second, Webster came to esteem the importance of classical teaching about God's immanent life and to work out the implications of that material for Christology. This led us into a brief discussion of the relation between narrative description and metaphysical ambition in the Christological task. For Webster, the latter does not supplant the former but rather is its ground and condition of possibility. A theological metaphysics of God *in se* is developed in order to register not only the asymmetry between the divine

---

155. *GWM* I:51.
156. *GWM* I:57.

and human natures of Christ but also the divine depth and salvific efficacy of his human history.

In this way, the argument of this chapter has begun to demonstrate the explanatory power of two elements of the heuristic framework given in Chapter 1. First, it has drawn attention to the significance of the two primary developmental shifts in Webster's thought – from Christocentric to Trinitarian, and from Trinitarian to Theocentric – for his understanding of the hypostatic union. Second, it has demonstrated how the doctrines of divine perfection and of creation (especially teaching about mixed relations) exercised a governing function in Webster's mature theology, even in Christology. But this chapter also raised a question that introduced some complexity into our understanding of Webster's mature thought on the relation between theology and economy, and therefore between God and creatures: How are we to understand the language of 'inclusion'?[157] It was introduced in our discussion of the relation between the divine processions and missions, and as we will see in the next chapter, it is significant for understanding how Webster construes the relation between divine perfection and the church.

---

157. This suggests that Webster's movement from Barth to Thomas was slightly more complex than the distilled narrative of Chapter 1 originally intimated.

Chapter 3

ECCLESIOLOGY

3.1 Introduction

This chapter will explore John Webster's ecclesiology. It will seek to expound the way in which Webster construes the relation between God and the church, and how this influences his characterization of ecclesial action.[1] The main argument will be laid out in four sections followed by a conclusion. The first and fourth sections will analyse Webster's early and mature ecclesiology respectively; the second and third sections will map the crucial theological moves that precipitated the development from the former to the latter.[2] My thesis is a fairly simple one: Webster's understanding of the relation between God and the church shifts from an emphasis on coinherence and continuity to an emphasis on distinction and asymmetry. Moreover, the way in which Webster articulates the distinction and asymmetry between God and the church develops as the doctrines of divine perfection and creation take on increased prominence in his theology, resulting in a positive account of ecclesial action and mediation.

In this way, the argument of this chapter will seek to demonstrate the explanatory power of two elements of the heuristic framework given in Chapter 1. First, it will draw attention to the significance of the two primary developmental shifts in Webster's thought – from Christocentric to Trinitarian, and from Trinitarian to Theocentric – for his understanding of the church. Second, it will demonstrate how the doctrines of divine perfection and of creation (especially teaching about mixed

---

1. One might expect a focus on questions related to ministerial order, sacraments or liturgical practices in a chapter on ecclesiology, but discussion of such topics is curiously sparse in Webster's writings. A notable exception is his discussion of episcopal order in 'The Self-Organizing Power of the Gospel of Christ: Episcopacy and Community Formation' (*WC*, 191–210). He devotes the majority of his attention to analysing the theological accounts of the God-creature relation that undergird particular ecclesiological proposals.

2. A note about sources and periodization: my discussion of Webster's early ecclesiology will draw from his writings in the 1980s, my discussion of his mature theology will draw primarily from *DW* and *GWM*, and my identification of the key transitions in his ecclesiology will draw from essays published in the 2000s (*WC*, 191–230; *HS*, 42–67; *Holiness*, 53–76; *CG*, 153–93).

relations and moved movement) have a governing function in Webster's mature theology, particularly in his account of ecclesial being and action. But this chapter will also raise a question that will introduce some complexity to the understanding of Webster's doctrine of divine perfection as it was laid out in Chapter 1: How are we to understand the distinction he makes between 'inclusive' and 'exclusive' accounts of divine perfection in relation to the church? Thus, we will continue our analysis of the language of 'inclusion', which began in the previous chapter with reference to the relation between processions and missions, in an effort to provide a more nuanced picture of the evolution of Webster's theology of divine perfection and its implications for his understanding of the God-creature relation.

3.2 Early ecclesiology: Coinherence and continuity

In Chapter 1, I suggested that Webster's early thought (1980s) is marked by a thoroughgoing Christocentrism. In Chapter 2, I argued that the Christology which was the governing force of Webster's thought during this period of time had at its core an understanding of the hypostatic union that emphasized the 'identity' and 'indivisibility' of the divine and human natures of Christ. As we now turn to his early ecclesiology, we see a similar emphasis. Though it was not a primary locus of concern for the early Webster, he did touch on ecclesiological matters on two occasions, and what we have is brief yet highly suggestive. Their significance is found in the contrast they provide to many of Webster's later writings on the subject, precisely because they speak of the 'coinherence' and 'continuity' between Christ and the church. We will take a brief look at each of these concepts in turn.

In 'Atonement, History and Narrative' (1986), Webster argues that the doctrine of the atonement cannot analyse the work of Christ by itself apart from its effects in history but must depict Christ's work in relation to the history of the church. A doctrine of the atonement is adequate only to the extent that it 'incorporates a sense of the sheer phenomenality of both the *illic et tunc* of Jesus' past and also the *hic et nunc* of the present context of understanding, and especially of the church'.[3] It is this balance and interrelation between Christ (atoning history) and the church (histories of the atoned) that Webster wanted to achieve through the concept of 'coinherence'. He states,

> My third argument builds on the second by emphasising the coinherence of the history of Jesus and the history of the church. We have already noted that part of the logical architecture of Jesus' history is the history of its effects. The dogmatic counterpart of this observation is the way in which the person and work of Christ are interwoven with the reality of the church.[4]

---

3. Webster, 'Atonement, History and Narrative', 115–6.
4. Webster, 'Atonement, History and Narrative', 129.

Webster is not suggesting that ecclesial action completes the work of Christ, so that the latter is in some sense contingent upon the former for its realization.[5] This is made clear in the 'second' argument, in which he describes ecclesial action as a matter of the subjective 'discovery', 'application' and 'appropriation' of the objective meaning of Christ's atoning work. This language is intended to safeguard the soteriological sufficiency of Christ's work.[6] Yet, Webster is quick to note, the relation between Christ and the church cannot be distinguished so neatly, nor should it be construed as merely extrinsic. Why? Because the history of the atonement 'includes' the histories of those who make up the church; the story of Jesus offers an identity description of 'not only the agent of salvation but also its recipients'.[7]

This depiction of the relationship between Christ and the church is a far cry from Webster's later emphases on the externality of Christ in relation to the church and on the ontological *perfectum* of Christ's work apart from the church. In these early writings, his focus is squarely on the interconnectivity between the 'atoning history' and the 'histories of the atoned'; neither has identity in isolation from the other, precisely because the latter is intrinsic to the former. A driving motivation behind this articulation of the matter seems to be found in Webster's concern to avoid theological abstraction and idealism by attending to the particularities of history via the help of narrative categories, a concern we discussed at some length in the previous chapter. While Webster is quite comfortable emphasizing the irreducible and finished nature of Christ's work, he also insists that without a due emphasis on the subjective, 'the objective would remain abstract' and therefore disconnected from and meaningless for the details of our present historical lives.[8] One way to ensure that such 'abstraction' does not creep into the doctrine of the atonement is to articulate the ways in which the present history of the church is a 'further constitutive element' of God's salvation in Christ.[9] At this point, it would seem that Webster is, somewhat surprisingly, committing himself to some version of the *totus Christus*, but his discussion of the 'coinherence' between Christ and the church comprises barely over two pages, and so we are left with only a few hints and more than a few questions.

We are given a bit more help from an article written a few years earlier, 'The Identity of the Holy Spirit' (1983), in which Webster speaks of the 'continuity' between Christ's redemptive action and the church's Spirit-enabled mission. Though the article is concerned primarily with pneumatological issues in Trinitarian theology, it concludes with a few brief comments about areas of divine

---

5. Webster, 'Atonement, History and Narrative', 128.
6. Webster, 'Atonement, History and Narrative', 129–30.
7. Webster, 'Atonement, History and Narrative', 130–1.
8. Webster, 'Atonement, History and Narrative', 124.
9. Webster, 'Atonement, History and Narrative', 125 (quote from Edward Schillebeeckx, *Jesus: An Experiment in Christology* (London: Collins, 1979), 62).

action that are the distinctive purview of the Holy Spirit, the second of which has to do with the relation between the work of Christ and the mission of the church. According to Webster, the Spirit extends Christ's kingdom and continues Christ's work through the church's agency. He states, '[T]he giving of the Spirit by the exalted Christ enables the mission of the church as *the agent through which Christ's kingdom is extended*.'[10] This link between the Spirit and ecclesial mission brings to the fore the distinctive nature of the Spirit's ministry as one who 'does not merely "remind" the church of Christ but also *continues this work through its agency*'.[11] The comments are admittingly brief, but the wording is significant. By the activity of the Spirit, the church is enabled to 'extend' Christ's kingdom and empowered to 'continue' Christ's work in the world. The focus is resolutely on the church as active agent. Drawing from the Lukan writings of the New Testament, Webster interprets what God has done in Christ and what the Spirit is doing through the church in terms of the continuity of salvation history. Unfortunately, because his primary focus in this article is pneumatology, not ecclesiology, these claims are not fleshed out in any further detail.

So what are we to make of these brief yet suggestive remarks in Webster's early writings? Well, it is important not to make too much of them, nor to read into them much by way of metaphysical structure, although it is tempting to do so when the latter article shows so many signs of social Trinitarian thought, especially that of John Zizioulas. That being said, it is worth taking stock of these early forays into ecclesiology because they provide a backdrop against which to highlight the contrasting themes and emphases that we encounter in the 2000s, when Webster begins to devote significant attention to ecclesiology as a doctrinal locus in its own right. As we will see, there is a notable shift from an emphasis on 'coinherence' and 'continuity' to that of 'distinction' and 'asymmetry'. Yet a crucial question for understanding Webster's ecclesiology rises to the surface at just this point: How does he articulate the distinction and asymmetry between God and the church? Which doctrines and conceptual resources does he employ, which does he critique or avoid, and what does this tell us about his understanding of the relation between God and creatures? My argument in the following sections will seek to identify and explicate the key points of development in Webster's ecclesiology, and in so doing, the hope is that some of the structural and material similarities with the developments we have already noted in his Christology will become evident. The main developments are as follows: First, Webster attempts to ground ecclesiology in the doctrine of the Trinity; and second, he discovers the importance of classical teaching about divine perfection and its implications for ecclesiology.

---

10. Webster, 'The Identity of the Holy Spirit', 7 (emphasis mine).
11. Webster, 'The Identity of the Holy Spirit', 7 (emphasis mine).

3.3 Ecclesiology in transition: Trinitarian deduction

In the early 2000s, ecclesiology emerges in Webster's theology as a doctrinal locus in its own right. His first essays on the matter attempt to ground all that is said about the church in the doctrine of the Trinity, or more specifically, a triune account of divine action.[12] These essays are somewhat reactive and highly polemical, sparked by what he considered to be the ills of much modern ecclesiology: the church is considered the 'first truth' of all Christian teaching; an overinflated account of ecclesial practices overwhelms talk of divine action; an improper grasp of the distinction between God and the church leads to a mis-characterization of the nature of ecclesial action and mediation. Like some of his contemporaries (e.g. Jenson, Gunton, Volf), Webster turned to the doctrine of the Trinity for solutions to what he perceived to be modern ecclesiology's problems. Yet Webster differed from his contemporaries in the *manner* in which he grounded ecclesiology in Trinitarian theology.

Thus, a key question for Webster's ecclesiology can be articulated as follows: How does one move from the doctrine of the Trinity to the doctrine of the church? He was consistently suspicious of attempts to do so based on a single concept or analogy – communion, relation or participation – preferring instead to give a descriptive account of the economic actions of the divine persons: the Father elects, the Son reconciles and the Spirit perfects. From these divine acts, Webster developed a threefold description of the church's being: the society of the elect, the creature of the Word and the spiritually visible community. Approaching matters in this way enabled Webster to highlight the distinction between the Trinity and the church and to keep the creative priority of divine action over ecclesial action at the forefront of his ecclesiology. In this section, I will offer an exposition of Webster's initial attempts at a 'trinitarian deduction' of the church, followed by a discussion of two ways in which his Trinitarian ecclesiology underwrites a particular account of the nature of ecclesial action.[13]

Webster begins his Trinitarian ecclesiology with the doctrine of election. The Father elects a people to be his creaturely covenant partner, thus fulfilling the oft-repeated divine resolve: 'I will be your God, and you shall be my people.' For Webster, the being of the church is grounded primarily in the divine will, which is expressed in covenant-making action. Therefore, the doctrine of election functions as the bridge between the doctrine of the Trinity and the doctrine of the church. By

---

12. Cf. *WC*, 191–230; *HS*, 42–67; *Holiness*, 53–76; John Webster, 'The Church as Witnessing Community', *Scottish Bulletin of Evangelical Theology* 21 (2003): 21–33.

13. The language of 'trinitarian deduction' comes from Webster's essay 'In the society of God' – 'Dogmatics arrives at the doctrine of the church by trinitarian deduction' (*GWM* I:181) – and seems to be an oblique challenge to Milbank's argument for the 'ecclesiological deduction' of the incarnation and atonement (John Milbank, *The Word Made Strange: Theology, Language, Culture* (Oxford: Blackwell, 1997), 159).

construing matters in this way, Webster is consciously swimming against the tide of some major currents in contemporary ecclesiology.

Primary among these currents is *communio* ecclesiology, which has enjoyed unique prominence in ecumenical discussions following the Second Vatican Council. Robert W. Jenson articulates the basic insight of communion ecclesiology as follows: 'The church is founded in the triune life of God because the church anticipates being taken into that life, and because, as the gospel interprets reality, it is precisely what creatures may *anticipate* from God that is their deepest being.'[14] For Jenson, the ontology of the church is derived from Trinitarian theology and eschatology, mediated through the doctrines of perichoresis and theosis, whereby God opens up 'room' within his life for creatures.[15] The being of the church, understood as a social communion, is constituted by its participation in God's inner communion. Similar theological judgements can be found in the writings of Jean-Marie Tillard and John Zizioulas.[16] As Nicholas M. Healy aptly stated, for these theologians 'communion' is a master-concept that is 'applied to inner-Trinitarian *koinonia*, the church's relation to God, the relation among the church's members, the relations between the churches and, not infrequently, to the relations between the church and other religious and non-religious bodies. Communion thus describes the church's essential nature, it functions, institutions, and practical life'.[17] A different though related example can be found in the mature ecclesiology of Colin Gunton. Although he raised a caution about the dangers of 'arguing directly to the Church from the immanent Trinity', and avoided dependence on a doctrine of metaphysical participation, he nonetheless developed a theology of perichoretic relations which functioned as the key analogy between God and the church.[18] Gunton offered this explanation of his 'ecclesiology of perichoresis': 'The Church is called to be the kind of reality at the finite level that God is in eternity …. [T]he doctrine of the Trinity is being used to suggest ways of allowing the eternal becoming of God – the eternally interanimating energies of the three – to provide the basis for the personal dynamics of the community.'[19] Jenson,

---

14. Robert W. Jenson, 'The Church as *Communio*', in *The Catholicity of the Reformation*, eds. Carl E. Braaten and Robert W. Jenson (Grand Rapids, MI: Eerdmans, 1996), 2.

15. Jenson, 'The Church as *Communio*', 3.

16. Cf. J.-M.-R. Tillard, *Church of Churches: An Ecclesiology of Communion*, trans. R. C. De Peaux (Collegeville, MN: The Liturgical Press, 1992); idem., *Flesh of the Church, Flesh of Christ: At the Source of the Ecclesiology of Communion*, trans. Madeleine Beaumont (Collegeville, MN: The Liturgical Press, 2001).

17. Nicholas M. Healy, 'Ecclesiology and Communion', *Perspectives in Religious Studies* 31:3 (2004): 273.

18. Colin Gunton, 'The Church on Earth: The Roots of Community', in *On Being the Church: Essays on the Christian Community*, eds. Colin E. Gunton and Daniel W. Hardy (Edinburgh: T&T Clark, 1989), 68; John Zizioulas, *Being as Communion: Studies in Personhood and the Church* (Crestwood, NY: St. Vladimir's Seminary Press, 1985).

19. Gunton, 'The Church on Earth', 78.

3. Ecclesiology

Tillard, Zizioulas and Gunton all have their distinctive ways of making the point, but in each case the link between the Trinity and the church is articulated through a master-concept or analogy such as 'communion' or 'perichoresis'.

Webster finds this approach to grounding the church in the Trinity problematic in two ways. First, they often have a slender account of divine freedom: '[S]uch accounts of the life of the Church as participation in or image of the relatedness of God characteristically give insufficient attention to the free majesty of God.'[20] Second, they risk drifting into 'divine immanence'.[21] The result of both these errors, according to Webster, is that the relation between divine and ecclesial action (and consequently, the characterization of ecclesial action) is distorted:

> [S]uch ecclesiologies characteristically stress the continuity between the action of God and the action of the Church, in a manner which can easily jeopardize our sense of the freedom and perfection of God's work. Such ecclesiologies can place excessive emphasis upon the Church as agent, and, correspondingly, underplay the passivity which is at the heart of the Church as a creature of divine grace.[22]

Interestingly, Webster's criticisms here are directed at the very emphases that were central to his early ecclesiology (as noted in the previous section). His understanding of the church's relation to God has shifted from an emphasis on continuity and activity to an emphasis on distinction and passivity. These themes will be developed in a moment, but what I want to highlight at this point is the theological logic that undergirds this shift. Webster ties together the freedom of God, the nature of the church as a creature of grace and the passivity of the church. Each link of the chain is predicated upon the former.

By grounding the church in the doctrine of the Trinity via the doctrine of election, Webster was attempting to articulate the theological link between God's freedom and the being of the church as a creature of grace, themes which were seldomly mentioned in contemporary ecclesiological discussions. The doctrine of election highlights the fact that the being of the church is radically contingent, predicated upon an antecedent divine decision. The church is not grounded (via participation) in the intra-divine communion or perichoresis; rather, it is grounded (via election) in the divine will, whose gracious turning towards creatures is uncaused by anything outside of God. Hence, the doctrine of election allows Webster to accentuate God's freedom in relation to the church. As a creature of God's free grace, the church is 'in no sense self-generated', being dependent on the will and work of God 'at every moment of its existence'.[23] Thus, passivity is at the heart of the church. This is the 'chain link' logic I noted in the previous paragraph: divine freedom – church as creature of grace – ecclesial passivity.

---

20. *Holiness*, 55.
21. *Holiness*, 55.
22. *Holiness*, 55.
23. *Holiness*, 60.

Along with the doctrine of election, Webster turns to another classically Reformed piece of ecclesiology – the church as *creatura verbi divini* – in order to register many of the same themes. Here the focus is on the way in which the church is constituted: '[T]he church is that human assembly generated and kept in life by the continuing, outgoing self-presentation ("Word") of Jesus Christ.'[24] If the church is constituted by the self-revelation of the divine Word, and the human correlate to divine revelation is faith, then the Christ-church relation is to be understood in terms of the Word-faith relation.[25] Just as faith has its generative source in the Word and exists as an act of trust in that Word, so also the church, as *congregatio fidelium*, has its generative source in Christ's self-revelation and exists as it continually hears and trusts his voice. For Webster, as for the Reformers, this Word is mediated primarily through the words and witness of Holy Scripture. Hence, the church is constituted and continues to exist only as it hears the divine address through Scripture. In this way, Webster sought not only to prioritize divine action in his account of the church's being, but also to characterize the nature of that divine action as an external Word and Address.[26] The church's being is constituted by an external, outgoing divine speech-act, rather than an incorporative act. This Reformed emphasis on the church as *creatura verbi divini* marks a significant shift from Webster's prior emphasis on the 'coinherence' of Christ and the church. It highlights the externality of Christ's relationship to the church, which is expressed in the way the church's identity is tethered to the hearing of Scripture. Scripture is the alien, intrusive voice of Christ (*viva vox Christi*) who calls the church into being.[27]

24. WC, 195–6.
25. HS, 44. Along these lines, Christoph Schwöbel argues that for the Reformers 'the true character of the Church consists in the Word of God and in true faith. Both constitute the *communio sanctorum* as the relationship of divine and human action in the church. According to this view, the church can be viewed from two perspectives. In trying to determine the nature of the church one has to talk about what makes the church possible, i.e. the Word of God, and what is made possible in the church, i.e. true faith' ('The Creature of the Word: Recovering the Ecclesiology of the Reformers', in *On Being the Church: Essays on the Christian Community*, eds. Colin E. Gunton and Daniel W. Hardy (Edinburgh: T&T Clark, 1989), 126–7).
26. HS, 45.
27. Webster's penchant for a Word-focused ecclesiology is developed in contrast to a major current of contemporary ecclesiological reflection which takes the theology and practice of the Eucharist as its starting point. For the former, the divine Word makes the church; for the latter, the Eucharist makes the church. The seminal Roman Catholic work which articulates this eucharistic ecclesiology is Henri De Lubac's *Corpus Mysticum: The Eucharist and the Church in the Middle Ages: A Historical Survey*, trans. Gemma Simmonds CJ, Richard Price, and Christopher Stephens (Notre Dame, IN: University of Notre Dame Press, 2007). For examples of de Lubac's influence on both Roman Catholic and Protestant ecclesiologies, see Paul McPartlan, *Sacrament of Salvation: An Introduction to Eucharistic Ecclesiology* (Edinburgh: T&T Clark, 1995); Hans Boersma, 'The Eucharist Makes the Church', *CRUX* 44:4 (2008): 2–11; idem., *Heavenly Participation: The Weaving of a Sacramental Tapestry* (Grand Rapids, MI: Eerdmans, 2011), 101–19.

Why does Webster's emphasis shift from 'coinherence' to 'externality'? The answer is related to his overall concern to register the asymmetry between divine and human action. But what is behind this concern? It is the conviction that without a robust theology of divine freedom, which is the ultimate ground of this 'asymmetry', ecclesiology will be prone to moralism. Webster argues,

> [W]e need to talk of the church as the creature of the Word, in order to retain the fundamental asymmetry between divine and human action. To talk of the church in these terms is to insist that at its heart the church is passive, a community whose life has as its core activity the listening to the apostolic Word of reconciliation. Ecclesiologies which centre on Word customarily have greater success in articulating the transcendent freedom of the object of Christian faith, and are customarily more resistant to moralization of the gospel, in which God's reconciling deed takes up residence in institutional forms or patterns of moral practice.[28]

If the doctrine of election was Webster's way of offering resistance to the dangers of ecclesiological immanentism, then the characterization of the church as *creatura verbi divini* is Webster's way of offering resistance to ecclesial moralism, and both theological concepts do so by emphasizing the transcendent freedom of God in relation to the church.

Similar concerns underwrite Webster's characterization of the church's visibility as a 'spiritual visibility'. Once again, we see a marked contrast to ecclesiologies that accentuate the institutional and social-historical visibility of the church. Communion ecclesiology tends to focus on the church as a communion of visible communities, which are united by their common participation in the inner-Trinitarian communion, which in turn is mediated and represented by a visible episcopal structure.[29] For those ecclesiologies that are more ethically oriented, the emphasis on visibility is often expressed through the idiom of practice, habit and virtue.[30] Webster resists both of these ecclesiological trends because he believes they mute the creative sufficiency of divine grace. Communion ecclesiology does so by making the episcopacy in some sense constitutive of ecclesial communion and unity; ethically oriented ecclesiologies do so by focusing on the density and phenomenality of ecclesial action in such a way that risks displacing the priority of God's reconciliatory action.

---

28. *WC*, 228.
29. See, for example, Robert W. Jenson, *Systematic Theology*, vol. 2 (Oxford: Oxford University Press, 1999), 220–49.
30. A paradigmatic example can be found in Stanley Hauerwas, *The Peaceable Kingdom: A Prier in Christian Ethics* (London: SCM, 1984), 96–115. For a critical engagement with Hauerwas's ecclesiology at a dogmatic level, see Nicholas M. Healy, *Hauerwas: A (Very) Critical Introduction* (Grand Rapids, MI: Eerdmans, 2014). For a more sympathetic evaluation that seeks to situate Hauerwas's ecclesio-moral discourse in the context of his intellection roots and cultural milieu, see John B. Thompson, *The Ecclesiology of Stanley Hauerwas: A Christian Theology of Liberation* (New York, NY: Routledge, 2016).

Now, at this point it is important to clarify the constructive purpose behind Webster's critiques: he is not seeking to minimize the visibility of the church (its existence as a social-historical form), but rather to offer a particular characterization of that visibility (what *kind* of visibility). He wants to highlight the unique way in which the church has its socio-historical existence, namely by virtue of the creative agency of divine grace. In other words, Webster is searching for ways to articulate a Reformed metaphysics of grace as the ground of the church's visibility. Hence, the term 'spiritual' is not pitted against 'visibility' as its contrary, but employed as its descriptor, in order to speak about the visibility of the church in relation to the creative agency of the Holy Spirit in particular. The church's visibility is ontologically constituted by the work of the Holy Spirit and epistemologically (or hermeneutically) discerned by the illumination of the Holy Spirit.[31] Much like Webster's use of the doctrine of election and identification of the church as *creatura verbi divini*, the purpose of this theologoumenon is twofold: first, to draw attention to the transcendent freedom and gratuity of God's action in relation to creaturely action, and consequently, to avoid both immanentism and moralism in giving an account of the church's action.

Having drawn attention to the particular way in which Webster grounds ecclesiology in the doctrine of the Trinity, we now turn to an analysis of how it underwrites a particular characterization of ecclesial action. How does (to use the language of Christoph Schwöbel) 'the way in which the Church is constituted by divine action determine the character and scope of human action in the Church'?[32] The answer is twofold. First, Webster's Trinitarian ecclesiology funds a passive and ecstatic characterization of ecclesial action. The shape of the church's action gives expression to the fact that the church receives her being *ab alio*. The church's acts point beyond themselves to the being and action of another (the triune God); they are indicative and ostensive. This leads Webster to speak of ecclesial action primarily in categories of speech: the church 'indicates', 'witnesses', 'testifies', 'attests' and 'confesses';[33] the church 'acknowledges', 'declares', 'prays' and 'praises'.[34] The emphasis on speech is not an arbitrary choice on Webster's part; it derives from the nature of the church's being as *creatura verbi divini*. As a human society constituted by a divine act of speech (the divine Word mediated through the scriptural word), the church's most 'natural' form of action is a responsive word of faith. Placing the accent on verbal action also has the added benefit of serving Webster's overriding purpose of rehabilitating 'a sense of the proper transcendence and uniqueness of the divine act' in relation to ecclesial action.[35] The church's acts do not mediate,

---

31. *Holy Scripture*, 47–50; *CG*, 179–183. Cf. *CD* IV.1, 643–62.
32. Swchöbel, 'The Creature of the Word', 122.
33. *WC*, 201–6, 222.
34. *Holiness*, 73–6.
35. *WC*, 222. For a creative attempt to reappropriate the *solas* in response to recent critiques of the Protestant Reformation, see Kevin J. Vanhoozer, *Biblical Authority after Babel: Retrieving the* Solas *in the Spirit of Mere Protestant Christianity* (Grand Rapids, MI: Brazos Press, 2016).

realize, embody or extend God's redemptive acts, which are perfect and complete in themselves. Rather, the church's acts merely point and testify to that perfect reality which lies outside the church's competence. For Webster, this emphasis on the passive and ecstatic nature of ecclesial action is the ecclesiological derivative of his commitment to the Reformed *solas*.[36]

Second, Webster's Trinitarian ecclesiology funds a negative or apophatic account of ecclesial mediation. Worried that many accounts of ecclesial mediation give insufficient attention to the finished and self-realizing nature of divine action, Webster suggests

> that the Christological ἐφάπαξ and its drastic curtailment of the *soteriological* significance of human ecclesial activity may best be safeguarded by a theology of mediation which is more *apophatic* in character .... Apophatic mediation is at heart *indicative*; the mediating reality – object, activity, person, word – does not replace or embody or even represent that which is mediated, but is as it were an empty space in which that which is mediated is left free to be and act.[37]

Here Webster's insistence on the essential passivity of the church is at its strongest: mediating realities are 'empty space' for divine action. At a later point in this chapter (Section 3.5), I will explain why Webster's theology of ecclesial mediation becomes profoundly more positive in later years, but our concern here has to do with what motivated this rather negative account of ecclesial mediation in 2001. It has to do, once again, with a desire to safeguard the perfection and freedom of Christ's person and work, a perfection and freedom which Webster believes requires a strong sense of the externality of Christ in relation to the church. Without a robust account of 'Christ's transcendence of [the] moral community, the sheer freedom of his presence to the church,'[38] Webster argues, a theology of the church will fail to register the fundamental asymmetry between divine and human action and in turn risk collapsing the former into the latter (immanentism) or supplanting the former with the latter (moralism). Either way, the error is to be resisted by focusing on the 'incommunicable and non-representable' nature of Christ's agency.[39] There can be no transfer of agency, authority or status from Christ to the church.[40]

36. *WC*, 227.
37. *WC*, 226.
38. *WC*, 229.
39. *WC*, 199. This is a significant reason why Webster rejected the doctrine of the *totus Christus*. According to Ralph Del Colle, the *totus Christus* model, as it has been articulated in Catholic ecclesiology since the Second Vatican Council, looks to the hypostatic union as an analogy for the church. A close link is forged between the nature of the divine-human relation in Christ and the divine-human relation in the church, leading to a characterization of the church as *sacramentum gratiae* – 'it effects what it signifies' and thus mediates the saving agency of God ('The Church', in *The Oxford Handbook of Systematic Theology*, eds. John Webster, Kathryn Tanner, and Iain Torrance (Oxford: Oxford University Press, 2007), 257–60).
40. *WC*, 200, 204, 205.

In this section, I have sought to elucidate Webster's first attempts to ground ecclesiology in the doctrine of the Trinity as well as the implications of this 'trinitarian deduction' for his account of ecclesial action. I drew attention to the way he resisted ecclesiological proposals that ground the church in the Trinity through a coordinating concept such as communion or perichoretic relation. Instead, Webster sought to ground his ecclesiology in a Trinitarian account of divine action via the doctrine of election as well as teaching about the self-revealing activity of Christ and the converting, illuminating work of the Spirit. This gave rise to an account of the God-church relation that accentuated 'distinction' and 'asymmetry', the free and gratuitous nature of divine action, and the passive, ecstatic and apophatic nature of ecclesial action. Webster states,

> An evangelical ecclesiology will thus have a particular concern to emphasise the asymmetry of divine and human action: God's work and the work of the church are fundamentally distinguished. But they are so distinguished, not in order to bifurcate them (which would undermine the fact that the church is indeed ingredient within the economy of God's saving purpose) but in order to accord priority to the gracious action of God, through which the church's action is ordered to its proper end in conformity with the will of God. The *distinction*, in other words, is for the purpose of *right relation*. They are also distinguished in order to specify with the right kind of theological determinacy the respective characters of divine and human churchly action. Divine action is sheerly creative, uncaused, spontaneous, saving and effectual; human, churchly action is derivative, contingent and indicative. All churchly action – cultic, moral, diaconal – is thus characterized by 'creative passivity', an orientation towards that perfect work which has been done and continues to be done for the church and to the church.[41]

The logic of Webster's ecclesiology is on full display in this quote: the specific order and emphasis of the doctrinal material (Trinity – election – grace – church) are designed to register the 'distinction' and 'asymmetry' between God and the church, the purpose of which is to clarify that the God-church 'relation' is grounded in the freedom and creativity of divine grace, which in turn leads to a characterization of ecclesial action as 'creative passivity'.

Before moving on to discuss another significant point of material development in Webster's ecclesiology, it is worth stepping back from detailed exposition for a moment and making a comment about the material structure of Webster's thought in the early 2000s and how it leads to a thin account of creaturely action and therefore ecclesial mediation. At this point in his development, Webster has made the shift from Christology to the doctrine of the Trinity as the 'material epicentre' and 'heuristic key' of all Christian teaching. Hence, all other doctrines, including ecclesiology, are derived from and governed by the doctrine of the

---

41. *WC*, 196.

Trinity. Yet Webster's doctrine of the Trinity is almost exclusively oriented towards the economy of grace. Very little is said about the immanent life of the Trinity (essence and processions), nor is much said about the works of nature (creation and providence). As I argued in Chapters 1 and 2, the lack of attention to matters of God's inner life is, in part, rooted in a conviction that talk about God *in se* apart from the economy of his works will lead to an abstract doctrine of God, which will in turn lead to a distorted understanding of God's relation to creatures[42] – far better to limit the focus of theological reason to God's works and self-revelation in the economy of grace. The lack of attention to the works of nature, on the other hand, is rooted in a conviction that the errors of naturalism, immanentism and moralism are best countered through an eschatological theology of grace. God's gracious action is uncaused, creative and intrusive, something that can never be anticipated by the creature and for which the creature has no natural capacity. Grace is a divine action *tout court*, not a created effect; therefore, grace can never become a possession or settled aspect of ecclesial culture.

What we see at this point in Webster's thought is an account of divine creativity that is expressed almost exclusively through an eschatological and intrusive theology of grace – a point which will receive further explanation in Chapters 4 and 5. Hence, Webster uses the language of creation *ex nihilo* primarily in reference to God's redemptive act of new creation rather than his original act of creation.[43] Added to this is his frequent use of 'event' language to describe the church's being, thereby following Barth's insistence that the church's existence is never a settled, self-possessed reality, but always contingent upon ever-fresh acts of divine redemption.[44] Webster himself recognizes that there is a danger in describing the church's being as an 'event', and so he is quick to clarify that this does not mean 'the human Christian community is unstable, liminal, and so incapable of sustaining a coherent historical and social trajectory'.[45] And yet, one may ask how exactly describing the church's mediating realities as 'empty space' for the action of God really does justice to the church as 'a coherent historical and social trajectory'? In other words, it seems that Webster's early attempts to articulate the fundamental distinction and asymmetry between God and the church, by relying primarily on a doctrine of election and an eschatological theology of grace, occasionally and unwittingly lead him into a competitive or contrastive account of their relation. Divine action and human action are understood as being inversely proportional, resulting in a passive account of ecclesial action and negative account of ecclesial

---

42. Cf. *Holiness*, 31–52.
43. *WC*, 215.
44. *WC*, 197–8, 202, 208; *HS*, 47. Cf. *CD* IV.2, 614–27. For a positive analysis of Barth's occasionalist ecclesiology, see Christopher R. J. Holmes, 'The Church and the Presence of Christ: Defending Actualist Ecclesiology', *Pro Ecclesia* 21:3 (2012): 268–80. For a critical evaluation, see Nicholas M. Healy, 'The Logic of Karl Barth's Ecclesiology: Analysis, Assessment and Proposed Modifications', *MoTh* 10:3 (1994): 253–70.
45. *WC*, 197.

mediation as the correlates of divine freedom and creativity. At times, Webster seems to interpret any kataphatic account of ecclesial mediation as an inherent threat to the perfection and primacy of divine grace, which makes one wonder if he has slipped into thinking of divine and human action as if they are operating on the same ontic plane of reality. With these concerns in mind, we turn to the second major development in Webster's ecclesiology.

3.4 Ecclesiology in transition: Divine perfection

The second major catalyst of development in Webster's ecclesiology is his discovery of the importance of a theology of divine perfection for articulating the ordered relation between theology and economy in general, and the redemptive relation between God and the church in particular. Beginning with his essay 'On Evangelical Ecclesiology' (2005), there is a gradual shift in focus from economy to theology proper as he seeks to show not only how ecclesial action is grounded in God's triune action, but also how God's triune action is grounded in the perfection of his inner being. Throughout this process many of Webster's Reformed ecclesiological emphases remain essentially the same: a preference for the doctrine of election as opposed to a doctrine of participation; an emphasis on the church as *creatura verbi divini* as opposed to a eucharistic communion; an insistence on *solus Christus*, whose identity is non-extendable, being is impartible, and work is non-transferable; and a focus on the church's 'spiritual visibility'. However, what does change is his starting point for the doctrine of the church – God's triune perfection, which is the ground of his salvific action towards the church. Webster now argues that approaching one's ecclesiology from the doctrine of the economic Trinity would be a mistake, precisely because 'adoption of this starting point can lead to [a] misconstrual of the relation-in-distinction between the gospel and the church'.[46] What I want to demonstrate in this section is how this shift in 'starting point' impacts Webster's understanding of the relation-in-distinction between God and the church. Then, in the following section, I will explain how this development opens space in Webster's thought for a positive account of ecclesial mediation.

The key question for Webster's ecclesiology has to do with the nature of divine perfection: '[I]s God's perfection an *inclusive* or an *exclusive* perfection?'[47] I touched on this topic in the previous chapter when discussing the relation between processions and missions; here I will show that it is of some significance for his understanding of the relation between God and the church as well. Webster outlines the difference between 'inclusive' and 'exclusive' perfection as follows:

> To speak of inclusive perfection would be to say that the fullness of God includes as an integral element of itself some reality other than God – that,

---

46. *CG*, 157.
47. *CG*, 158.

because creatures are in some way called to participate in God's life, his life is co-constituted by their participation. To speak, on the other hand, of exclusive perfection would be to say that the fullness of God is *a se* and *in se*. God's relations to that which is other than himself are real; but they are the expression of God's freedom, not of a lack, and in these relations creatures do not participate in God but are elected for fellowship and therefore summoned into God's presence.[48]

On the one hand, this quote displays continuity with Webster's writings from a few years earlier (i.e. *Holiness*): the covenantal categories of 'election' and 'fellowship' are contrasted with the metaphysical category of 'participation', thereby revealing one of the major fault lines in contemporary theological proposals regarding the God-creature relation.[49] On the other hand, this quote displays some discontinuity with Webster's previous writings, namely the way in which he traces this fault line back to differing conceptions of divine perfection. It is a matter of one's doctrine of God *in se*. This, he now believes, is the real underlying issue that determines the trajectory of one's ecclesiology. For Webster, the decision seems clear: God's perfection is exclusive. It is 'the repleteness of his life, the fullness or completeness of his being, the entirety with which he is himself. As the perfect one, God is utterly

---

48. *CG*, 158.
49. Radical Orthodoxy (RO) locates the development of modern secularism and nihilism in the loss of a participatory metaphysics (Cf. Simon Oliver, 'Introducing Radical Orthodoxy: from participation to late modernity', in *The Radical Orthodoxy Reader*, eds. John Milbank and Simon Oliver (London: Routledge, 2009), 3–27; James K. A. Smith, *Introducing Radical Orthodoxy: Mapping a Post-secular Theology* (Grand Rapids, MI: Baker Academic, 2004)). The Protestant Reformation is interpreted as one step within a larger process of secularization, and its theology is critiqued for espousing a voluntarist doctrine of God and extrinsicist theology of grace (Cf. Boersma, *Heavenly Participation*, 89–94). The proposed answer to these theological ills is quite simply to recover the participatory metaphysics of the pre-modern Christian tradition. The reaction to this genealogical narrative among certain Reformed theologians has been equally trenchant: critiquing RO for its reliance on a Platonic notion of participation (*metathexis*), which, it is argued, overwhelms the covenantal categories used to depict the Creator-creature relation in Scripture. Thus, certain Reformed theologians have sought to develop a fully fledged covenantal ontology derived from a forensic doctrine of justification and thereby eliminate any remaining vestiges of the medieval notion of participation (Cf. Bruce L. McCormack, 'What's at Stake in Current Debates over Justification? The Crisis of Protestantism in the West', in *Justification: What's at Stake in the Current Debates*, eds. Mark Husbands and Daniel J. Treier (Downers Grove, IL: InterVarsity Press, 2004), 81–117; Michael S. Horton, 'Participation and Covenant', in *Radical Orthodoxy and the Reformed Tradition: Creation, Covenant, and Participation*, eds. James K. A. Smith and James H. Olthuis (Grand Rapids, MI: Baker Academic, 2005), 107–32; idem., *Covenant and Salvation: Union with Christ* (Louisville, KT: Westminster John Knox Press, 2007), 127–310). For these theologians, the participatory metaphysics

realized, lacks nothing, and is devoid of no element of his own blessedness. From all eternity he is wholly and unceasingly fulfilled'.[50]

There are two important implications of this account of divine perfection for Webster. First, it allows him to develop a non-comparative account of God's transcendence and otherness in relation to creatures. A prime example can be found in an extended quote from Webster's essay 'The Holiness and Love of God' (2004):

> The act in which God fulfils his holy being as Father, Son and Spirit differentiates him from every other being; as God enacts his majestic identity, he is entirely himself. Like all God's acts, this act of personal self-differentiation is wholly effortless, uncaused and perfect, requiring nothing for its fulfilment beyond

---

of RO and the covenantal theology of the Reformers are seen as mutually exclusive metaphysical paradigms. Other theologians are seeking to integrate covenant and participation within an overall theological vision or system. John Milbank argues that, although Calvin's doctrine of participation is restricted to a Christological context, there is space in his thought for a wider notion of participation with regard to the metaphysics of creation. According to Milbank, the notion of covenant can be integrated within the larger framework of a participatory metaphysics, although it does pose some challenges to the Reformed understanding of justification as imputation ('Alternative Protestantism: Radical Orthodoxy and the Reformed Tradition', in *Radical Orthodoxy and the Reformed Tradition: Creation, Covenant, and Participation*, eds. James K. A. Smith and James H. Olthuis (Grand Rapids, MI: Baker Academic, 2005), 27–37). Another proposal can be found in Justin S. Holcomb, 'Being Bound to God: Participation and Covenant Revisited', in *Radical Orthodoxy and the Reformed Tradition: Creation, Covenant, and Participation*, eds. James K. A. Smith and James H. Olthuis (Grand Rapids, MI: Baker Academic, 2005), 243–62. Holcomb argues that RO's theology of participation can give Reformed theology a much-needed lever by which to offer a cultural critique of modernity, and conversely, Reformed theology's emphasis on covenantal history can help RO avoid undue abstraction and idealism. Finally and most recently, Jared Michelson has argued that RO's genealogy of modernity does not adequately account for examples of Reformed scholastic theologians (e.g. Stephen Charnock and Herman Witsius) who held a Thomist participatory metaphysics alongside of a robust covenantal theology and that there is good theological reason to believe that a Reformed doctrine of justification as imputation can coexist with a participatory understanding of union with Christ and infused habits ('Reformed and Radically Orthodox?: Participatory Metaphysics, Reformed Scholasticism and Radical Orthodoxy's Critique of Modernity', *IJST* 20:1 [2018]: 104–28; 'Covenantal History and Participatory Metaphysics: Formulating a Reformed Response to the Charge of Legal Fiction', *SJT* 71:4 [2018]: 391–410).

50. *CG*, 157. Wittman comments, 'When set forth in this manner, God's perfection is not "inclusive", but "exclusive" perfection in that it does not have creatures as an integral aspect of the fullness is describes' ('John Webster on the Task of a Properly Theological *Theologia*', 109).

itself. God's 'otherness' is not something which God comes to have in rivalry between himself and others. The divine being is replete, and is involved in no agonistics. God's holiness is thus his transcendence of any possible relation in which he is merely one factor alongside another, even if it be the supreme or victorious factor.[51]

Precisely because God's otherness and uniqueness are grounded in his immanent perfection, and because the creature cannot possibly add to or subtract from the perfection of God's being, God's relation to creatures is neither competitive nor antagonistic. Hence, Webster seems to suggest that an 'exclusive' account of divine perfection is the ultimate ground for the non-competitive relation between God and creatures. This leads us to the second implication of divine perfection: it allows Webster to ground his Reformed ecclesiological distinctives – e.g. commitment to the *solas*, emphasis on the externality of God's relation to the church and preference for the concept of covenant fellowship over participation – in the doctrine of God. God alone is life in himself and 'does not receive his life at the hand of any other', nor can any other 'modify or extend his life'.[52] It is the exclusive nature of God's perfection that now grounds Webster's claims that God's being is 'imparticipable' and his saving agency non-transferable, claims he made previously based on the sufficiency of God's works.[53] In sum, God's perfection is beyond both creaturely competition and creaturely participation.

At this point, some proponents of *communio* ecclesiology (e.g. Henri de Lubac) would raise an important objection to this approach. Does a commitment to an exclusive account of divine perfection lead to a dualism between natural and supernatural, visible and invisible, whereby the relation between God and the church becomes 'purely extrinsic'?[54] To some extent Webster feels the weight of this critical question, yet he ultimately thinks it is misplaced, believing an element of externality is essential to any theology of grace which wants to avoid collapsing divine action into ecclesial action.[55] The way forward, he argues, is not found in an account of intrinsic perfection or a minimization of ecclesiology altogether.

---

51. *CG*, 117.
52. *CG*, 157.
53. *CG*, 163.
54. See, for example, Henri De Lubac's, 'Critiques of Protestant Ecclesiology', in *Catholicism: Christ and the Common Destiny of Man*, trans. Lancelot C. Sheppard (London: Burns & Oates, 1950), 21–2, 26–8; idem., *The Splendour of the Church*, trans. Michael Mason (Glen Rock, NJ: Paulist Press, 1963), 51–5. In contrast to Protestant 'extrinsicism', de Lubac seeks to develop an understanding of the church as the sacrament of God. On this topic, see Hans Boersma, *Nouvelle Theologie and Sacramental Ontology: A Return to Mystery* (Oxford: Oxford University Press, 2009), 242–65.
55. For a catalogue of Webster's various (mostly critical) engagements with Catholic ecclesiology, see Fergus Kerr, 'John Webster and Catholic Theology', *NB* 98 (2017): 457, 460–2, 464, 473–5, 480–1.

Rather, 'a more precise specification of God's perfection', out of which the church is generated, is needed.[56]

Webster seeks to offer this precision through recourse to the concept of 'motion', a point to which we will return in our discussion of Webster's mature account of ecclesial action and mediation. For our present purposes, it is important to note that divine perfection consists of a twofold motion. First and primarily, it is the internal motion of the Holy Trinity: 'the eternally mobile repose' of Father, Son and Spirit.[57] Second and derivatively, divine perfection 'includes a movement outwards', in which 'the fullness of God is the origin and continuing ground of a reality which is *outside* his own life'.[58] Yet this distinction raises a further question about the nature of divine perfection: What is the relation of the internal movement to the external movement? And how can theology articulate the relation between these movements in such a way that compromises neither the freedom and aseity of God nor the 'real'[59] and 'mutual'[60] nature of God's relation to creatures?

At this point in his development, Webster makes recourse to a Barthian influenced doctrine of election in an effort to hold together these two concerns. We have already noted how the doctrine of election plays a key role in Webster's ecclesiology, providing the link between the Trinity and the church. It remains pivotal for Webster's early conceptual formulations of divine perfection as well, because it can articulate the proper relationship between the first and second movements of that perfection, specifying how the second, external movement can be necessary for God without compromising his freedom and majesty in relation to creatures. Webster's argument is as follows:

> This second movement, in which God wills and provides for free creaturely being, is a necessary movement. It is not *externally* necessary, for then it would not be a divine movement but a divine reaction (and therefore not divine); rather, it is internally necessary, because it flows from the eternal divine counsel to be himself also in this second movement .... This movement is a movement of holy love .... God's holiness is loving because it is not mere divine self-segregation but God's self-election for integrity in loving fellowship with what is not God .... God's perfection is actual as his determination for fellowship. It is this movement which is the ground of the church.[61]

---

56. *CG*, 166.
57. *CG*, 167.
58. *CG*, 166–7.
59. *CG*, 158.
60. *CG*, 166, 170.
61. *CG*, 167. The distinction between external and internal necessity seems to have come from Barth's account of divine love and freedom in *CD* II.1, 272–321. As Eric J. Titus has argued, divine freedom for Barth 'is characterized by the idea that God is unconditioned by that which is external to God and is conditioned only by God's "own choosing and deciding, willing and doing"' ('The Perfections of God in the Theology of Karl Barth: A Consideration of the Formal Structure', *Kairos: Evangelical Journal of Theology* 4:2 [2010]: 207).

Note the language used here: 'internally necessary', 'self-election' and 'determination for fellowship'. The doctrine of election is not about the inscrutability of the divine will, nor is it about the election and retribution of individual human beings; rather, it is about God's sovereign 'self-determination' to be God for us; it is about the 'directedness of the being of God to us'.[62] In other words, it is about the nature of divine perfection. God's perfect actuality is internally orientated *ad extra*; therefore, divine freedom, majesty and aseity are expressed in covenant-making and fellowship-establishing action.[63] The doctrine of election is the means by which Webster attempts to affirm an exclusive account of divine perfection (i.e. the church is not constitutive of the divine life) while also claiming that God's saving action and relation to the church are not arbitrary or accidental or contingent, but grounded in the very nature of divine perfection.

It is this dual purpose that seems to give rise to a tension in Webster's early accounts of divine perfection. How can an external movement towards creatures be 'internally necessary' to divine perfection without that movement (and the consequent relation established with creatures) being in some sense constitutive of God's inner life? In other words, it is not exactly clear that Webster's early accounts of divine perfection in the mid-2000s are 'exclusive'. We could quote a number of examples on this score: 'God's integral perfection does not exclude but rather *includes* the movement of his perfect being toward creatures in works of love.'[64] Or again: 'God is perfect; but his perfection *includes* a movement outwards, a turning to that which is not God, as its lordly creator, reconciler and consummator.'[65] Or, the same thing expressed in the form of a question: '[H]ow can God's perfection *include* his relation to the world?'[66] My question is this: Is it consistent to deny that creatures co-constitute God's life while also affirming that God's action towards and relation to creatures is included in God's integral perfection? I am not sure that this distinction holds: the affirmation seems to imply that some aspect of God's perfection (no matter how small) is dependent on his relation to creation to some degree. It seems that there is a genuine tension in Webster's account of divine perfection at this point, a tension which arises as he seeks to affirm some version of an exclusive account of divine perfection while also specifying how God's redemptive relation to the church is grounded in the very nature of that perfection via a Barthian influenced doctrine of election. As Ian A. McFarland has argued,

---

62. *CG*, 168. Cf. *CD* II.2, 94–145.

63. We can see a similar logic at work in Webster's account of the relation between divine aseity and the church: 'God is essentially, to the depths of his triune being, God for us and God with us, the one whose mercy evokes the miracle of human fellowship with himself. There is always a double theme in Christian theology, a twofoldness in all its matter which corresponds to the identity of aseity and self-giving in the life of the Holy Trinity' (Holiness, 54).

64. Webster, 'God's Perfect Life', 145 (emphasis mine).

65. *CG*, 166 (emphasis mine).

66. Webster, 'God's Perfect Life', 151 (emphasis mine).

'The content of the divine will must be rooted in God's being, but (*pace* Barth) the two cannot be equated without muddying the distinction between Creator and creature.'[67]

Hence, our discussion of the relation between God's perfection and the church has added a bit of complexity to our heuristic framework in Chapter 1: it is true that a theology of divine perfection plays a central and governing role in the final 10–12 years of Webster's career, but it is also true that it is a doctrine which undergoes development during that period of time. Early articulations reflect a tension between inclusive and exclusive accounts of divine perfection, whereas later articulations opt for the latter more consistently. This transition is reflected in the way the language of 'inclusion' is replaced by that of 'cause'/'principle' and 'effect', which is indicative of the prominent role that the doctrine of creation came to play in articulating the relation between divine perfection and creatures. We will circle back to this point in a moment, but for now let us return to a discussion of Webster's ecclesiology.

As Webster's account of divine perfection and its implications for ecclesiology develop in the years following these original articulations in 2005–2006, the doctrine of election still provides a key means of grounding the doctrine of the church in the immanent life of God, but there are two changes, both of which are significant for our present discussion of Webster's understanding of the relation-in-distinction between God and the church. The first change is in the way the doctrine of election is articulated, moving from a broadly Barthian framework (God's self-election and self-determination for fellowship with humanity in Christ) to a broadly Reformed scholastic articulation (though not sharing their predilection for relishing in the inscrutability of the divine will) tied closely to the *pactum salutis*.[68] Secondly and more importantly, the doctrine of election (and the works of grace as a whole) is situated within the wider context of God's works of nature. The doctrine of creation comes to have pride of place as the primary hinge between theology and economy, between God's movement *ad intra* and his movement *ad extra*.[69] In order to elucidate the point, it is worth placing two quotes side by side:

---

67. Ian A. McFarland, 'Present in Love: Rethinking Barth on the Divine Perfections', *MoTh* 33:2 (2017): 247.

68. Cf. *GWM* I:183. Webster employed teaching about the *pactum salutis* as a way of grounding the economy of salvation in the divine will while attempting to avoid a potential implication of Barth's doctrine of election – namely that the humanity of Christ is essential to the eternal being of God.

69. Elsewhere, Webster identified the divine missions as the 'hinge' between theology and economy (*DW*, 146). But whether it is the doctrine of election or divine missions, the focus is on God's works of grace. Hence, the transition to the doctrine of creation as the 'hinge' is significant.

What ties together the realities of God in himself and God's economic presence is God's *will*, directed to creatures as sovereign decision and determination in their favor.[70]

[I]t [the doctrine of creation] is the bridge by which consideration of God *in se* passes over to consideration of God *ad extra*; it is the ground of the fact that Christian doctrine is responsible to attend not to a single but a double theme (God and all things).[71]

The first quote comes from an article in which Webster is raising some Reformed (Calvinist) reservations regarding the *analogia entis* and its undergirding participatory metaphysics. His emphasis on the divine will is designed to fund a particular construal of the economy, one which is grounded in divine decision rather than diffusion, and therefore, accents the moral nature of the relation between God and creatures.[72] Interestingly, Webster gives theological specificity to God's 'will' by turning to Ephesians 1, a passage that has the doctrine of election and the covenant established in Christ squarely in focus, making one wonder whether Barth still looms in the background. And yet, in the second quote (published three years later), we see a marked difference in emphasis: the doctrine of creation provides the 'bridge' between God *in se* and God *ad extra*. Created existence itself is the first effect of God's creative agency, and all other actions of God towards the creature presuppose that initial gift. The question raised by these quotes can be formulated as follows: Does creation set the context within which God enters into historical relations with creatures, or does covenant set the context within which God creates, and therefore creation is providing the necessary equipment for covenantal relation which is (in election) already established?[73] It seems to me that Webster eventually opted for the former: creation, not the covenant, is the most basic context within which God enters into historical relations with creatures. As a result, the relation between God's perfection and creatures is mediated first through the doctrine of creation (and derivatively the doctrine of

---

70. Webster, 'Perfection and Participation', 391.
71. *GWM* I:117.
72. It is the Pauline depiction of the God creature relation in terms of a *moral history* grounded in the divine will (Eph. 1:4 5, 9, 11) that leads Webster to resist the concept of metaphysical participation in his ecclesiology. Thus, the primary categories for his soteriology and ecclesiology are covenantal (sin and its redemption by a personal, historical and moral act of God the Son) not participatory (estrangement and its overcoming; diffusion of being and its return). When seen in this light, Webster's ecclesiological focus on 'covenantal fellowship' over against 'participation' is part and parcel of a Reformed emphasis, not only on the radical distinction and asymmetry between God and creatures, but also on the ethical nature of their relation.
73. This way of formulating the question was proposed to me in an email correspondence with Jared Michelson.

providence), which then provides the context and presupposition for the works of grace, including the doctrine of election.[74]

The impact of this doctrinal reconfiguration can be seen in Webster's ecclesiology in a number of ways. (1) The distinction between uncreated and created being becomes ecclesiologically fundamental and is articulated through the theory of mixed relations. The God-church relation is no longer depicted as 'mutual' and 'real' for God, but rather as 'non-reciprocal' and 'non-real'.[75] (2) The category of 'creatureliness' becomes foundational in giving an account of ecclesial being and action. (3) A scholastic account of creaturely action as a 'moved movement' is employed to develop a properly ordered yet definitively positive account of ecclesial mediation. While much could be said about each of these items, I will restrict the discussion in the following section to the way in which item one opens the logical and theological space for item three.

3.5 Mature ecclesiology: Distinction and mediation

Having devoted attention to Webster's theory of mixed relations in the previous two chapters, it is not necessary to repeat that material here. What is important to our current discussion is the fact that Webster applies this conceptuality to the relation between God and the church, thereby situating the God-church relation established by grace within the larger context of the Creator-creature relation established at creation, which in turn opens theological space for a positive account of ecclesial mediation. In order to demonstrate that this is the case, I begin with a brief discussion of the implications of the doctrine of creation *ex nihilo* for how Webster conceives of the Creator-creature relation.

According to Webster, the doctrine of creation *ex nihilo* has a unique pedagogical function in a theological system because it requires that theological reason attend to fundamental aspects of the Creator's perfection as well as the Creator-creature distinction. And it is precisely this perfection and distinction that enables a non-competitive account of divine and human action. In his essays on the doctrine of creation, Webster's material account of divine perfection is articulated in Thomist conceptual categories. This is particularly evident in Webster's insistence that God's being is not 'ordered to another' outside of himself, and that God is 'wholly outside the genus of that which is ordered to him'.[76] In other words, God is wholly realized life in himself apart from creatures, and he neither gains nor loses anything by the act of creation. Rather than speaking of God's relation to creatures as flowing from an 'internal necessity', he now highlights the fact that there is in God no *esse-ad* relation to anything outside himself. This account of divine perfection then governs what is said about the nature of God's act of creation – it is 'non-necessary'

---

74. *GWM* I:99–100, 117–9.
75. *GWM* I:181; Webster, 'Ressourcement Theology and Protestantism', 491.
76. *GWM* I:124.

– and illumines the nature of God's relation to creation – it is 'non-constitutive', 'non-reciprocal' and 'non-real'.[77] Where some may worry that such negations are bound to threaten the loving and intimate nature of the God-creature relation, Webster argues that the opposite is in fact true. It is only because God's relation to creation is non-constitutive and adds nothing to his perfection, that one can trust that the Creator's actions *ad extra* are devoid of self-interest and, therefore, acts of pure generosity – intended solely for the creature's benefit. Moreover, it is only because God is beyond relations of reciprocity and dialectic that his actions do not displace or compete with creaturely actions.[78] In other words, the non-reciprocal (i.e. mixed) and incommensurable nature of the relation between God and creatures, derived from a Thomistic account of divine perfection and creation *ex nihilo*, is precisely what undergirds their non-competitive relation.

And so, moving back to ecclesiology, we see a shift in Webster's account of the relation between divine and ecclesial action as it is situated within the wider context of the Creator-creature relation. Whereas earlier work suggested that the doctrine of creation *ex nihilo* implied that divine and human action are 'inversely proportional',[79] now Webster's mature account of the doctrine says otherwise: '[I]t is elemental to a scriptural metaphysics that the motion of God and the motion of creatures are not inversely but directly proportional: the more God moves the creature, the more the creature moves itself.'[80] Or again: 'The church is a society which moves itself as it is moved by God.'[81] The radical distinction and the mixed relation between uncreated and created being, mediated through the doctrine of creation, open the logical and theological space for Webster to develop a non-competitive account of divine and ecclesial action. In order to explore this dynamic in Webster's mature ecclesiology a bit further, we turn now to an analysis of Webster's use of the concept of motion and the implications this has for his account of ecclesial mediation.

The concept of motion is central to the material interconnectivity of Webster's essay 'In the Society of God' (2011) – his final essay devoted solely to ecclesiology. It is used to describe the immanent divine processions, the salvific mission of the Son and the social-historical acts of the church.[82] The intention behind this material interconnectivity is clear in Webster's work: it allows him to emphasize the priority of divine being and action in relation to creaturely being and action, the former being the ground and creative source of the latter. Ecclesial action derives its existence from and is in a constant state of ontological dependence upon divine action.[83] Thus, for Webster, the phenomenal particularities of the church cannot be understood on their own terms (i.e. as purely natural phenomena), but have 'to

77. *GWM* I:103, 107.
78. Cf. *GWM* I:113.
79. *CG*, 171.
80. *GWM* I:188.
81. *GWM* I:193.
82. *GWM* I:182, 185, 188.
83. *GWM* I:188, 193.

be traced back – reduced – to God as their exemplary, efficient and final cause.'[84] When theological reason devotes its attention to analysing the social-historical acts of the church, it seeks to understand those acts as 'moved movements'. This requires theological reason to follow a very particular logic of ascent: in order to understand ecclesial movement it must devote attention to that by which it is moved (variously described as the motion of divine providence, the divine missions, and 'the electing, calling, gathering, and sanctifying works of God'),[85] and in order to understanding the divine motion by which the church is moved it must contemplate the ultimate source of that motion (the self-moved mover), namely the immanent life of the triune God (the divine processions).

At this point, one may well ask how Webster's wide-ranging use of the concept of 'motion' is any different from Jenson and Tillard's use of the concept of 'communion' or Gunton's use of the concept of 'relation', both of which Webster was highly critical? To employ the concept of motion in the way that he has – i.e. to construe the material relations between God's inner life, God's external action and the church's action – seems to require an analogical use of the term.[86] And yet, Webster explicitly resists attempts to describe the relation between God and creatures via a mediating term such as 'communion' or 'relation'. The best example of this can be found in his critique of Colin Gunton: '[D]eploying "relation" (or, more abstractly "relationality") as a bridge term between God and creatures can prove precarious, effecting the passage from God to the church too comfortably, without securing an adequate sense of the unqualified gratuity of the church's created existence and of its difference from God who is the uncreated source of its life.'[87] So how is Webster's use of the concept of motion different? The answer is twofold.

First, the concept of motion is more serviceable for theology because of its ability to keep the focus on the priority of divine action in one's construal of the God-church relation. Webster states, 'The relation of theology proper and ecclesiology is best explicated not by setting out two terms of an analogy but by describing a sequence of divine acts both in terms of their ground in the immanent divine being and in terms of their creaturely fruits.'[88] In other words, the concept of motion is dynamic, keeping the theological focus on the creative priority of divine action and thereby on the distinction between God and the church in a way that the concepts of 'communion' and 'relation' have more difficulty achieving. Second, the concept of motion is able to articulate a non-competitive account of divine and ecclesial action without thereby collapsing the distinction between them. Some context may prove helpful in illuminating this point.

84. *GWM* I:189.
85. *GWM* I:193.
86. On the analogical use of the concept of motion, see Simon Oliver, *Philosophy, God and Motion* (London: Routledge, 2005), 2–3.
87. *GWM* I:182.
88. *GWM* I:182.

There have been a number of critiques in recent decades of dogmatic approaches to ecclesiology that seek to ground the being of the church in the inner life of God, arguing that they tend to offer idealized accounts of the church which bear a rather tenuous relation to the social-historical realties of its actual existence in time, particularly the church's sinfulness. Webster has received criticism along these lines from Christopher Craig Brittain: 'Essentially, the discussion begins with a theory of God, which is taken as definitive of the nature of the church, with the implication that this theoretical lens cannot be called into question by the empirical observations and experiences of members of historical churches.'[89] In other words, Webster locates the true being of the church at a level of invisibility and abstraction that ultimately makes any link to the visible and lived experience of the church's members tenuous at best. This renders social-scientific study insignificant for ecclesiology and makes it very difficult for the theologian to acknowledge, account for and critique the concrete sinful actions of the church.

A common response has been to make accounts of ecclesial practices the linchpin of ecclesiological reflection. While Webster acknowledges the potential threat of ecclesiological idealism, he is far more concerned with the theological and metaphysical underpinnings of the practice-oriented response to this idealism.[90] The implicit assumption, argues Webster, is that 'the real is the social-historical',[91] and what initially 'presents itself as a principle of non-competition between divine and social agents turns out to require us to fold language about divine action into language about the functions and codes of the Christian society'.[92] Webster wants to affirm the 'principle of non-competition' but do so in such a way that does not

---

89. Christopher Craig Brittain, 'Why Ecclesiology Cannot Live by Doctrine Alone: A Reply to John Webster's "In the Society of God"', *Ecclesial Practices* 1 (2014): 17.

90. While a full-length evaluation of Brittain's critique is beyond my purview in this chapter, his argument does bring to light the fact that Webster's ecclesiological writings are primarily theological-metaphysical in focus, not practical-pastoral. Brittain and Webster are talking about the church's sin in two different contexts or levels of discourse. If this is the case, then it is not that Webster's ecclesiology necessarily makes it difficult for him to speak of the concrete sins of the church, but rather that he is attempting to situate harmiotology within the larger context of a theological-metaphysics of nature and grace. The clearest example of this can be found in his essay 'Theology and the Peace of the Church' (2012), in which goodness and peace are identified as the natural (i.e. metaphysically basic) condition of creatures. Sin and conflict are then interpreted as that which is contrary to nature (*contra naturam*), and crucially, this 'contrariety' is articulated in terms of a metaphysical privation (*DW*, 156–7, 161). Such an account does not necessarily overlook the 'palpable *datum*' of the church's sins, although it can in fact do so, but rather seeks to give theological-metaphysical specificity to the '*kind* of reality' sin is (*DW*, 160).

91. *GWM* I:178.

92. *GWM* I:178–9.

collapse divine action into human action. This is precisely what his use of the concept of motion – especially 'moved movement' – is designed to achieve.

To see how this is the case, it is important to recognize that Webster is drawing upon a pre-Newtonian tradition of motion as it is articulated in the thought of Aquinas, where the concept of motion has not yet been restricted to the notions of physical force and efficient causality.[93] The pre-modern concept of motion is much more capacious, allowing for applicability not only to physical but also to moral and spiritual realities. Moreover, it is part and parcel of a hierarchical and teleological cosmology, where the universe consists of layers of interconnected and interdependent motions, all of which find their ultimate origin and goal in the perfect self-movement of the Creator. And so, on the one hand, Webster can describe the immanent life of God in terms of a motion that is radically different from creaturely motion:

> God the Holy Trinity is alive with self-moved life. This movement of his is unlike creaturely movement because it is *self*-movement, *a se*, not moved from beyond itself, and so in its very mobility a kind of perfect repose, a movement without agitation. As God moves himself, he does not come into being or stretch towards his fulfilment; his movement is not theogony but inexhaustible plenitude, the fullness of eternal life.[94]

Yet, on the other hand, it is precisely this divine self-motion (i.e. the divine processions) that causes creatures to live and move and have their being. It is manifest as 'creative love'.[95] Hence, a doctrine of divine perfection, mediated through the doctrines of creation and providence, grounds the characterization of creaturely action as a 'moved movement'. This forms an important backdrop to everything Webster goes on to say about ecclesial modes of action. God is not only the original 'principle' of creaturely being, but also the abiding 'source' of creaturely action; he is 'not an abyss into which the creature tumbles, but one who in conferring being also bequeaths act. The relation of creatureliness includes "non-passive receptivity", a given capacity for becoming through the enactment of created life'.[96] It is this 'non-passive receptivity'[97] and 'given capacity', implicit within the concept of 'moved movement', that opens the logical and theological space for a positive account of ecclesial action and mediation.

---

93. The following discussion of the concept of motion (especially as it appears in Aquinas' thought) is heavily indebted to the work of Simon Oliver, by whom Webster himself was influenced. Cf. Oliver, *Philosophy, God and Motion*, 85–137; idem., 'Trinity, Motion and Creation *Ex Nihilo*', 133–51.
94. *GWM* I:182.
95. *GWM* I:188–9.
96. *GWM* I:113.
97. This phrase is from Schmitz, *The Textual of Being*, 196.

We can demonstrate this claim by looking at two examples of Webster's mature theology of ecclesial mediation: (1) his depiction of the church as a social-historical phenomenon, and (2) his theology of baptism. We begin with Webster's discussion of the phenomenal forms of the church, 'the primary structures of its creaturely, social-historical existence'.[98] He mentions three in his essay 'In the Society of God': assembly, Scripture and order. At this point in our discussion, it is not at all surprising to find Webster referring to Scripture as that which mediates God's communicative presence to the church and thereby constitutes the church as *creatura verbi divini*. It is, however, quite new to find Webster speaking of the church's acts of assembling and ordering as in some sense mediatory. Webster begins with the church's act of assembling: '[T]he church is a human assembly or form of association. But its human act of assembly follows, signifies and mediates a divine act of gathering; it is a moved movement of congregation.'[99] Notice how the human acts of following, signifying and mediating are all comprised within the overarching notion of 'moved movement'. Ecclesial action is derived from a prior divine movement (follows), refers beyond itself to the self-moving being and work of God (signifies), and is itself a means by which God moves creatures towards their fulfilment (mediates).

The language of mediation appears in a somewhat different form when Webster discusses the church as an ordered society. He states,

> The basic signs of the church – Scripture and sacraments – are its primary instruments of order, but they are administered by derivative instruments: creeds and confessions, canon law, a publicly authorized ministry. Order *sanctifies* human common life, and so is a provision of divine goodness …. The order of the church, its existence in limitation, is a grace because it is essential to the healing of created society from the disarray by which it is overcome.[100]

Given the way in which Webster's essays in *GWM* have absorbed the language and conceptuality of scholasticism, and given the way he refers to Scripture and sacraments as the 'primary instruments of order', it makes his use of the phrase 'derivative instruments' resonate with sacramental overtones. Here, we are a long way from any sort of separation of nature and grace, or dualism between divine and human action. On the contrary, the confessional and institutional elements of ecclesial order – the church's public forms of life – are characterized as 'grace'. They are not only the result of grace, but they are a creaturely form of grace whose goal is the restoration of creatureliness: 'Healing comes by the restoration of creatureliness, that is, through the saving gift of determinate form.'[101] Ecclesial

---

98. *GWM* I:189.
99. *GWM* I:190.
100. *GWM* I:192.
101. *GWM* I:193.

order is not to be identified with divine action *tout court*, but neither is divine saving action without its creaturely, social-historical form.

This leads us, finally, to Webster's mature theology of baptism, where the shift towards a positive account of ecclesial mediation is on full display. In his essay 'Mortification and Vivification' (2014), Webster devotes a significant amount of space to discussing the relation between baptism and regeneration.[102] At the start, he makes a key distinction between the first cause of regeneration (God alone) and the instrumental cause of regeneration (baptism). Then he anticipates a common Reformed objection: 'Pietist Christians may worry that this attributes to the church's action of baptism what ought to be attributed to God alone, encouraging reliance on rite at the expense of personal faith.'[103] Webster may have the likes of John Owen in his sights here. Interestingly, Webster's doctrine of regeneration is deeply indebted to Owen's discussion of the matter in *Pneumatologia*, especially as it relates to the notion of infused habits of grace.[104] Webster shares Owen's Reformed emphasis on regeneration as the condition of possibility and source of the theological virtues, yet he differs from Owen in his evaluation of the role of baptismal in mediating this regenerative grace. In this regard, Webster follows Aquinas. He writes, 'But because baptism is the instrumental cause – not the source – its efficacy is derivative …. God alone effects regeneration, and does so applicatively through baptism, by means of which the divine gift of new life in Christ is distributed.'[105] Having made a clear distinction between divine and creaturely causality, Webster goes on to speak of the efficacy of baptism in rather active terms. Baptism 'bestows', 'effects', 'founds', 'initiates', 'communicates', 'inaugurates' and 'empowers'.[106] Moreover, baptism not only confers the remission of sins and effects union with Christ, but also bestows a new nature with new capacities, powers and habits. It is a means by which the Spirit infuses grace into the human person.[107]

---

102. Cf. *GWM* II:106–11.
103. *GWM* II:106.
104. Cf. John Owen, *The Works of John Owen*, ed. William H. Goold (Edinburgh: T&T Clark, 1850–5), 3:207–337. According to Owen, regeneration includes the communication of 'a new, spiritual, supernatural, vital principle or habit of grace, infused into the soul, the mind, will, and affections, by the power of the Holy Spirit, disposing and enabling them in whom it is unto spiritual, supernatural, vital acts of faith and obedience' (3:329). For a discussion of Owen's theology of infused habits, see Christopher Cleveland, *Thomism in John Owen* (New York, NY: Routledge, 2016), 69–120.
105. *GWM* II:106–7.
106. *GWM* II:107–8.
107. Webster is now defining grace in Thomistic terms as a divine action and its created effect. It is also worth noting that for Webster, like Aquinas, the divine motion by which creatures are moved internally towards their end is uniquely related to the person and work of the Holy Spirit. Thus, it is no mistake that in his essay 'In the Society of God' the characterization of the church's social-historical forms as 'moved movements' follows directly on the heels of a discussion the Holy Spirit as 'the divine agent of creaturely perfection' (*GWM* I:187). This way of reading Webster may ease some of Tom Greggs

At two crucial points in this discussion, Webster links baptism with the concept of motion, once in reference to creaturely motion and once in reference to divine motion. In the first instance, Webster speaks of the way in which baptism 'inaugurates and empowers – but does not perfect – the fallen creature's movement towards complete renewal'.[108] In the second instance, Webster quotes Aquinas, who is describing the effect of the grace and virtue bestowed through baptism as a 'spiritual motion':

> [T]here is no life if the members are not united to the head from which they receive feeling and motion. Thus it is necessary that a person be incorporated by baptism into Christ as a member of his. But as feeling and motion flow from the natural head to the members, so from the spiritual head, which is Christ, there flow to his members spiritual feeling, which is the knowledge of truth, and spiritual motion, which results from the impulse of grace.[109]

Baptism is an event of interlocking motions, divine and creaturely; irreversibly ordered yet non-competitively related. Grace is a motion that flows from Christ through baptism to the Christian and in turn propels a corresponding creaturely

---

critiques of his ecclesiology for having a muted and deficient pneumatology (cf. Tom Greggs, 'Proportion and Topography in Ecclesiology: A Working Paper on the Dogmatic Location of the Doctrine of the Church', in *Theological Theology: Essay in Honour of John B. Webster*, eds. R. David Nelson, Darren Sarisky, and Justin Stratis (London: Bloomsbury T&T Clark, 2015), 89–106). It also raises questions about Derek W. Taylor's diagnosis of Webster's ecclesiological deficiencies. According to Taylor, Webster's ecclesiology is plagued by a 'hermeneutical spiritualism', which is grounded in Christological deficiencies – namely an incipient 'Nestorianism' caused by Webster's commitment to the *extra Calvinisticum* (Derek W. Taylor, *Reading Scripture in the Wake of Christ: The Church as a Hermeneutical Space* (PhD diss., Duke University, 2017), 15–22, 37–46). The theological cogency of the *extra Calvinisticum* is a matter that can be debated in its own right, yet what is troubling about Taylor's critique is the way in which it is driven by imposing the limitations of his research question and methodology – Christ is the essence of Christianity and Christology is the cardinal Christian doctrine (Taylor, *Reading Scripture*, xl) – upon Webster's ecclesiology. For Webster, ecclesiology is a matter of 'trinitarian deduction', and yet Taylor pays almost exclusive attention to the connection between Webster's Christology and ecclesiology, offering very little discussion of the difference patriology and pneumatology make for Webster's thought. As a result, Taylor faults Webster's Christology for failing to provide the proper basis for a robust account of the social-historical practices of the church, when in fact Webster seeks to achieve this primarily through pneumatology. It may well be that Webster has a deficient account of the social-historical visibility of the church, but such a judgement ought not to be made based solely on an analysis of the relation between Christology and ecclesiology.

108. *GWM* II: 108.
109. *GWM* II:111 (quote from *ST* IIIa. 69.5 resp.).

movement towards perfection.[110] And crucially, this gracious divine movement is not a purely extrinsic force but moves creatures internally through the bestowal of new capacities, powers and habits (i.e. principles of motion).[111] Ecclesial mediation finds its proper context within this theology of grace, situated between its source (the efficacy of divine motion) and oriented towards its goal (the perfection of creaturely motion). In this way, ecclesial action is still relativized by divine action, but in such a way that upholds and fulfils the integrity of creaturely nature.

It has been my argument that this theology of ecclesial mediation was made possible by developments in Webster's account of divine perfection and, consequently, of the way in which he articulated the relation-in-distinction between God and creatures. The shift from a Barthian to a Thomist account of divine perfection was manifest in the way he turned from the doctrine of election to the doctrine of creation *ex nihilo* as the primary hinge between theology and economy. Consequently, Webster's account of the distinction between God and creatures became more radical, and his account of their relation became increasingly non-competitive. This opened the door for developing a positive account of ecclesial mediation without thereby diminishing the radical distinction between God and the church. And thus, in an interesting turn of events, Webster's mature theology (2010s) sought to give a robust account of ecclesial agency without having to employ the concepts of 'coinherence' and 'continuity' (the emphases of his ecclesiology in the 1980s) and without in any way compromising the perfection of God's being and Christ's work (the major concerns of his ecclesiology throughout the 2000s).[112]

As we conclude our discussion of Webster's mature ecclesiology, it is worth recapitulating its basic theological principles. First, ecclesiology is best approached by integrating the topic within a larger account of God's relation to creatures, and second, an account of the God-creature relation is to be governed by teaching about God's inner life. Hence, the basic dogmatic principle of ecclesiology: 'All

---

110. *GWM* II:120.

111. With regard to Aquinas' understanding of grace as motion, which provides the background to Webster's articulation here, Simon Oliver states, 'In addition to God moving humanity to its appropriate end, grace is also given as an "habitual gift," namely a form or nature by which humanity can move and be moved to the supernatural end appointed by God. As we have seen, God's providence extends to creatures not simply by moving them to their appropriate ends but also through the bestowal of forms and powers by which they make that motion their own. Similarly, God provides his grace by which humanity may make its motion to beatitude its own' ('Aquinas and Aristotle's Teleology', 865). The forms of habitual grace, according to Aquinas, are the theological virtues of faith, hope and love.

112. I am not claiming that Webster's description of the socio-historical dynamics of the church are sufficient (they are rather thin in fact), but that the deficiency is descriptive, not material. In other words, his mature essays on ecclesiology are putting the material structure and concepts in place that will ground and provide context for a thick description of ecclesial practices, which ideally would have been developed in a full-length systematic theology.

this extends into ecclesiology the principle – fundamental to the doctrine of creation, incarnation, and grace alike – that whatever is said of God's relation to creatures is grounded in God's antecedent perfection in himself.'[113] This implies that theological reason approaches the topic of the church's being and acts with a twofold movement of 'trinitarian deduction'[114] and 'trinitarian reduction'.[115] The movement of Trinitarian deduction follows the order of being, beginning with God's immanent life and showing how that life is the origin and sustaining source of the church's being and action. The movement of Trinitarian reduction follows the order of knowing, beginning with the social-historical forms and actions of church and tracing their motive force back to the act and being of God. Webster's focus is thoroughly theological and metaphysical. And yet, just as Webster's mature approach to Christology did not deny that it was a historical science, so also his mature approach to ecclesiology does not deny that it is an ethnographic science. His point, often polemically stated, is simply that historical and ethnographic sciences are penultimate and instrumental, and that they only serve theology well when situated within a larger theological ontology.[116] The ultimate goal of ecclesiology, like Christology, is contemplation of the being and works of the Holy Trinity.

3.6 Conclusion

My argument in this chapter has revolved around a comparative study of Webster's early and mature ecclesiology, focusing on his understanding of the relation between God and the church, and how this influences his characterization of ecclesial action. In Webster's early ecclesiology, we saw an emphasis on the coinherence between Christ and the church and on the church as an agent whose Spirit-enabled activity continues and extends Christ's work in the world. We argued that his early ecclesiology was driven by a desire to resist theological abstraction and idealism. In Webster's mature ecclesiology, we discovered a rather different picture. He used conceptual resources from a Thomist account of divine perfection and doctrine of creation to emphasize the radical distinction and non-competitive relation between God and the church, thereby opening space for a positive account of ecclesial action and mediation without employing the

---

113. Webster, 'Ressourcement Theology and Protestantism', 492.
114. *GWM* I:181.
115. *GWM* I:193.
116. *GWM* I:193–4. Along similar lines, Nicholas M. Healy exposes some of potential pitfalls, both practical and theological, of the renewed focus on ecclesial practices in recent decades and suggests the solution is to reintegrate an account of ecclesial practices within a doctrine of the economic Trinity ('Practices and the New Ecclesiology: Misplaced Concreteness?', *IJST* 5:3 [2003]: 287–308). Webster would agree and add that the doctrine of the economic Trinity needs to be grounded in a doctrine of the immanent Trinity.

categories of 'coinherence' and 'continuity'. We argued that his mature ecclesiology was driven by a desire to manifest the asymmetry between God and the church: the social-historical forms of the church rest upon the perfection of God's self-movement as their metaphysical and salvific ground, and so the temporal is suspended from the eternal. I also sought to pinpoint two theological shifts from the 2000s that acted as catalysts for the development between Webster's early and mature ecclesiology. First, Webster recognized the need to ground ecclesiology in the doctrine of the Trinity in such a way that maintains a proper sense of the distinction and asymmetry between God and the church. Second, Webster made the doctrine of divine perfection the starting point for his ecclesiology, and eventually gave the doctrine of creation pride of place over the doctrine of election in making the transition from theology proper to economy.

In this way, the argument of this chapter has sought to provide further demonstration of the explanatory power of two elements of the heuristic framework given in Chapter 1. First, it has drawn attention to the significance of the two primary developmental shifts in Webster's thought – from Christocentric to Trinitarian, and from Trinitarian to Theocentric – for his understanding of the church. Second, it has demonstrated how the doctrines of divine perfection and of creation (especially teaching about mixed relations and moved movement) have a governing function in Webster's mature theology, even in his account of ecclesial being and action. But this chapter also raised a question that introduced some complexity into our understanding of Webster's mature thought on the relation between theology and economy, and therefore between God and creatures: How are we to understand his use of the language of 'inclusive' and 'exclusive' when describing the nature of divine perfection? The question proved to be of some significance for our understanding of the evolution of Webster's theology of divine perfection and its implications for his understanding of the God-church relation. Having explored the hypostatic relation between the divine and human natures of Christ in Chapter 2 (Christology) and the redemptive relation between God and the church in Chapter 3 (ecclesiology), we turn now to consider the communicative relation between God and creatures (bibliology).

Chapter 4

BIBLIOLOGY

4.1 Introduction

This chapter will explore John Webster's bibliology. It will seek to expound the way in which Webster construes the relation between God and Scripture, and how this influences his characterization of Scripture's readers and the act of reading. The main argument will be laid out in two composite sections followed by a conclusion. Each section corresponds to a discernible phase in Webster's bibliology. Here I am following the insight of Michael Allen:

> It is worth noting two major phases of reflection here: the cluster of writings that led to and were marked by the publication of his *Holy Scripture* (2003), including essays in part 1 of *Word and Church*, and then the essays that make up part 1 of *Domain of the Word* (2012) as well as the more recent essay on the doctrine of inspiration.[1]

The first section of this chapter will offer an analysis of *Holy Scripture*, and the second section will highlight the key bibliological developments in *Domain of the Word*. My thesis is that Webster's bibliology is driven by a consistent concern to resist the secularization of Scripture and interpretive activity without thereby diminishing the creaturely integrity of text and reader. Thus, he seeks to articulate a non-competitive account of the relation between God's self-revealing activity and creaturely activities and products. Yet the way in which he articulates this non-competitive relation evolves as teaching about God's inner life, providence and pneumatology take on prominence in his thought, resulting in a more robust account of the creaturely coordinates of divine revelation.

In this way, the argument of this chapter will seek to demonstrate the explanatory power of two elements of the heuristic framework given in Chapter 1. First, it will draw attention to the significance of the second primary developmental shift in Webster's thought – from Trinitarian to Theocentric – for his understanding of Scripture and its readers. This will be seen in the way Webster grounds the economy of grace (including God's revelatory missions) in the immanent life of

---

1. Allen, 'Toward Theological Theology', 225 n.45.

God. Second, it will demonstrate how the works of nature provide the context for understanding the works of grace in Webster's mature theology. This will be seen in the way the Spirit's work of inspiration and illumination is coordinated with teaching about God's providential ordering of history. But this chapter will also add nuance to the interpretation of Webster's doctrine of God laid out in Chapter 1. An analysis of Webster's doctrine of revelation will allow us to capture the personalist elements in his doctrine of God – God is a self-revealing Subject – and see how they fund a particular understanding of the God-creature relation, one which stresses its personal and communicative as well as moral and spiritual dynamics.

4.2 Holy Scripture *(2003)*

Originally delivered as the *Scottish Journal of Theology* lectures at the University of Aberdeen in 2001 and slightly revised for publication in 2003, *Holy Scripture* is one of Webster's most influential works. In its pages we begin to hear the distinctiveness of his theological voice come to the fore, the prime example of this being his resolve to flesh out the implications of designating the doctrine of the Trinity as the cardinal Christian doctrine. He states, 'Christian theology has a singular preoccupation: God, and everything else *sub specie divinitatis*. All other Christian doctrines are applications or corollaries of the one doctrine, the doctrine of the Trinity, in which the doctrine of the church, no less than the doctrine of revelation, has its proper home.'[2] As I argued in the previous chapters, Webster's doctrine of the Trinity (in the early 2000s) is resolutely focused on God's acts in the economy. What I want to demonstrate here is that by approaching the doctrine of Scripture through this lens, Webster's argument in *Holy Scripture* follows a very particular logic.

How does Webster grant the doctrine of the Trinity a governing role in his bibliology? First, Scripture and its readers are located in the economy of grace, which is constituted by the revelatory and reconciliatory missions of the Son and the Spirit. Second, a theological ontology of Scripture and an ecclesiology and anthropology of its readers are derived from their place and function in this economy. Third, a theological ethics of the act of reading is derived from the ontology of Scripture and anthropology of its readers. We begin our discussion with the dogmatic location of Scripture and its readers.

4.2.1 Dogmatic location of Scripture and its readers

Holy Scripture can be read as an extended exercise in dogmatic relocation.[3] Webster attempts to situate Scripture, including both the processes of its production and

---

2. *HS*, 43.
3. *HS*, 3.

the activities of its reception and reading, within the triune economy of grace. As we noted in Chapter 1, formal questions about 'dogmatic location' take on a particular prominence in Webster's thought around the turn of the twenty-first century, and this is seen most clearly in his bibliology. The concept of location provides an important way of contextualizing speech about creaturely realities (Scripture, church, reader) within an overall account of God-creature relation, and a way of grounding that relation in the freedom and gratuity of divine action. Creaturely being and acts are what they are only in relation to God's originating, reconciling and perfecting acts as Father, Son and Holy Spirit. Therefore, one of the primary agendas of *Holy Scripture* is to diagnose the 'mislocation' of Scripture and its readers in modern theology and to reintegrate them into their proper dogmatic 'location'.

Webster offers many examples of the mislocation of Scripture in modern theology, but two are particularly noteworthy.[4] The first example has to do with the implicit textual ontology of historical-critical methods: the text is abstracted from its place in the economy of God's revelatory and reconciliatory action and viewed as part of a purely immanent world of human communication. This naturalization or secularization of Scripture often assumes that talk of divine action is not essential, but merely ancillary, to giving an account of what the scriptural texts *are*. If the first example has to do with the problem of a naturalized ontology of Scripture, then the second example has to do with the claim that Scripture has no ontology, or at least that its ontology is determined primarily by human use. A theological version of this to which Webster is particularly sensitive is the way the term 'Scripture' can be used to refer to the communal use of a set of texts rather than their divine use.[5] In other words, the doctrine of Scripture is domesticated and construed as a product of ecclesial action rather than as a servant of divine revelation. For Webster, the reintegration of Scripture into its proper 'setting in trinitarian, pneumatological and ecclesial doctrine' is intended to guard against both the naturalization (i.e. the atrophy of divine action) and the domestication (i.e. the inflation of ecclesial action) of Scripture.[6]

The concept of location clarifies the nature of the scriptural texts (and their readers) by situating them within a field of divine action, requiring the theologian to understand them in terms of their wider transcendental context. The divine economy is the 'atmosphere or sustaining context of what creatures are and do', and so an ontology of Scripture and anthropology of its readers must proceed

---

4. The two examples given below come from *HS*, 6–8. For more examples, see *WC*, 9–10, 22–5; John Webster, 'Review Article: Canon and Criterion: Some Reflections on a Recent Proposal', *SJT* 54 (2001): 223–5.

5. See, for example, David H. Kelsey, *The Uses of Scripture in Recent Theology* (London: SCM Press Ltd, 1975).

6. *WC*, 10.

by way of a theological description of God's action.⁷ This is part of the reason why one does not find extended discussions of exegetical methods or practical solutions to hermeneutical issues in Webster's writings. Rather, he offers a dogmatic description of the 'location, character and ends of exegetical labour'.⁸ Webster does not intend to eclipse or replace the detailed work of exegesis, but to contextualize it: 'A doctrine of Scripture offers a theological ontology of Scripture and an ecclesiology and anthropology of its readers, in terms of which Christian exegetes can understand their place in the divine economy and so more fittingly perform the task to which they are appointed.'⁹ In the next section I will examine the theological ontology of Scripture that emerges from Scripture's location in the economy of grace, and then turn my attention to the ecclesiology and anthropology of reading in the following section.

4.2.2 Theological ontology of Scripture

Scripture's ontology is derived from its location in the economy of grace – the 'dynamic and purposive field of relations between the triune God and his creatures'.¹⁰ Therefore, the content of the term 'Holy Scripture' can 'only be thoroughly mapped by seeing this set of texts in connection with purposive divine action *in its interaction with* an assemblage of creaturely events, communities, agents, practices and attitudes'.¹¹ In other words, bibliology is a species of one's theology of the God-creature relation; in particular, it articulates the personal and communicative dynamic of that relation. And so, Webster's bibliology reflects a larger theme in his theology: a desire to develop a properly ordered and non-competitive account of the relation between God and creatures, where the freedom and priority of divine action are the ground of creaturely being and action.

In *Holy Scripture*, Webster looks to the doctrine of the Trinity as the key to articulating these elements of the God-creature relation. And, as I noted in the previous chapter, *how* creaturely realities are grounded in the doctrine of the Trinity is a matter of great importance, for it often underwrites a particular

---

7. *DW*, 128. Lewis Ayres summarizes Webster's theological approach well: '[O]ne of the most significant moves John makes ... is to argue that Christian thinking is actively undermined by general epistemological prolegomena. Our accounts of how Christian thinking proceeds must be firmly grounded in talk of how the Triune God acts to create, reveal and save. An account of what Scripture is and how it should be read must also, then, begin in Trinitarian reflection – wherever else it also takes us' ('The Word Answering the Word: Opening the Space of Catholic Biblical Interpretation', in *Theological Theology: Essays in Honour of John B. Webster*, eds. R. David Nelson, Darren Sarisky and Justin Stratis (London: Bloomsbury T&T Clark, 2015), 37).
8. *HS*, 3.
9. *CG*, 36.
10. *WC*, 28.
11. *HS*, 5 (emphasis mine).

account of the nature of those realities. This was true of Webster's ecclesiology: the doctrine of election grounded the church in the Trinity, resulting in a passive account of ecclesial action and apophatic account of ecclesial mediation. When it comes to Webster's bibliology, it is the doctrine of revelation that provides the key link to Trinitarian theology:

> [W]hat is said about the sanctification and inspiration of Scripture is an extension of what is said about revelation; but what is said about revelation is an extension of what is said about the triune God. What Scripture is as sanctified and inspired is a function of divine revelatory activity, and divine revelatory activity is God's triune being in its external orientation, its gracious and self-bestowing turn to the creation.[12]

Webster's bibliology follows a very definite material order: Trinity – revelation – sanctification and inspiration. So I will unpack his theological ontology of Scripture through a brief analysis of three terms – revelation, sanctification and inspiration – each of which describes an aspect of the triune God's gracious action towards creatures.

Webster begins by clarifying the dogmatic location of the doctrine of revelation: Trinitarian theology and soteriology. Why is this necessary? According to Webster, the doctrine of revelation has suffered distortion in modern theology as it has migrated from its native soil in the material claims of the Christian faith into the realm of epistemology. As its location has changed, so also has its function: it 'has to take on the job of furnishing the epistemological warrants for Christian claims'.[13] In other words, the concept of revelation is employed to provide the procedural and authorial foundations for doctrine, rather than articulating the internal logic of God's self-communication. What Webster finds problematic with this modern tendency is that it distorts the proper order of the relation between God and creatures: the doctrine of revelation revolves around the epistemic conditions of the knowing subject rather than the self-revealing action of the divine Subject. The solution, according to Webster, is to weave together the doctrine of revelation and the doctrine of the Trinity, showing how the former derives from the latter. Like Barth, Webster leverages Trinitarian theology in an effort to develop a *theocentric* doctrine of revelation: God is known through God himself.[14] He offers the following definition: '*[R]evelation is the self-presentation of*

---

12. *HS*, 9.
13. *HS*, 12.
14. John Webster, 'Texts: Scripture, Reading and the Rhetoric of Theology', *Stimulus* 6:4 (1998): 12. Karl Barth states, '*God* reveals Himself. He reveals Himself *through Himself*. He reveals *Himself*' (*CD* I/1, 296). For an excellent discussion of Barth's doctrine of revelation, see Trevor Hart, 'Revelation', in *The Cambridge Companion to Karl Barth* (Cambridge: Cambridge University Press, 2000), 37–56. Following Barth in this regard, Webster distances himself from postliberal approaches to Scripture, which tend to locate Scripture primarily within the doctrine of the Church, seeing Scripture as a part of the immanent and

the triune God, the free work of sovereign mercy in which God wills, establishes and perfects saving fellowship with himself in which humankind comes to know, love and fear him above all things.'[15]

This definition draws together both sides of the God-creature relation. First, God himself is the personal agent and content of the act of revelation.[16] The key point here is that Webster highlights the priority of divine action in relation to the knowing subject through a personalist account of divine revelation. Katherine Sonderegger has argued persuasively that 'Webster follows the Personalist school in his insistence that God is known only by Self-disclosure'.[17] God always remains the personal Subject of the act of revelation. As such, he never becomes 'commodified' – an object available on creaturely terms. This means that Scripture is not to be conceived as God's 'revealedness'.[18] (I will note the implications of this conviction in my discussion of Webster's doctrine of inspiration.)

Second, divine self-revelation is purposive, creating and sustaining fellowship with humans. In other words, the creaturely reception of revelation is established by the act of revelation itself. Here we see another element of Barth's influence: Webster claims that 'revelation and reconciliation are the self-same reality, viewed under different aspects'.[19] Reconciliation and revelation are not entirely different divine actions, one being soteriological and the other epistemological. Rather, revelation is the 'communicative force' of God's reconciliatory actions in Christ and by the Spirit.[20] Therefore, the cognitive element of revelation cannot be separated from the moral and relational dynamics of reconciliation, nor can it be separated from the self-mediating presence of God. This proves to be a key point not only for Webster's ontology and teleology of Scripture – Scripture serves the 'fellowship-establishing trajectory' of God's self-revelation[21] – but also for his ecclesiology and anthropology of reading – soteriological and moral categories take precedence

---

intertextual world of ecclesial practice and self-understanding. Webster's earliest writings on the nature of theology and Scripture were more sympathetic to postliberal approaches (see John Webster, 'Locality and Catholicity: Reflections on Theology and the Church', *SJT* 45 [1992]: 1–17; idem., 'The Church as Theological Community', *ATR* 75 [1993]: 102–15), yet he always remained critical of the tendency to make Scripture a function of ecclesial use. For Webster, the voice of Scripture is not primarily that of the church, but an alien voice which interrupts and arrests the church, and this is because Scripture is the servant of God's self-revelation.

15. *HS*, 13.
16. *HS*, 13–5; *WC*, 65–6.
17. Sonderegger, 'God-Intoxicated Theology', 33.
18. *HS*, 15.
19. John Webster, 'Reading Scripture Eschatologically (I)', in *Reading Texts, Seeking Wisdom: Scripture and Theology*, eds. David F. Ford and Graham Stanton (London: SCM Press, 2003), 249. Cf. *HS*, 16; *WC*, 27.
20. *HS*, 16.
21. *HS*, 17.

over hermeneutical ones.[22] It is this personalist account of revelation, with its close ties to the doctrines of the Trinity and of reconciliation, that provides the theological context for Webster's discussion of the concepts of sanctification and inspiration.

If the doctrine of revelation seeks to highlight the priority of divine action in relation to Scripture and its readers, then the doctrine of sanctification is intended to specify how that revelatory action does not stunt or compromise but rather hallows 'creaturely processes', appointing and ordering them for divine service.[23] Sanctification has a broad referent, denoting God's relation to all the creaturely processes that surround the scriptural text, from pre-textual production to textual reception and interpretation. Webster's use of the concept of 'sanctification' in the realm of bibliology is admittedly unusual. One may expect to find the term in its more usual locus in the doctrine of salvation, particularly in relation to the doctrine of justification, or in sacramental theology (rather than referring to the 'hallowing' of the scriptural canon). So it is worth asking why Webster makes recourse to this particular concept in his bibliology. The answer has to do with its ability to address 'in a direct way the relation of divine activity to creaturely processes, without sliding into dualism'.[24]

In other words, the concept of sanctification enables Webster to answer a question which lies at the heart of modern bibliology: How are we to conceive of 'the relation between the biblical texts as so-called "natural" or "historical" entities and theological claims about the self-manifesting activity of God'?[25] According to Webster, modern responses to this question often fall into one of two problems, both of which are fuelled by a competitive understanding of the relation between the transcendent and the historical. The first problem is identified as the 'historical naturalism' of modern biblical criticism. The natural history of the scriptural texts is

---

22. See the discussion in Section 4.2.3.
23. *HS*, 17–8.
24. *HS*, 10. Webster surveys a range of other terms that could have been used to construe the relation between the biblical text and divine revelation: (1) the notion of divine 'accommodation or condescension', (2) the analogy of the hypostatic union, (3) the Barthian concept of 'prophetic and apostolic testimony', (4) the sacramental idea of a 'means of grace', and finally, (5) Berkouwer's emphasis on the 'servant-form' of Scripture (*HS*, 22–5). He argues that options 1–2 are problematic because they lean towards a 'transcendentalism' that does not do justice to the creatureliness of texts but that options 3–5 are helpful for resisting 'the drift into dualism' whereby the scriptural texts are abstracted from their location and function in the economy of God's self-revelation (*HS*, 26). Webster's judgements are indicative of the underlying concern of his bibliology: to hold together the creatureliness of the text and its role in God's self-revelation.
25. *HS*, 18. For a perceptive discussion of the issues undergirding this question, see Wolfhart Pannenberg, *Basic Questions in Theology*, trans. George H. Kehm (Philadelphia, PA: Fortress Press, 1970), 137–210.

affirmed, but in such a way that abstracts them from their location in the economy of God's self-revelation. Therefore, 'creaturely forms (language, action, institutions) [are] denied the capacity to indicate the presence and activity of the transcendent God'.[26] The second problem is identified as 'ahistorical supernaturalism' (Webster's exact target remains unnamed, but at this point in his career, it was likely Reformed Orthodox doctrines of inspiration and their contemporary evangelical proponents). The Bible's relation to divine revelation is affirmed, but in such a way that the text assumes semi-divine properties which seem to strip them of their historical contingency and 'creatureliness'.[27] In very different ways, both problems suffer from the same essential flaw: they operate within a competitive account of the relation between the transcendent and the historical.

According to Webster, this problem is the result of the loss of a Trinitarian account of God's relation to the world. Once talk of the salvific divine missions (i.e. Christ's presence in the world by the power of the Holy Spirit) recedes, then God's relation to creaturely realities is construed as one of external, causal will, 'unconnected to the creation'.[28] Webster's proposed solution is to replace this dualistic understanding of divine causality with a theology of God's 'continuing free presence and relation to the creation' through the missions of the Son and Spirit.[29] The work of sanctification is an aspect of the mission of the Spirit in particular. For Webster, much hinges on the creedal identification of the Spirit as the Lord *and* the Giver of life, for this allows him to affirm that the Spirit's vertical lordly action (the transcendent) gives rise to horizontal creaturely life (the historical). In other words, pneumatology offers a critical corrective to the modern dualism between the transcendent and the historical by clarifying that the Spirit's work of sanctification 'establishes and does not abolish creatureliness', which in turn opens the theological space for the idea that 'the creature (in this case, the text) can be a means of divine action without cost to its own substance'.[30] And this principle applies not only to the text, but also to the agents (authors, redactors, readers) and actions (production, reception, interpretation) in which the text is situated.

---

26. *HS*, 19–20. Cf. *WC*, 11–17, 73.

27. *HS*, 20.

28. *HS*, 21. In this respect, Webster's diagnosis of dualism as a major problem of modern theology and his identification of the need for a renewed Trinitarian ontology bears many similarities to the work of Colin Gunton. For all their differences, both looked to the economic missions of the Son and the Spirit as the key to an account of the God-creature relation (although Webster diverged from this in his mature theology). See, for example, Colin E. Gunton, *A Brief Theology of Revelation* (Edinburgh: T&T Clark Ltd, 1995); idem., *The Triune Creator: A Historical and Systematic Study* (Grand Rapids, MI: Eerdmans, 1998); idem., *The Christian Faith: An Introduction to Christian Doctrine* (Oxford: Blackwell Publishers, 2002).

29. *HS*, 21.

30. *HS*, 30, 28.

This non-competitive account of the relation between divine action and creaturely processes provides the context for a discussion of the doctrine of inspiration. According to Webster, inspiration is the 'textual application' of sanctification, the Holy Spirit's work in relation to the text specifically, which raises an interesting question.[31] Is there a potential tension here between the language of 'sanctification' (suggesting posterior action/consecration) and 'inspiration' (suggesting prior action/causation)? Whatever one's judgement of the matter, it is clear that Webster sees no tension, and the reason has to do with his theology of grace. As we noted in our discussion of Webster's ecclesiology, his account of divine creativity in the early 2000s is still tied primarily to God's works of grace. Grace creates *ex nihilo*.[32] This leads Webster to an ontology of creatureliness that is primarily eschatological: creatures are what they become by the gracious action of Christ and the Spirit. Little is said about the doctrines of creation or providence at this point in Webster's thought. Therefore, when Webster uses the language of 'sanctification', he is not coordinating it with a prior doctrine of created nature, but rather specifying God's hallowing action as that which is most basic about creaturely realities in the economy of grace. In other words, sanctification does not merely perfect created nature but creates and establishes it. Thus, both sanctification and inspiration are the same sort of divine action – a prior, causative action – the only difference being that the latter has a narrower, textual referent.

Webster unpacks the doctrine of inspiration through a conceptual expansion of 2 Peter 1:21 – 'those moved by the Holy Spirit spoke from God' – drawing upon the concept of divine motion to develop a non-competitive account of the relation between divine revelation and the authors and text of Scripture. But this focus on divine motion also leads Webster to argue that the doctrine of inspiration is not to be identified primarily with the activity of an author, community or reader, nor is it to be identified with a 'textual property'; rather, inspiration refers to the 'communicative function of texts' in the movement of God's self-revelation. Inspiration is a matter of God's continued use of the text, not simply its production. Once again, Webster is motivated by a desire to avoid the secularization of Scripture (its abstraction from the economy of God's self-revelation) as well as the divinization of Scripture (the elimination of its creatureliness). Human authors are moved by God and their texts are used by God, but in such a way that establishes, and does not diminish, their creaturely integrity.

In the case of texts, creaturely integrity includes verbal form: '[T]he Spirit generates language.'[33] Therefore, Webster affirms a doctrine of verbal inspiration: 'What is inspired is not simply the *matter* (*res*) of Scripture but its verbal *form* (*forma*).'[34] The driving impulse behind this affirmation is a desire to draw out the theological implications of a non-competitive relation between the Holy

---

31. *HS*, 30.
32. *HS*, 71.
33. *HS*, 37.
34. *HS*, 38.

Spirit and the human authors. The texts do not need to be abstracted from their natural history, nor does one need to revert to a theory of dictation, in order to affirm the dual causality of Scripture.[35] Rather, the activity of the Spirit and of the human author are 'directly, not inversely, proportional' and 'concursive rather than antithetical'.[36] These theological moves will become much more pronounced in a latter phrase of Webster's bibliology, but their presence here is somewhat qualified or at least held in tension with another theme that we find in Webster's early bibliology – namely a dialectic between God's eschatological transcendence and the biblical text.[37]

Webster states, 'Scripture, sanctified and inspired, is the vessel which bears God's majestic presence, and is broken in so doing.'[38] It is not simply that God's presence transcends the creatureliness of the scriptural text, but that it breaks it, meaning there is a permanent 'tension between "Spirit" and "letter" [that] may never be completely dissolved'.[39] Yet, one may well ask, if the Spirit's activity and human authorship are 'directly, not inversely, proportional', then why this 'tension'? Although D. A. Carson's interpretation of Webster's doctrine of Scripture is generally unreliable, he is right to question him on this point: 'Webster sets the *product* over against the *activities of the divine agent.* Why the antithesis? Why not rather say that *because* of the activities of the divine agent, the product is what it is?'[40] This tension in Webster's bibliology may be caused in part by the eschatological character of his doctrines of grace and revelation in the early 2000s, where an emphasis on the intrusive and unilateral nature of God's action is a means by which he seeks to register the distinction between God and creatures. But it may also be that the root cause of this tension is to be found even further back, in his personalist doctrine of God. It is important to remember the Barthian background of his thought here: the doctrine of the Trinity is expressed in close conjunction with the doctrine of revelation, and the latter is developed in such a way that seeks to safeguard the freedom and subjectivity of the former. Revelation always remains a free divine act, never becoming a created effect or settled object.

In order to better understand these theological intuitions and judgements, it is worth taking a brief foray into Barth's *CD* I. Barth's critique of those who equate God's revelation with textual availability is twofold: not only does it threaten to compromise the 'unconditional freedom'[41] of God's revelation, which 'always implies a choice in relation to man',[42] but also it runs the risk of shifting

---

35. *HS*, 39.
36. *HS*, 38–9.
37. Cf. Allen, 'Toward Theological Theology', 236–7.
38. *HS*, 40.
39. *HS*, 41.
40. D. A. Carson, 'Three More Books on the Bible: A Critical Review', in *Collected Writings on Scripture* (Wheaton, IL: Crossway, 2010), 253.
41. *CD* I/1, 157.
42. *CD* I/1, 159.

the epicentre of the doctrine of revelation from divine action to the Bible *as text*. Divine revelation becomes a stabilized and objectified textual deposit, thereby losing its character as a mysterious and gracious event. According to Barth (and Webster), this leads to a characterization of Scripture as 'divine revealedness' or 'direct impartation', rather than human words that continually *become* witnesses to God's Word by ever-fresh acts of revelation.[43] God's action in and through the Bible is mistakenly translated into 'a statement about the Bible as such' (i.e. an attribute or property of Scripture); the Word of God is identified with a textual 'state or fact' instead of a divine work and act.[44]

The underlying worry is that this sort of doctrine of verbal inspiration will inevitably distort the spiritual and moral posture of the exegete, placing the interpreter in a position of control over the event of revelation. In other words, the God-creature relation will become disordered. The Word of God will be conceived as something 'universally present and ascertainable',[45] something latent within the biblical text that awaits extraction or realization via the exegetical activities of human reason. Hermeneutics will become naturalized and over-inflated. Thus, both Barth and Webster emphasize the fact that God is the 'Lord of the wording of His Word'.[46] The reception of revelation is always a pneumatically achieved reality, never generated by a particular 'method of scriptural exegesis'.[47] So readers cannot assume, but always remain dependent upon, God's act of self-revelation when interpreting Scripture. Humans don't control this event but pray for it with thankfulness (recollection) and hope (expectation). Therefore, the proper posture of the exegete before Scripture is one of waiting on the Lord, trusting his promise and anticipating his gift. Reading is an act of spiritual dependence, not merely intellectual competence.

These theological and moral intuitions are the driving force behind Webster's ontology of Scripture and his anthropology of reading in the early 2000s. And so, I want to suggest that he is motivated by a desire not only to give a properly ordered yet non-competitive account of the relation between God's self-revelation and the biblical text, but also to develop a moral and spiritual account of Scripture's readers and the act of reading. I also want to suggest that his initial attempts at achieving these goals seem to create some tensions in his thought, the first being a tension between God's eschatological presence and the biblical text. With this in mind, we turn to a discussion of Webster's ecclesiology and anthropology of reading.

---

43. *CD* I/2, 107–8. See also *CD* I/1, 109–18.
44. *CD* I/2, 527.
45. *CD* I/1, 158.
46. *CD* I/1, 139 (quoted in *HS*, 15). Cf. Brent A. Rempel, '"A Field of Divine Activity": Divine Aseity and Holy Scripture in Dialogue with John Webster and Karl Barth', *SJT* 73:3 (2020): 203–15.
47. *CD* I/1, 183.

4.2.3 Ecclesiology and anthropology of reading

Since Scripture is the servant of God's communicative self-giving, the *viva vox Dei*, then the relation between Scripture and the (ecclesial and individual) reader is viewed by Webster as a species of God's relation to creatures. A strong emphasis on the ontological and epistemological creativity and efficacy of the divine Word is combined with a characterization of the reader's activity as an aspect of the passivity of faith. Therefore, the act of reading is construed in moral and spiritual rather than technical and hermeneutical categories.

We begin with Webster's ecclesiology of reading. According to Webster, the proper relationship between Scripture as the *viva vox Dei* and the church as *creatura verbi divini* is to be perceived from the vantage point of the doctrine of the Trinity. Since, as we noted in the previous section, the doctrine of revelation is (for Webster as for Barth) a close correlate of the doctrine of the Trinity, and the doctrine of Scripture is grounded in the doctrine of revelation, then Scripture cannot be construed as an immanent element of ecclesial life. Thus, Webster highlights the transcendent reference of Scripture by connecting its textual visibility primarily to God's self-revelation instead of its ecclesial use or context. There are times when, as Brad East has argued, the logic of Webster's thought may be read as flowing in the opposite direction: since the church is constituted by hearing the divine address through Scripture, then Scripture is 'not the presence of an immanent ecclesial entity', but an interruption of the church from the outside.[48] In other words, Webster follows Barth's intuition that Reformed bibliology is in some sense an extrapolation of a Reformed doctrine of the church.[49] While there may be some merit to this reading of Webster, its weakness seems to be its inability to account for the way he construes the Scripture-church relationship as a subset of the Word-faith relationship. The nature of the Word is not extrapolated from the nature of faith, but rather the nature of faith is derived from the nature of the Word. The same logic seems to hold for the Scripture-church relation. While the formal order of Webster's doctrinal claims may fluctuate occasionally, the material order remains unidirectional: Trinity – revelation (Word) – bibliology (servant of the Word) – ecclesiology (creature of the Word). The church's relation to divine revelation is not direct but mediated through Scripture, and the church's fundamental posture towards Scripture is one of faith. Far from abstracting Scripture from the life of the church, this dogmatic arrangement intends to offer a particular characterization of their relation: 'Scripture is not the word of the church; the church is the church of the

---

48. *HS*, 46.
49. Bradley Raymond East, *The Church's Book: Theology of Scripture in Ecclesial Context in the Work of John Howard Yoder, Robert Jenson, and John Webster* (PhD diss., Yale University, 2017), 179–86.

Word.'⁵⁰ Therefore, the definitive action of the church in relation to Scripture is that of 'faithful hearing'.⁵¹

We can see this emphasis at work in Webster's account of the 'spiritual visibility' of the church. In Chapter 3 we argued that, when used as an ontological descriptor, this phrase refers to the unique nature of the church's visibility – a visibility whose origin and ground are the invisible realities of divine action (election, reconciliation, calling). Because the church's being is grounded in God's fellowship-creating activity, then it is not primarily 'a visible social quantity' but rather 'the invisible new creation … [a] spiritual event'.⁵² Webster claims that this statement is not intended to deny the natural, historical and social visibility of the church, but to suggest that its visibility is secondary and derivative. And yet, when we come to his discussion of the church's 'apostolic history', the relation between divine and ecclesial action seems to slip from one of derivation to one of competition: 'Apostolicity … is predicated of the church on the basis of divine action rather than on the basis of any human dynamic: talk of apostolicity is primarily talk of the church's Lord rather than of the Lord's servants'.⁵³ For Webster, this translates into a strong distinction between Scripture and tradition, where the latter is 'conceived as a *hearing* of the Word rather than a fresh act of *speaking*'.⁵⁴ His accentuation of the asymmetrical relation between Scripture and the church results in a characterization of the church's action in the presence of divine speech that is limited to faith as hearing.⁵⁵

His accounts of Scripture's authority and the process of canonization continue this emphasis on divine activity and ecclesial passivity.⁵⁶ Scripture's authority is

---

50. *HS*, 44.
51. Here Webster differs from R. W. L. Moberly, who claims that the church is the 'plausibility structure' of faith and therefore the 'presupposition' of a theological interpretation of Scripture (see 'Theological Interpretation, Presuppositions, and the Role of the Church: Bultmann and Augustine Revisited', *Journal of Theological Interpretation* 6:1 [2012]: 1–22). In response to Moberly, David W. Congdon argues that the main problem with this approach is not so much the claim that the church functions as a presupposition to interpretation but rather its implicit assumptions about what the 'church' is (see 'The Nature of the Church in Theological Interpretation: Culture, Volk, and Mission', *Journal of Theological Interpretation* 11:1 [2017]: 101–17). Is it primarily a social-cultural entity or an eschatological community? On this point, Webster would agree with Congdon that it is the latter.
52. *HS*, 47.
53. *HS*, 50.
54. *HS*, 51. Webster spends relatively little time (here or elsewhere) discussing the nature of the church's history and tradition. His article 'Purity and Plenitude' (*GWM* I:195–210) is the notable exception. Most of it is devoted to description and critique of Yves Congar's *Tradition and Traditions*, leaving little room for Webster to develop his own constructive proposal.
55. *HS*, 52.
56. For a critique of Webster on this score, see East, *The Church's Book*, 200–2.

not conferred or ascribed by the church, but 'confessed' and 'acknowledged' – activities which respect and reflect the ontological priority of God's action and speech.[57] Even the church's involvement in the messy and complex process of canonization is 'generated and controlled by Christ's self-utterance'.[58] It is a matter of Spirit-enabled 'perception', 'acceptance', 'approval' and 'assent' – receptive modes of activity whose significance are epistemological rather than ontological.[59] The church's acts are primarily ostensive, referring beyond themselves to the prevenient action of God, and its posture is properly passive, one of hearing before speaking.[60] God's action, and derivatively Scripture's authority, takes centre stage. The church does not share or participate in this divine action and authority, which is self-mediating, but only confesses and acknowledges its 'supreme dignity, legitimacy and effectiveness'.[61] It is only on the basis of God's continued presence and power (in Christ and by the Spirit) that there is a canon and a church, a divine speaking and a human hearing. In the order of being, knowing and acting, the priority of God and subservience of the church are strictly observed.

Webster's approach to the relation between Scripture and the individual reader follows a similar trajectory. He attempts to highlight the priority of God's action in such a way that establishes the human act of reading in its proper theological setting and spiritual posture. Thus, he proposes the following definition of reading:

> It is an intellectual activity in a determinate field or space, the space made in human time, culture and reason by God's reconciling presence as Word and Spirit. Within that space, to read holy Scripture is to participate in the history of sin and its overcoming; to encounter the clear Word of God; and to be a pupil in the school of Christ.[62]

Webster makes his argument in two movements: First he locates the reader in the economy of grace, and then he develops a theological ethics of the act of reading which derives from the reader's location. I will discuss each move in turn.

First, the reader is located in the economy of grace, where human knowing is restored and ordered towards God. It is important to remember that Webster's account of the economy of grace (the missions of the Son and the Spirit) is characterized by the inseparability of revelation and reconciliation: '[R]evelatory grace *includes* the sanctification of the human knower.'[63] God's self-revealing

---

57. *HS*, 52–3; Webster, 'Texts', 13.
58. *HS*, 60.
59. *HS*, 60–3.
60. *HS*, 65–6.
61. *HS*, 6.
62. *HS*, 87. Webster prefers to use the language of 'reading' rather than 'interpretation' because he believes the former is better suited to the nature of God's self-revelation and less prone to becoming entangled in the complexities of hermeneutical theory (cf. *HS*, 86; *WC*, 77; Webster, 'Reading Scripture Eschatologically', 247).
63. *HS*, 71.

activity redeems human knowing activity, the former initiating and evoking the latter. Therefore, the act of reading Scripture is an aspect of the reader's restored covenantal fellowship with God, a conviction which leads Webster to depict the act of reading in moral and spiritual categories rather than hermeneutical ones. In so doing, he is resisting the notion that Scripture should be read just like any other book and therefore that the act of reading Scripture is to be conceived as a species of a more general hermeneutical theory.[64] But even more fundamentally, Webster is resisting the anthropological ideals that he believes undergird modern hermeneutical theories, namely the prioritization of 'intellectual originality' as well as 'immediacy and autonomy'.[65] We will discuss this subject in further detail in the following chapter, but here we simply note that Webster finds these ideals ill-suited for a Christian description of reading precisely because they marginalize theological and soteriological language. There is little space for teaching about the prophetic office of Christ and the regenerative work of the Spirit, both of which are central to Webster's depiction of the space and act of reading. For Webster, the nature of human reading is determined by the personal nature of divine self-revelation, and therefore it involves a unique spiritual posture of 'active passivity and passive activity'.[66]

In fact, Webster is so focused on the ways in which God's self-revealing activity conditions and determines the activities of the reader, that he pays very little attention to social and ecclesial aspects of the reader's hermeneutical situation.[67] He devotes significant space to developing a theology of ecclesial action but gives almost no indication of the ways in which being located in the church might shape the reader's activity. In previous writings he had spoken of the ecclesial 'culture' of reading, but it seems that by the time he wrote *Holy Scripture*, worries about the tendency of such language to overshadow talk of God's action caused him to drop it altogether.[68] Instead, we see him shift away from any semblance of a postliberal emphasis on textuality, culture, practices or tradition (common features of Webster's writings in the 1990s). It is replaced by a thoroughly Barthian account of the *munus propheticum Christi*. While one could very well critique Webster for espousing a form of hermeneutical individualism or spiritualism, as Derek W.

---

64. This is a key point where Webster differs from approaches to the theological interpretation of Scripture that are heavily indebted to philosophical hermeneutics, whether it be Austin's speech-act theory (see Kevin Vanhoozer, *Is There a Meaning in This Text?: The Bible, the Reader, and the Morality of Literary Knowledge* (Grand Rapids, MI: Zondervan, 1998)) or Gadamer's fusion of horizons (see Jens Zimmermann, *Recovering Theological Hermeneutics: An Incarnational-Trinitarian Theory of Interpretation* (Grand Rapids, MI: Baker Academic, 2004)).
65. *HS*, 73.
66. *HS*, 72. Cf. Webster, 'Reading Scripture Eschatologically', 245.
67. Apart from a brief side comment about the reader's activity sharing in the spiritual visibility of the Church in which it is located (*HS*, 92).
68. Cf. Webster, 'Texts', 12; *WC*, 16, 20–22, 29, 85–6.

Taylor has done, it is important to keep in mind the motivation behind his (at times exclusive) emphasis on Christ's self-revealing activity.[69] It was a conviction, learned from Barth, that modern hermeneutical theories tend to abstract Scripture and its readers from the economy of God's self-revealing activity, and therefore (mis)construe the act of reading as an act of historical reconstruction or textual constitution.[70] The central problem, according to Barth and Webster alike, is the posture the exegete is encouraged to adopt towards the scriptural text and thus God's self-revelation. In other words, the implicit anthropology of reading espouses a distorted understanding of the relationship between God and creatures and promotes a disfigured spiritual posture towards Holy Scripture.

Webster looks to Calvin and Bonhoeffer as resources for describing the proper spiritual posture of the reader: 'a certain brokenness', 'teachable, self-mortifying and piously heedful of the Lord's voice', 'reverence and obedience towards the divine self-witness' and 'reverent attention'.[71] Reading is depicted as a 'self-forgetful reference to the prevenient action and presence of God'.[72] It is a spiritual (as opposed to technical) exercise of '*listening* or *attention*',[73] one which 'demands an attitude of ready submission and active compliance'.[74] Exegesis does not make present but rather attends to the axiomatic presence and activity of Christ as he announces himself through the scriptural text.[75] In other words, Lessing's gap is non-existent, or at least it is bridged by divine revelatory activity, not human interpretive activity. And so, exegetical objectivity is not identified primarily with a particular historical or literary method but with 'awareness of and dependence upon a divine movement'.[76] For Webster, Calvin and Bonhoeffer's emphasis on the reverent and submissive spiritual posture of reading is a direct consequence of a theological ontology of Scripture where the text is construed as a field of divine activity. The ontology of Scripture determines what is involved in reading Scripture.[77]

This leads us to the second movement of Webster's argument: developing a theological ethics of the act of reading. He does this in three stages: (1) reading is an episode in the history of salvation, (2) reading is an encounter with the clear Word of God, and (3) reading is an act of pupils, not masters.

(1) Reading Scripture 'is an episode in the history of sin and its overcoming'.[78] As I argued above, the act of reading Scripture, because it takes place in the economy of grace, is an aspect of reconciled fellowship with God. Thus, reading is a spiritual

---

69. Cf. Taylor, *Reading Scripture in the Wake of Christ*, 37–72.
70. WC, 94.
71. HS, 74–8.
72. WC, 43.
73. HS, 83; WC, 104.
74. HS, 80.
75. HS, 81–2; WC, 101–2.
76. WC, 93.
77. Webster, 'Reading Scripture Eschatologically', 246–7; WC, 95–7.
78. HS, 87. Cf. Webster, 'Texts', 13; idem., 'Reading Scripture Eschatologically', 247, 254; WC, 78.

and moral as well as an intellectual practice, requiring the reader to become a certain kind of person.[79] At this point, where many champions of a theological interpretation of Scripture would turn to a discussion of the reader's virtues as shaped by ecclesial practices,[80] Webster describes God's redeeming activity. He wants to construe reading as a moral act without falling into a form of hermeneutical or ecclesiological moralism; thus, he uses theological and soteriological categories to develop his ethics of reading. If exegetical reason is going to attain its end in fellowship with God, it must be rescued from ignorance and idolatry. Reading Scripture requires personal transformation and 'hermeneutical conversion'.[81] And crucially, only God can bring this about. This is where the doctrine of regeneration enters the picture for Webster: it is a firm affirmation of *sola gratia* in the realm of hermeneutics. This affirmation does not necessarily require one to avoid the language of readerly virtue altogether, but it does lead Webster to accentuate the adventitious nature of the virtues necessary for reading. They are the fruit of regeneration, God-given capacities, part of the Spirit's restoration and illumination of exegetical reason.[82] The reader's virtues are cast in a highly eschatological register at this point in Webster's career.[83] The combination of a strong sense of human depravity and of the intrusive nature of divine revelation leads him to an interceptive account of reason's transformation. So, for example, Webster states, '[R]eason's regeneration, its eschatological transformation, involves the *overthrow* of one "ruling principle" – reason as an autonomous guide to the conduct of life – and its *substitution* by the personal presence and activity of the Spirit.'[84] Note the language used here: 'overthrow' and 'substitution', not (as in Webster's mature theology) 'restoration' and 'perfection'. This is part of the reason why he favours virtues of receptivity: 'teachableness', 'humility', 'repentant listening' and 'focused attentiveness'. They all involve an element of passivity.[85] This is the *kind* of human activity that is appropriate in relation to the textual servant of God's self-revelation, and it is the *kind* of activity that only the Spirit can produce.

(2) Reading Scripture is an encounter with 'the clear Word of God'.[86] Webster's discussion of the clarity of Scripture bears many parallels to his doctrine of inspiration. He seeks to prioritize the sovereignty and efficacy of divine revelation in such a way that avoids identifying it with a textual property or with the interpretive authority of a reader (whether individual, ecclesial or scholarly), while also developing a non-competitive account of the relation between divine revelation and human reading. He does this by arguing that Scripture's clarity is

---

79. *HS*, 87; *WC*, 78, 83, 109.
80. See, for example, Stephen E. Fowl, *Engaging Scripture* (Oxford: Blackwell Publishers, 1998).
81. *HS*, 88-9.
82. *HS*, 89-91; Webster, 'Reading Scripture Eschatologically', 254-6.
83. Cf. *WC*, 84, 109; Webster, 'Reading Scripture Eschatologically', 248.
84. Webster, 'Reading Scripture Eschatologically', 252 (emphasis mine).
85. Webster, 'Texts', 14.
86. *HS*, 91.

a function of God's self-revealing action: '[I]t is that which the text *becomes* as it functions in the Spirit-governed encounter between the self-presenting saviour and the faithful reader.'[87] *Claritas scripturae* is a spiritual event – not a spiritual possession or interpretive tradition or enlightened state of being, but a God-given perception of God's self-revelation in concrete acts of reading. Thus, clarity is not something that can be guaranteed or possessed by the creature apart from the actual event of divine revelation. Here Webster is straining to avoid any hint of 'hermeneutical Pelagianism' whereby human acts of interpretation might replace or co-constitute divine acts of self-revelation.[88] To characterize *claritas scripturae* as a spiritual event is to once again situate the act of reading in the Word-faith relation, where 'faith [as hearing] is the reader's primary act' since faith's object is a self-interpreting Subject.[89]

(3) Reading Scripture 'is not the work of masters but of pupils in the school of Christ'.[90] Here Webster clarifies that a passive spirituality of reading does not mean inactivity, but a particular kind of activity marked by teachableness: '[B]eing led by Word and Spirit, learning the doctrine of God, asking God for light, above all, being taught.'[91] It is an active receptivity to God. Interestingly, it is within this context that Webster himself raises a question about the role of critical methods in biblical interpretation, showing that his concerns are moral and spiritual as well as theological. Historical critical methods should not be rejected *tout court*, but evaluated based on their ability to promote 'childlike' readings of Scripture, where exegetical reason is exercised as deference before the divine teacher, not merely as technical mastery or competence.[92] This point is connected to the dialectical 'tension' in Webster's thought between the Spirit and the text, which was motivated, in part, by the conviction that to erase this tension would lead to an exegetical posture of mastery. Here we see a similar concern: Webster is interested in the spiritual posture fostered by a critical method more than with the details of its methodology. Ultimately, he is concerned with how humans relate to God through the mediation of Scripture, for acts of reading are acts of fellowship. This is why the real difficulty in reading Scripture, according to Webster, is not primarily exegetical; rather, it is 'our defiance of grace', our ignorance, idolatry and rebellion.[93] Hence why prayer is closely wed to the activity of reading Scripture: reading is 'a spiritual

---

87. *HS*, 95.
88. *HS*, 100.
89. *HS*, 99.
90. *HS*, 101.
91. *HS*, 102.
92. *HS*, 104–5. On the polemical and ideological freight behind use of the term 'historical criticism', see Francis Watson, 'Does Historical Criticism Exist? A Contribution to Debate on the Theological Interpretation of Scripture', in *Theological Theology: Essays in Honour of John B. Webster*, eds. R. David Nelson, Darren Sarisky, and Justin Stratis (London: Bloomsbury T&T Clark, 2015), 307–18. For the most part, Webster is careful to avoid dismissive overtones.
93. *HS*, 106; Webster, 'Reading Scripture Eschatologically', 249.

affair'.[94] It is about rightly ordered relationship with God, a relationship which is established, sustained and perfected by divine activity.

While the voicing of these themes is understandable (maybe even necessary) within contexts where the nature and interpretation of Scripture have suffered from acute secularization, Webster's theological proposal can be one-sided at times. There seems to be a tension in his thought between God's revelatory activity and the reader's activity, whether ecclesial or individual. He emphasizes the priority of God's self-revealing activity in such a way that places the human reader in a predominantly passive or receptive posture before the text: they are hearers not speakers, readers not interpreters. Yet, one may well ask, if it is true that God's revelatory grace '*includes* the sanctification of the human knower' and that this sanctification includes the bestowal of 'genuine and inalienable creaturely substance', then why does Webster limit the human response to divine revelation to receptivity alone instead of receptivity *and* moved activity? Angus Paddison was right to critique him on this point:

> But surely this is to imply that interpretation cannot itself be sanctified by God, in the same manner that the human texts of the Bible are enlisted into the service of the gospel? One is left wondering precisely what is left for human agency aside from receptivity (which, I agree with Webster, is not passive). By hindering his readers from exploring how we *learn* to read Scripture through the time God gives us, Webster ends up not sufficiently protecting himself from the risks of a one-sided account of interpretation. In other words, Webster falls into the same trap he had earlier warned against, of pitting human agency in competition with divine agency.[95]

While this is a strongly worded critique, it does identify an internal tension in Webster's thought in the early 2000s. As with his account of Scripture, so also with his account of reading: his articulation of the freedom and efficacy of God's self-revealing activity and his attempts to develop a non-competitive account of divine and human agency seem to pull in opposite directions at times. This is an area where Webster's thought develops in later years as he recognizes and seeks to resolve this tension. How this unfolds in his bibliology will be a topic for the next section, but first a brief summary of my argument thus far.

4.2.4 Summary

Our discussion of *Holy Scripture* has highlighted four key elements of Webster's bibliology in the early 2000s. First, Scripture and its readers (ecclesial and individual) are situated within the economy of grace, the field of relations between

---

94. *WC*, 47.
95. Angus Paddison, *Scripture: A Very Theological Proposal* (London: T&T Clark, 2009), 22.

the triune God and his creatures. Second, the key to understanding the character of the economy of grace (and thereby God's relation to the world) is an economically oriented doctrine of the Trinity, particularly the revelatory mission of the Son and the sanctifying mission of the Spirit. Third, the missions of the Son and the Spirit are described as *opera gratiae liberae* and often cast in an eschatological register, which gives rise to a tension between God's eschatological presence and the biblical text. Fourth, the relation between God and the authors of Scripture is active on both the divine and creaturely side, but the relation between God (via Scripture) and the Church or reader is active on the divine side and receptive on the creaturely side. The act of reading is depicted in primarily passive terms.

4.3 Domain of the Word *(2012)*

When compared with the dogmatic sketch of *Holy Scripture*, we see both continuity and development in Webster's mature bibliology and hermeneutics. The core logic remains essentially the same: Scripture and its readers are located within the economy of grace (construed as a field of Trinitarian action); this dogmatic location then generates a theological ontology of Scripture as well as an ecclesiology and anthropology of its readers; and finally, this ontology and anthropology gives rise to a theological ethics of the act of reading. In this way, every aspect of the nature and interpretation of Scripture is guided by teaching about the triune God and his relation to creatures.

While the general logic of Webster's bibliology does not change in his mature theology, some elements of its material content evolve in an effort to register the divine depth and ground of God's self-revealing action as well as develop a more robust account of the integrity of the creaturely coordinates (textual, ecclesial, anthropological) of revelation. The key shifts for Webster's mature bibliology and hermeneutics are twofold. First, he seeks to ground the triune economy of grace (including God's revelatory missions) in the immanent life of the Trinity. Second, he situates God's revelatory missions within the wider context of the works of nature (creation and providence). In the remainder of this chapter, I will seek to demonstrate the significance of these theological shifts for Webster's theological ontology of Scripture and his ecclesiology and anthropology of reading. But first, I begin with a brief discussion of the dogmatic location of Scripture and its readers in Webster's mature theology.

4.3.1 Dogmatic location of Scripture and its readers

As I argued in Section 2.1, the concept of 'dogmatic location' is employed by Webster to clarify the nature of the scriptural texts, their readers and acts of reading by situating them within a field of divine action. By locating Scripture and its readers in the 'economy of grace', Webster is drawing attention to the salvific missions of the Son and the Spirit as the ultimate ground and context for creatures, their acts and their relation to God. The impulse to locate Scripture and its readers in this way remains throughout Webster's mature theology, but what develops is a conviction that the nature of the economy of grace will be misunderstood if it is not 'reduced' or 'traced back' to its ground and cause in the immanent life of God.[96] Webster states, 'Created being, time, action and culture are given shape, made into an order, by the purposive activity of the triune God. Created being and activity are grounded in these *opera dei externae*, which are themselves grounded in the unfathomable plenitude of God's being in himself.'[97] As a result, theology proper is called upon to illuminate the character of God's works, which in turn illuminate the nature of creaturely realities. And so, Webster's mature essays on bibliology seek to ground what is said about the revelatory missions of the Son and Spirit in teaching about the eternal life of God.

A prime example of this new focus can be seen in Webster's mature account of the *munus propheticum Christi*.[98] 'Holy Scripture and its interpretation', argues Webster, 'are elements in the domain of the Word of God. That domain is constituted by the communicative presence of the risen and ascended Son of God who governs all things. His governance includes his rule over creaturely intelligence: he is Lord and therefore teacher.'[99] Here Webster claims that Christ's prophetic ministry is a form of his governance and rule over creatures in the wake of the resurrection and ascension – Webster has already made this point in *Holy Scripture*. But in the essay 'Resurrection and Scripture', he goes one step further, grounding the resurrection and ascension of Christ in God's triune being. He does so by offering a dense description of the relation between Jesus' resurrection and divine aseity. He states, 'The resurrection of Jesus is thus part of the material definition of God's aseity: in and of himself, in free self-determination, God is and acts *thus*. Jesus' reality as the risen one is that than which nothing greater can be conceived.'[100] For the moment, I will leave aside questions raised by this quote about the nature of divine perfection.[101] What interests me here is the way Webster incorporates

---

96. *DW*, 54.
97. *DW*, 7.
98. Another example can be found in Webster's doctrine of illumination, where the deity and personhood of the Holy Spirit ground what he goes on to say about the work of the Spirit in relation to human acts of interpretation. I will say more about this in Section 4.3.3. On the continuing significance of Barth's exposition of the prophetic office of Christ for Webster's mature bibliology, see Fred Sanders, 'Holy Scripture under the Auspices of the Holy Trinity: On John Webster's Trinitarian Doctrine of Scripture', *IJST* 21:1 (2019): 14–17; Sarisky, 'The Ontology of Scripture', *IJST* 21:1 (2019): 62–3, 71–2.
99. *DW*, 3. For an exploration of the theology of language implicit in Webster's use of spatial metaphors – location, space, sphere, domain – see R. David Nelson, 'Webster and Ebeling on Christian Texts: A Placeholder for a Theological Theology of Language', in *Theological Theology: Essays in Honour of John B. Webster*, eds. R. David Nelson, Darren Sarisky, and Justin Stratis (London: Bloomsbury T&T Clark, 2015), 203–18.
100. *DW*, 35.
101. For a discussion of the notion of 'inclusive perfection' in Webster's theology, see Chapters 2–3.

the resurrection into the definition of divine aseity in order to fund a particular understanding of the risen Christ's relation and presence to creation: '[H]e is not contingent but absolute, transcending and comprehending all creaturely reality.'[102] Jesus' resurrection is the temporal enactment of his antecedent divine life (i.e. his eternal relation to the Father) and lordship; therefore, it reveals to us that Jesus Christ enacts a 'transcendent relation to creaturely reality'.[103] Webster's logic can be summarized as follows: the risen and ascended Christ participates in God's aseity and infinity, which means he is absolute and beyond creaturely determination, and therefore he can be communicatively present to creatures without restriction.

This point is particularly important for our discussion of Webster's mature bibliology, for it reveals the dual motivation behind grounding God's work of revelation in his inner being: not only does it register the divine depth, efficacy and gratuity of God's economic activity, but also it enables a particular characterization of God's relation to creatures whereby divine transcendence does not compete with but is the very condition of possibility for God's personal, communicative presence. Teaching about God's aseity and infinity, far from construing God as a remote causal power, specifies the ground of God's personal and communicative relation to creatures. Only from the vantage point of its divine ground can the character of this communicative relation and its creaturely coordinates be discerned.

This proves to be a foundational piece of Webster's mature ontology of Scripture. Scripture is the creaturely means by which the risen and ascended Christ makes himself communicatively present to creatures, and what is revealed through Scripture is not simply an immanent feature of this world but rather 'a share in God's knowledge of himself and of all things'.[104] According to Webster, this does not require one to overlook the historical and cultural features of the text, but to recognize that they are theologically grounded in the person and self-revealing action of the risen Christ, and via Christ in the eternal self-knowledge of God. (Webster often quotes Matthew 11:27 on this score.) In other words, there is a divine depth to the creaturely features of the text.

This way of grounding Scripture in the inner life of the Trinity functions in Webster's thought as resistance to the secularization of Scripture and its interpretation. But it also gives rise to an important question for our understanding of Webster's mature bibliology: How does he attempt to resist the secularization of Scripture without thereby diminishing the creaturely features of the text and the human dynamics of its interpretation? In answering this question, which will be my purview in the next two sections, I will draw attention to the second major development in Webster's bibliology: he situates God's revelatory missions within the wider context of the works of nature (creation and providence).

---

102. *DW*, 34.
103. *DW*, 34.
104. *DW*, vii.

4.3.2 Theological ontology of Scripture

The aforementioned question – how does one resist the secularization of Scripture while also affirming its creaturely integrity? – lies at the heart of the developments in Webster's mature theological ontology of Scripture. He formulates the question by forging together the language of Augustine and Barth: 'How may we speak of Scripture as the temple from which God makes his divine utterances, without compromise either of the integrity of natural speech-and-text-acts, or of the principle that "God is known through God himself"?'[105] Before exploring Webster's answer to the question, it is worth surveying two contemporary answers he avoids and why.

First, Webster does not employ the language of participation. A significant strand of contemporary theology has suggested that the answer to the above question lies in a metaphysics of participation. The breakdown of the relationship between 'sign' (creaturely text) and 'reality' (divine action) was, it is argued, precipitated by the rise of fourteenth-century nominalism and the loss of a patristic-medieval participatory ontology. As a result, the relationship between divine action and temporal realities (history, text, reader) was conceived in extrinsic rather than intrinsic terms, and therefore modern thought was forced to choose between one or the other. The solution to this distorted account of the God-creature relation is to be found in rehabilitating a medieval participatory ontology. This is Matthew Levering's argument in *Participatory Biblical Exegesis*:

> When the participatory dimension of reality is lacking, either anthropocentric readings of Scripture or, conversely, theocentric readings that deny the human dimension altogether, take over. By contrast, in participatory biblical exegesis one can integrate conceptually divine and human agency. On the one hand, everything comes from the triune God, the one in whom all finite things participate (metaphysically and Christologically-pneumatologically) .... On the other hand, the participatory relationship means that God's action and human action are not in competition.[106]

While Webster shares many affinities with Levering's desire to resist the secularization of Scripture and to mend the competitive account of the God-creature relation that undergirds it, he believes that the doctrine of providence is better suited for these purposes. Moreover, it has the added benefit of maintaining a stronger sense of the distinction between uncreated and created being as well as the prevenient nature of divine action.[107]

---

105. *DW*, 11.
106. Matthew Levering, *Participatory Biblical Exegesis: A Theology of Biblical Interpretation* (Notre Dame, Indiana: University of Notre Dame Press, 2008), 14.
107. Cf. *DW*, 11–12.

Second, Webster does not employ the analogy of the hypostatic union.[108] This analogy is influential among some contemporary English-speaking Reformed and evangelical theologians, although its history dates back to the Cappadocians. It envisages the relation between the divine Word and the human words of Scripture in terms analogous to the relation between the divine and human natures of Christ. This analogy can be employed for diverse purposes, both to resist the secularization of Scripture and to affirm its 'true humanity'.[109] While Webster shares both concerns, he argues that the hypostatic union is *sui generis* and that to employ it as an analogy for Scripture stems from a failure to properly 'distinguish instrumentality from incarnation'.[110] Instead of leveraging an analogy to characterize the relation between divine Word and scriptural text, Webster describes a series of divine actions. (I noted a similar pattern in my discussion of his ecclesiology in the previous chapter.) The goal is to provide a dynamic picture of the God-creature relation in which the priority of divine action takes centre stage.

Webster lays out three types of divine action as if they form a series of concentric circles, moving from the most general to the most specific: (1) providence describes God's action in relation to history, (2) sanctification describes God's action in relation to the biblical authors and traditions, and (3) inspiration describes God's action in relation to the biblical text.[111] The most obvious point of difference in comparison to Webster's theological ontology in *Holy Scripture* is the replacement of 'revelation' with 'providence' as the most general form of divine action. Webster's intention is not to displace or diminish the role of the doctrine of revelation in his bibliology, but rather to situate God's revelatory activity within the wider framework of God's works of nature. This allows him to accomplish two things simultaneously: to resist the secularization of Scripture and to develop a non-competitive account of divine and creaturely action. Teaching about God's providential ordering of history is employed to outflank the secularization of Scripture by developing a theology of created nature in which divine action is its constitutive ground. In other words, the concept of 'pure nature' is resisted by showing how natural and cultural realities are grounded in God's sustaining and directing activity. For Webster, the main problem with an ontology of 'pure nature' is the way in which it conceives of divine agency as 'consequent rather

---

108. For notable examples of pushback against Webster on this point, see Allen, 'Toward Theological Theology', 225 n.45; Carson, 'Three More Books on the Bible', 248–50.

109. For a representative example of the latter, see Peter Enns, *Inspiration and Incarnation: Evangelicals and the Problem of the Old Testament* (Grand Rapids, MI: Baker Academic, 2005). For a critical analysis of the use of the incarnational analogy in reference to Scripture, see Lewis Ayres and Stephen E. Fowl, '(Mis)Reading the Face of God in Interpretation of the Bible in the Church', *Theological Studies* 60:3 (1999): 513–28; Stephen E. Fowl, 'Scripture', in *The Oxford Handbook of Systematic Theology*, eds. John Webster, Kathryn Tanner, and Iain Torrance (Oxford: Oxford University Press, 2007), 346–7.

110. *DW*, 14.

111. *DW*, 14–7.

than initiatory'.[112] Recourse to divine action is not considered necessary for a description of what the texts are; instead, the texts are described as natural realities on their own terms. In the early 2000s Webster resisted this idea via the doctrine of revelation, but now he does so by conceiving of providence as 'a necessity of nature'.[113]

This shift in doctrinal focus provides Webster with an opportunity to articulate a key principle that then forms the context for how he goes on to talk about God's works of sanctification and inspiration – namely the principle of 'internal motion'. We already discussed this principle in relation to the concept of 'dual causality' in Chapter 1 and of 'moved movement' in Chapter 3. In the context of bibliology, Webster unpacks the matter in terms of 'interior' and 'exterior' principles of action. Creatures are moved by both principles of action, the 'exterior' being the cause and enabling source of the 'interior'. He states,

> God's providential activity does not force created realities against their natures, but orders those natures in such a way that they move themselves to their true end .... Applied to the biblical writings this means that God's providential ordering of the history of the biblical writings is not a deviation from natural history, properly understood, but an *interior movement* in which God accomplishes his will for creatures by creatures.[114]

Webster's doctrine of inspiration in *Holy Scripture* made recourse to the concept of divine motion, but it was underdeveloped and did not specify its nature as an 'interior' motion. Here Webster makes much of this point because he wants to give expression to a non-dualist and non-competitive account of divine and human agency, and to highlight the integrity and efficacy of creaturely acts in particular. God so moves the creature that the creature moves itself towards its appointed end – this is the fulfilment and perfection of the creature. This is a point which Darren Sarisky's otherwise excellent discussion of Webster's bibliology seems to miss. Like Derek Taylor, Sarisky believes that Webster's bibliology does not sufficiently overcome the modern dualism between the transcendent and the historical, and that this problem is rooted in the nature of his Christology (epitomized in his affirmation of the *extra Calvinisticum*). While there may be some merit to the claim that 'there is something of a de facto disjunction between the text's theological function and analysis of its mundane or immanent features',[115] both Taylor and Sarisky overlook the important function of the doctrine of providence (and pneumatology) in Webster's mature bibliology, which is, in part, seeking to fill the

---

112. *DW*, 6. On the origins of the concept of 'pure nature' and its impact on theology, see Louis Dupré, *Passage to Modernity: An Essay in the Hermeneutics of Nature and Culture* (Yale, CN: Yale University Press, 1995), 1–90, 167–89.
113. *DW*, 15 (quote from *ST* Ia.103.1 ad 1).
114. *DW*, 15 (emphasis mine).
115. Sarisky, 'The Ontology of Scripture', 70.

very lacuna they have identified. I am arguing that one of the chief functions of the doctrine of providence in Webster's bibliology is that it provides him with the resources by which to affirm that God's action is constitutive of creaturely realities without thereby compromising the integrity and efficacy of creaturely acts.

This claim can also be demonstrated by looking at the ripple effect of the principle of 'interior motion' in Webster's mature doctrine of inspiration. It opens the logical and theological space for a more robust affirmation of the 'verbal and plenary' inspiration of Scripture, which in turn opens space for a fuller development of the textual properties of Scripture and the textual mediation of revelation.[116] This is a topic where the developments in Webster's understanding of the relation between God and the biblical text are on full display. Problems in one's doctrine of inspiration, argues Webster, most commonly arise from a competitive understanding of the God-creature relation, which is expressed in metaphysical assumptions about divine causality and motion. He states,

> Once the concept of divine motion is detached from a Christian theological construal of the nature and ends of God's acts toward creatures, it is quickly reduced to efficient causality, making its application to the work of the mind well-nigh impossible: how can the work of the mind be properly human if driven by extrinsic force? (Anxieties on this score commonly surface in modern treatments of revelation and of the inspiration of Scripture.)[117]

In his essay 'On the Inspiration of Holy Scripture' (2015), Webster responds to this situation by clarifying the relationship between divine and authorial causality. To speak of the activity of the prophets and apostles as caused by divine activity is not to violate their creaturely integrity, precisely because God is not on the same causal plane as creatures but rather the enabling origin of all creaturely causes. 'God is not one of an array of causes, but the cause of causes, the cause by virtue of which there is created causality. As cause of causes, God is not in competition with the causes that he creates. God wills creaturely causes.'[118] Following Aquinas, Webster identifies God as the primary and principal cause of Scripture, the prophets and apostles as secondary and instrumental causes.[119] But the crucial point is this: divine causation is not an extrinsic compulsion, but an internal motion that preserves the structure of created nature and provides creatures

---

116. John Webster, 'Holy Scripture', in *Between the Lectern and the Pulpit: Essays in Honour of Victor A. Shepherd*, eds. Rob Clements and Dennis Ngien (Vancouver, BC: Regent College Publishing, 2014), 176.

117. John Webster, 'Editorial', *IJST* 14:4 (2012): 379. Cf. John Webster, 'ὑπὸ πνεύματος ἁγίου φερόμενοι ἐλάλησαν ἀπὸ θεοῦ ἄνθρωποι: On the Inspiration of Holy Scripture', in *Conception, Reception, and the Spirit: Essay in Honor of Andrews T. Lincoln*, eds. J. Gordon Mcconville and Lloyd K. Pietersen (Eugene, OR: Cascade Books, 2105), 242, 248-9.

118. Webster, 'On the Inspiration of Holy Scripture', 248.

119. Webster, 'On the Inspiration of Holy Scripture', 244, 248.

'with power to act'.[120] In other words, revelatory grace enables and animates action (including the production of scriptural texts); it 'intensifies creaturely movement'.[121] The Spirit moves authorial movement interiorly; therefore, divine and authorial actions are directly, not inversely, proportional.

This account of divine causality and motion is what enables Webster to affirm the verbal and plenary inspiration of Scripture without feeling the need to then qualify such statements by claiming that there is an eschatological tension between the Spirit and the letter (as he did in *Holy Scripture*). Here we see the mature Webster shedding his earlier Barthian reserve and siding wholeheartedly with Aquinas and the Reformed Scholastics. He no longer thinks (as did Barth) that this account of verbal inspiration may objectify divine revelation into a textual deposit; rather, it 'simply indicates one kind of action that God performs in relation to Scripture'.[122] Consequently, Webster's mature essays on the nature of Scripture are scattered with expositions of the properties – clarity, unity, sufficiency, authority, perspicuity – Scripture acquires as a result of the Spirit's inner work of inspiration, without any concern that this will somehow compromise or mute the freedom of God's self-revelation by objectifying it.[123] The text does not simply bear witness to God's act of self-revelation but is itself 'an act of God's self-disclosure'.[124] Nor does he think this understanding of inspiration falls into the trap of minimizing authorial activity, because 'verbal inspiration is an instance of inner motion rather than mechanical efficient causality'.[125] In other words, the concept of 'interior motion', as expounded in the doctrine of providence, provides Webster with the conceptual recourses by which to articulate a doctrine of inspiration that compromises neither the priority of divine action nor the integrity of authorial action. Thus, Fred Sanders is only half right when he argues that '[t]he trinitarian grounding of his doctrine of Scripture enabled Webster to retrieve the Protestant orthodox doctrine of Scripture's inspiration'.[126] It is also due to the fact that Webster sought to situate his understanding of the Spirit's work of inspiration within a larger account of God's providential ordering of history.

A significant by-product of this development is the way in which Webster begins to conceive of the scriptural text as a 'sign'. Drawing upon Books 1–2 of Augustine's *De Doctrina Christiana*, Webster argues that Scripture is a tapestry of 'word-signs' whose function is to mediate and direct rational creatures to the *res* of God's self-revelation.[127] Given that Webster draws a parallel to the relation between *signum* and *res* in the Lord's Supper elsewhere, it seems that he is beginning to think

---

120. Webster, 'On the Inspiration of Holy Scripture', 238, 245, 249.
121. Webster, 'On the Inspiration of Holy Scripture', 249, 243.
122. Webster, 'On the Inspiration of Holy Scripture', 246.
123. See, for example, *DW*, 17–9, 59–60.
124. Webster, 'Jesus Christ', 61. For Webster, this is a key reason why exegesis should be concerned primarily with the text itself, not with reconstructing what lies behind the text.
125. Webster, 'On the Inspiration of Holy Scripture', 246.
126. Sanders, 'Holy Scripture under the Auspices of the Holy Trinity', 4.
127. *DW*, 10.

of the scriptural text as functioning in a sacramental manner.[128] And given that Webster begins to speak of the ability of natural and cultural realities to 'signify' their divine cause, it seems that once again a theology of creation is opening space for a positive account of creaturely mediation.[129] Now, Webster is careful to point out that the textual mediation of divine revelation is something 'divinely instituted' (he often uses the Reformed language of election and calling), lest one forget the freedom of God's self-revelation and the fact that scriptural signs are set apart from the sign-nature of all creation because they have a unique function in the realm of Christ's salvific and prophetic work.[130] Yet, with this qualification in place, Webster employs the language of 'sign' in order to articulate a theology of the textual mediation of revelation.

Before moving on to discuss the implications of these developments for Webster's mature ecclesiology and anthropology of reading, it is worth summarizing the argument of the last two sections. I have argued that, for Webster, the dogmatic location of Scripture in the economy of grace continues to provide the key to the ontology of Scripture. Yet, in comparison to *Holy Scripture*, he has developed his understanding of the divine economy in two directions: (1) the divine economy is grounded in the immanent life of the Trinity, and (2) the divine economy is situated within the wider context of God's works of nature (creation and providence). These dogmatic moves allow Webster to employ the concept of 'interior motion' as well as a theology of textual mediation in order to articulate a non-competitive understanding of the relation between God and Scripture, one which still espouses the priority and creativity of divine action (against any secularizing tendencies) but is now better equipped to describe the creatureliness of the biblical text.

4.3.3 Ecclesiology and anthropology of reading

When it comes to the interpretation of Scripture, the dogmatic moves of Webster's mature theology mirror those made in *Holy Scripture*: he locates Scripture's readers and the act of reading within the economy of grace; he focuses on developing an ecclesiology and anthropology of reading rather than addressing specific hermeneutical issues; he characterizes the reader's activity primarily in terms of hearing rather than interpreting; he remains uneasy with accounts of theological interpretation of Scripture that are 'burdened by large-scale hermeneutical theory or an inflated ecclesiology';[131] he seeks to maintain a firm sense of the distinction between God and creatures; he accords much weight to a theology of the missions

---

128. *DW*, 121. For a recent study of the patristic notion of Scripture as sacrament, see Hans Boersma, *Scripture as Real Presence: Sacramental Exegesis in the Early Church* (Grand Rapids, MI: Baker Academic, 2017).
129. *GWM* II:166.
130. *DW*, 10, 95–8.
131. John Webster, 'Being Constructive: An Interview with John Webster', *Christian Century* 125 (2008): 34.

of the Son and the Spirit; and finally, he depicts the act of reading Scripture in moral and spiritual terms. However, his new focus on the divine ground and depth of the economy as well as his new concern to situate the works of grace within the works of nature allows for a more robust theology of the reader's activity, in which interpretation is construed as a creaturely answer to God's act of revelation. I will seek to demonstrate how this is the case by looking at Webster's account of the relation between the Spirit and the individual reader in his doctrine of illumination, but first a word about the relation between bibliology and ecclesiology.

It is, in my estimation, one of the regrettable features of Webster's mature theology that discussion of the ecclesial location of Scripture and reason are rather sparse.[132] In a few exceptions to this trend, we are given small hints that change is under way in Webster's understanding of the relation between Scripture and the church, especially its exegetical and theological tradition. He speaks of creeds, canon law and authorized ministry as 'derivative instruments' which administer the grace of Scripture and the sacraments.[133] He describes the preacher as one who speaks on behalf of Christ and whose public speech is 'a mode of the Word's reconciling presence'.[134] He even develops a notion of *claritas scripturae* in which clarity is 'ecclesiologically realized', emerging 'over time in the common life and practices of the Christian community' under the guidance of the Holy Spirit.[135]

One might expect such statements to flower into an affirmation of the ecclesial mediation of revelation, yet Webster's mature theology still insists on making a firm distinction between Scripture and the church's tradition. A significant reason for this distinction is found in Webster's doctrine of inspiration.[136] He states, 'The words which the Spirit provides and employs are a *settlement* of the divine Word.'[137] According to Webster, the inscripturation of revelation marks the end of inspiration and the beginning of the church's receptive hearing. It signals a new phase in God's providential activity whereby the church no longer speaks afresh but now listens to what has been spoken. Tradition, therefore, is

---

132. Matthew Levering and Stephen R. Holmes have highlighted the deficiencies of Webster's bibliology in this regard, arguing that the ecclesial and liturgical location of Scripture is important for understanding its nature. See Matthew Levering, *Engaging the Doctrine of Revelation: The Mediation of the Gospel through Church and Scripture* (Grand Rapids, MI: Baker Academic, 2014), 60–74; Stephen R. Holmes, 'Scripture in liturgy and theology', in *Theologians on Scripture*, ed. Angus Paddison (London: Bloomsbury T&T Clark, 2016), 110 n.9.
133. *GWM* I:192.
134. *DW*, 25.
135. *DW*, 23.
136. Another reason has to do with the sinfulness of Scripture's readers. For Webster, the church's tradition is not an infallible reception or mediation of the divine Word, but rather an episode in the history of sin and its redemption. It reflects the fact that 'God's Word addresses sinful creatures, and enters into conflict with them' (*DW*, 20).
137. *DW*, 17.

defined as Spirit-guided attentiveness to and hearing of the gospel in Scripture.[138] Webster's mature theology still enjoins a predominantly passive and subordinate account of tradition (and ecclesial action generally) in relation to Scripture.[139] One may well wonder about the implications of Webster's mature theology of divine illumination had they been developed in relation to ecclesiology, not just the individual reader. Would this have caused adjustments in his theology of tradition and understanding of its relation to Scripture and the act of interpretation? We are not given enough detail to know, because he tends to focus on the Spirit's work in the individual reader.

In his essay 'Illumination' (2011), Webster offers a theological exposition of the person and work of the Holy Spirit in relation to the act of receiving and reading Scripture. This is a topic where, like his discussion of inspiration, the developments in his understanding of the relations between God and creatures are on full display. Webster takes John Owen as his muse, suggesting two guiding pneumatological principles: 'that the Spirit directs creaturely intelligence and that the Spirit operates "in and by the faculties of our own minds"'.[140] Understanding the nature of this relationship between the operation of the Spirit and the faculties of the human mind is the crux issue in his exposition of illumination. He approaches the topic indirectly, beginning with the doctrine of God (*ad intra* and *ad extra*), moving on to the works of God (*opus naturae* and *opus gratiae*), and only then venturing a direct discussion of the Spirit's work of illumination. Here we see the same logic at work in his pneumatology that we noted earlier in our discussion of Christ's prophetic office, namely that the nature of divine perfection illumines the nature of God's revelatory mission and communicative relation to creatures. When discussing the prophetic ministry of the Son, Webster drew attention to its ground in divine aseity and infinity in order to emphasize the transcendent nature of Christ's relation to creatures. When discussing the illuminating ministry of the Spirit, Webster draws attention to its ground in God's fullness and goodness in order to emphasize the benevolent nature of God's relation to creatures.

It is part of the nature of divine goodness, which is self-sufficient and lacks nothing, to give, preserve and perfect creaturely being and powers. Webster states, 'He bestows and preserves creaturely being with its own proper powers and freedoms. In the Spirit's superintendence of creation, God works to quicken the forms of created life, and to move creatures to self-movement towards their

---

138. *CG*, 57–8.

139. This remains a key source of grief for Catholic theologians. See, for example, Lewis Ayres, '"There's Fire in That Rain": On Reading the Letter and Reading Allegorically', *MoTh* 28:4 (2012): 624–6; Gavin D'Costa, 'Revelation, Scripture and Tradition: Some Comments on John Webster's Conception of "Holy Scripture"', *IJST* 6:4 (2004): 337–50; Matthew Levering, *Engaging the Doctrine of Revelation: The Mediation of the Gospel through Church and Scripture* (Grand Rapids, MI: Baker Academic, 2014), 59–85, 139–74.

140. *DW*, 52 (quote from Owen, *Works*, 3:204).

perfection.'[141] Notice the phrase 'quicken the forms of created life'. The Spirit not only gives creaturely life, but also works to preserve the integrity of the forms given to that creaturely life. In other words, the Spirit works in creatures in accordance with the structure of their nature: 'The Spirit cherishes created realities and powers, offering no violence to them but so moving them that their integrity and dignity are preserved.'[142] Crucially, this means that primary and final causes do not overwhelm but rather establish and perfect secondary causes; the Spirit enables and sustains the operations of the created mind.[143]

Therefore, when Webster turns to the Spirit's work of illumination, he describes it as a work of grace which restores and perfects human nature, especially intelligence. Whereas earlier writings described the Spirit's works of grace in a highly eschatological register, emphasizing their intrusive nature ('overthrow' and 'substitute'), here Webster situates the Spirit's works of grace within a larger theology of creation and providence. The upshot is that the work of illumination unfolds in ways that are fitting to created nature and give occasion for the exercise of its powers. Thus, illumination establishes in creatures an active intelligent movement towards God's self-revelation in Scripture.[144] How does this happen? Once again, we see Webster's mature theology shift away from the Barthian language of spiritual 'event' to the Thomist language of infused 'habit'. He states, 'This subjective enlightenment involves the impartation by the Spirit of principles and habits which enable us to complete the circle of revelation by meekness, reverence and deference in seeking the knowledge of God from Holy Scripture.'[145] Revelation is conceived as a 'compound event' which includes a human act of interpretation, enabled and guided by the Spirit's work of illumination.[146] Here we see Webster combining a teleology of God's self-revelation with a teleology of created nature: revelatory grace restores and perfects nature, directing it towards its appointed end in rational and moral fellowship with God. Interpretation of Scripture is part of this movement towards perfection; it is an aspect of the Christian's vivification.

Just as the telos of God's self-revealing and illuminating works is coordinated with the telos of human nature, so also the telos of acts of reading is coordinated with the telos of Scripture. The goal is both contemplative (to know the mind of God) and practical (to obey the will of God).[147] According to Webster, the implications for the act of reading are twofold. First, the task of reading requires attention to the *res* of the scriptural *signum*. The human characteristics of the text (literary and historical) will necessarily require the interpreter's careful attention, but only as instrumental signs ordered towards God's self-revelation. That is, reading is a matter of discerning the connection between the details of the textual *signum* and

---

141. *DW*, 7.
142. *DW*, 54–5.
143. *DW*, 55–6; Webster, 'Editorial', 379–80.
144. *DW*, 57.
145. *DW*, 61.
146. *DW*, 60.
147. Webster, 'Holy Scripture', 178.

its divine *res*.[148] Distortion occurs where the *signum* is either overlooked or seen as the ultimate end of interpretive activity:

> If Augustine is correct to remind us that God does not 'broadcast direct from heaven', we are required to use philological, semantic, literary and historical arts, but to do so in a way which respects the fact that the text is *signum*, not *res*. What must be checked is the confusion of sign and matter, and the elevation of sign into the final object of interpretive labour.[149]

For Webster, the interpretation of Scripture (relation between textual *signum* and reader) is to be guided by the ontology of Scripture (relation between divine *res* and textual *signum*).

Second, the art of reading requires spiritual graces. The Spirit fosters spiritual activities, habits of the soul – prayer, conformity, obedience, growth, patience, fortitude – which train the reader to discern the divine *res* of the textual *signum*.[150] The movement from *signum* to *res* is the heart of exegetical labour, and the human intellect requires divine grace to enact this movement. As we have seen, this theme is a consistent feature of Webster's theological ethics of reading from beginning to end. Reading is a spiritual and moral as well as an intellectual endeavour.

4.4 Conclusion

My argument in this chapter has revolved around a comparative study of Webster's *Holy Scripture* (2003) and *Domain of the Word* (2012), focusing on his understanding of the relation between God and Scripture, and how this influences his characterization of Scripture's reader and the act of reading. I argued that Webster's bibliology was driven by a consistent concern to resist the secularization of Scripture and interpretive activity without thereby diminishing the creaturely integrity of text and reader. In other words, he seeks to articulate a non-competitive account of the relation between God's self-revealing activity and creaturely activities and products. In our discussion of Webster's early bibliology, I noted the way in which he sought to do this by locating Scripture and its readers within the triune economy of grace. Then he developed a theological ontology of Scripture fitting to its location through the concepts of revelation, sanctification and inspiration. And finally, he constructed an ecclesiology and anthropology of reading that took its cues from the personal nature of God's self-revelation. We also identified two tensions in Webster's early bibliology: (1) a tension between

---

148. Cf. Darren Sarisky, 'A Prolegomenon to an account of Theological Interpretation of Scripture', in *Theological Theology: Essay in Honour of John B. Webster*, eds. R. David Nelson, Darren Sarisky, and Justin Stratis (London: Bloomsbury T&T Clark, 2015), 253.
149. *DW*, 29. Cf. *DW*, 100.
150. *DW*, 63.

God's eschatological presence and the biblical text, and (2) a tension between God's self-revealing activity and the reader's interpretive activity. As we turned to a discussion of Webster's mature bibliology, we highlighted the ways in which Webster sought to resolve these tensions: first, by grounding the economy of grace in the immanent life of the Trinity, and second, by situating the economy of grace (especially the Spirit's work of inspiration and illumination) within a theology of the works of nature (especially providence). While gaps in his bibliology still remain, particularly in relation to ecclesiology, the overall intent of these developments was to offer a more robust account of the creaturely coordinates (textual and anthropological) of divine revelation.

In this way, the argument of this chapter has sought to provide further demonstration of the explanatory power of two elements of the heuristic framework given in Chapter 1. First, it has drawn attention to the significance of the second primary developmental shift in Webster's thought – from Trinitarian to Theocentric – for his understanding of Scripture and its readers. Second, it has demonstrated how the works of nature (especially the doctrine of providence) provide the context for understanding the works of grace in Webster's mature theology, including his account of Scripture's inspiration and the reader's illumination. But this chapter has also brought to the surface a significant thread in Webster's doctrine of God that was not thoroughly explored in Chapter 1, namely his personalist account of God as a self-revealing Subject. This theme was central to his doctrine of revelation and funded an understanding of the God-creature relation which stressed its personal and communicative as well as moral and spiritual dynamics. As we will see in the next chapter, this aspect of Webster's doctrine of God also has widespread implications for his understanding of the nature and operations of theological reason.

Chapter 5

THEOLOGICAL THEOLOGY

5.1 Introduction

This chapter will explore John Webster's account of theological reason. It will seek to expound the way in which Webster construes the relation between God and the theologian, and how this influences his characterization of the nature and operations of reason. The main argument will be laid out in two composite sections followed by a conclusion. The first section will offer an analysis of the Thomas Burns Lectures (1998) as a representative example of his early account of 'theological theology', and the second section will highlight the key developments in his thought as they appear in *God without Measure* (2016). My thesis is that Webster's account of 'theological theology' is driven by a consistent concern to register the ontological and epistemological priority of God in relation to the activities of the knowing subject. He seeks to articulate how the theologian's reasoning is conditioned and defined by God's presence and action. Yet the way in which he articulates this divine 'priority' and 'conditioning' evolves as teaching about God's inner life, creation and pneumatology takes on prominence in his thought, resulting in a reordered anthropology of the theologian and theology of grace, which facilitate a more robust account of the creaturely integrity and dynamics of reason.

In this way, the argument of this chapter will seek to demonstrate the explanatory power of two elements of the heuristic framework given in Chapter 1. First, it will draw attention to the significance of the overarching development of Webster's thought – from Christocentric to Theocentric – for his understanding of theological reason. This will be seen in the way the ultimate ground of the activities of theological reason shifts from God's eschatological presence in Christ to God's immanent perfection, particularly divine omniscience and goodness. Second, it will demonstrate how the works of nature provide the context for understanding the works of grace in Webster's mature theology. This will be seen in the way the Spirit's work of regeneration and sanctification is coordinated with teaching about the nature and ends of reason, which are derived from God's original ordering of creation. But the topic of this chapter will also provide an opportunity to explore further the impact of the personalist elements of Webster's doctrine of God and, moreover, to analyse aspects of Webster's theology of grace that I was not able to explore sufficiently in Chapter 1. A key question for Webster is as follows: Is grace to be identified primarily with divine freedom, construed eschatologically as an interruption of human life, and characterized as God's ever-fresh act of giving? Or is grace to be identified primarily with divine goodness, coordinated with an ontology and teleology of created nature, and construed as a created effect as well as a divine act? As I will demonstrate below, these questions are of no little significance for Webster's understanding of the relation between God and the theologian.

5.2 Thomas Burns Lectures *(1998)*

Since their delivery at the University of Otago in 1998, Webster's Thomas Burns Lectures (TBL) have remained by and large unknown. Yet they offer a much fuller account of Webster's early understanding of the nature of 'theological theology' than his famous inaugural address 'Theological Theology' at the University of Oxford.[1] The order and topics of the lectures are as follows:

Lecture 1: 'Culture: The Shape of Theological Practice'
Lecture 2: 'Texts: Scripture, Reading and the Rhetoric of Theology'
Lecture 3: 'Traditions: Theology and Public Covenant'
Lecture 4: 'Conversations: Engaging Difference'
Lecture 5: 'Criticism: Revelation and Disturbance'
Lecture 6: 'Habits: Cultivating the Theologian's Soul'[2]

In these lectures, we see the final vestiges of a Webster for whom Christology (focused on the resurrection and cast in a highly eschatological register) is the material epicentre of Christian doctrine. He has not yet acknowledged the doctrine of the Trinity as the *articulus stantis et cadentis ecclesiae*, and yet the logic of his argument anticipates that found in *Holy Scripture* (2003), which I analysed in the previous chapter. First, the theologian and her intellectual activities are located in the culture of Christian faith and practice, which is constituted by the eschatological presence of God. Second, a theological anthropology of the theologian is derived from her eschatological location. Third, the 'eschatological existence' of the theologian gives rise to a depiction of reason's activities in moral terms as responsibility before its object – the eschatological presence of God, who is self-revealing Subject. We begin our discussion with the dogmatic location of reason.

---

1. The phrase 'theological theology' comes from Jüngel's *God as the Mystery of the World*. After describing contemporary suspicion regarding the possibility of theology (i.e. human speech about God), Jüngel argues that the theologian ought not to be debilitated by lament but rather to see the present crisis 'as an opportunity for more theological theology' (4).

2. The lectures were subsequently published in two instalments: lectures 1–3 in *Stimulus* 6:4 (1998): 2–23 and lectures 4–6 in *Stimulus* 7:1 (1999): 2–20. A recent republication of the lectures along with an excellent introduction by Ivor Davidson can be found in John Webster, *The Culture of Theology*, eds. Ivor J. Davidson and Alden C. McCray (Grand Rapids, MI: Baker Academic, 2019).

5.2.1 Dogmatic location of reason

The TBL can be read as an extended exercise in dogmatic relocation. Webster attempts to situate the theologian and the activities of theological reason within the 'space' created by the eschatological presence of God. As I noted in the previous chapter, formal questions about 'dogmatic location' take on a particular prominence in Webster's thought around the turn of the twenty-first century, and this can be seen in his attempts to develop a theological account of the nature of theology. The concept of location provides an important way of contextualizing speech about creaturely realities (reason, culture, practice) within an overall account of the relation between God and creatures, and a way of grounding that relation in the freedom and gratuity of divine action. Creaturely being and acts are what they are only in relation to God's eschatological interruption and renewal of all things in Christ and by the Spirit. Therefore, one of the primary agendas of the TBL is to diagnose the 'mislocation' of reason in modern theology and to reintegrate it into a proper dogmatic 'location'. Webster's argument unfolds in two steps.

First, Webster argues that reason is in fact located. It is not to be understood as a natural, generically human, capacity, but rather as a historically and socially embedded practice.[3] Theological reason, like all aspects of human existence, is a 'practice' in a particular 'culture'.[4] Culture is defined by Webster as a historical and social 'space' within which human actions take place, giving them coherence, meaning, purpose and intelligibility. Practice is defined as 'a set of activities through which human beings pursue complex, socially-established goals'; they are a means of inhabiting a 'cultural space'.[5] Reason is a practice in a culture, and therefore regionally and locally defined, receiving its shape and orientation from its particular standpoint in time and space. In defining reason in this way, Webster is drawing upon the insights of postmodern philosophy and postliberal theology in order to gain critical leverage against Enlightenment ideals of rationality,[6] which, he believes, are still deeply engrained in the modern research university and to

---

3. Webster, 'Habits', 16.
4. Webster, 'Culture', 2, 4–5.
5. Webster, 'Culture', 4.
6. For an example from postmodern philosophy, see Pierre Bourdieu, *Outlines of a Theory of Practice*, trans. Richard Nice (Cambridge: Cambridge University Press, 1977), and from postliberal theology, see George A. Lindbeck, *The Nature of Doctrine: Religion and Theology in a Postliberal Age* (London: SPCK, 1984). For an explanation of the diverse cultural contexts that shaped the argument of Lindbeck's *The Nature of Doctrine*, see Mike Higton, 'Reconstructing *The Nature of Doctrine*', *MoTh* 30:1 (2014): 1–31. There is a debate as to whether Lindbeck's theory of doctrine is indebted primarily to a sociological theory of religion (see Mike Higton, 'Frei's Christology and Lindbeck's Cultural-Linguistic Theory', *SJT* 50:1 [1997]: 83–95) or Christology (see Mike Higton, 'George Lindbeck and the Christological Nature of Doctrine', *Criswell Theological Review* 13:1 [2015]: 47–61).

which theology has all too often assimilated.⁷ Those Enlightenment ideals can be described as follows: reason is the capacity of the individual subject – Descartes's '*ego*' – to abstract oneself from all local particulars (e.g. faith commitments, communal confessions, institutional or statutory authorities, historical and cultural contingencies), make value-free or neutral (and therefore objective) representations of the world, and offer critical judgements concerning local particulars and beliefs on this basis. In other words, reason is a transcendental capacity for judgement which is not affected by or embedded in a local context – it is 'pure reason'.

According to Webster, when theology adopts this account of reason, the results are numerous and deleterious: (1) theology becomes detached from its local culture, including the faith, practices and textual tradition of the church; (2) the anthropological ideals of freedom and originality become the prime theological virtues; and finally, (3) theological reason adopts a moral and spiritual posture (competence and control) that is out of sync with the nature of its object – in other words, the priority of God's self-revealing activity is eclipsed by the activities of the subjective knower. I will return to a discussion of items 2 and 3 in a moment, but my intention here is to show how the first step of Webster's argument in the TBL is to rectify item 1. He does this by suggesting that the activities of theological reason need to be recast as practices within the local culture of Christian faith:

> All intellectual acts take place in a particular space or region; that is to say, reflective activity is best understood, not by exquisite analysis of modes of consciousness, but by observing the practices of a cultural world. Christian theology's culture is that of Christian faith – its store of memories, its lexical stock, its ideas, its institutions and roles, its habits of prayer and service and witness, the whole conglomeration of activities through which it offers a 'reading' of reality. That culture precedes and encloses reflective theological enquiry, and it is within, not in isolation from, that sphere that Christian language and concepts acquire their intelligibility.⁸

Rational activity is contextual, embedded in social and historical space. This basic conviction then allows Webster to make a twofold claim: (1) Enlightenment

---

7. According to Webster, this can be seen in the way the logic of *Wissenschaft* (embodied primarily in mathematics and the natural sciences) became the universal standard of rationality for all disciplines (including history, philosophy and theology) in the modern university. For an analysis of the logic and historical development of *Wissenschaft*, see Nicholas Wolterstorff, 'The Travail of Theology in the Modern Academy', in *The Future of Theology: Essays in Honor of Jürgen Moltmann*, eds. Miroslav Volf, Carmen Krieg, and Thomas Kucharz (Grand Rapids, MI: Eerdmans, 1996), 35–46; Hans W. Frei, *Types of Christian Theology*, eds. George Hunsinger and William C. Placher (New Haven, CT: Yale University Press, 1992), 95–132.

8. *CG*, 29.

notions of rationality do not carry universal authority or applicability but are matters of cultural convention, and (2) the rational activities of Christian theology ought to inhabit the particular cultural world of the church. The theologian is a skilled 'practitioner within the Christian tradition' and therefore practises of 'textuality' as well as worship and piety are central to the operations of theological reason.[9] But once Webster has employed the language of culture and practice to establish the ecclesiological embeddedness of reason over against notions of 'pure reason' (in ways reminiscent of postliberal theology), he then turns the tables, raising a critical question regarding the limitations of that language. His question is driven by a concern to safeguard the freedom and transcendence of God: How can one conceive of Christian theology as a regional activity without collapsing into immanence?

This question leads us to the second major step in Webster's argument: the culture of Christian faith is not a stable space, but an eschatological space. It is a culture which arises from (and is called into question by) the eschatological presence of God. Here Webster draws upon themes from the early Barth (particularly his lectures in the 1920s) to reconfigure the language of culture and practice around God's acts of judgement and grace, thereby gaining critical leverage against the tendency of postliberal theology to view them as determinate, stable realities. Webster's concern is that postliberal theology may be repeating the same error that the young Barth identified in liberal theology, namely 'the reduction of the divine to a mere aspect or function of the world of human moral and cultural endeavour'.[10] In contrast, he wants to register the ontological and epistemological priority of divine action in relation to the activities of the knowing subject. Theological reason is not only conditioned by its cultural location, but even more fundamentally by its theological and spiritual location.

This is where Martin Westerholm's essay on Webster's account of 'theological theology' is both remarkably insightful and slightly misleading. He makes the observation, as I have here, that for Webster 'theological work must, like any other human activity, be understood in terms of the history in which it is situated'.[11] Then he goes on to argue, accurately in my estimation, that a key shift for Webster occurs when he views theological reason as situated primarily within the history of salvation rather than the history of ideas. For Westerholm, this shift marks the fundamental difference between Webster's account of 'theological theology' in the Oxford lecture (1997) and in *God without Measure* (2016). It is this last point that my reading of the TBL seems to problematize. In these lectures from the late 1990s, Webster is already attempting to locate theological reason within the

---

9. George Schner, *Education for Ministry: Reform and Renewal in Theological Education* (Kansas City: Sheed & Ward, 1993), xiii (quoted in Webster, 'Culture', 1: 8).
10. Webster, 'Culture', 6.
11. Westerholm, 'Practice of Theological Theology', 448.

history of salvation much like his mature theology does.[12] The key differences have more to do with his theological construal of the history of salvation and the way he conceives of that history as grounded in divine action. These differences will become clear in the second half of this chapter, but for now I want to demonstrate the way in which Webster appeals to eschatology and Christology as the primary doctrines through which he depicts the cultural space in which theological reason is located.

Much like Barth in the 1920s, Webster's eschatology in the TBL is not tied primarily to the future *parousia*, but rather expresses a conception of ultimate reality. Eschatology 'refers to that single, perfect reality which is the basis and end of all realities, that absolute which, as the origin of all that is, is pure, free, ungraspable, approachable only by virtue of its own prior approach to us in a kind of loving devastation'.[13] In other words, eschatology gives voice to the radical otherness of God, who is the ground and context of all creaturely realities (including reason) yet transcends any form of assimilation into them. And crucially, the eschatological presence of this transcendent God is identified Christologically with the resurrection of Jesus Christ and his presence by the power of the Holy Spirit. 'He, the risen Jesus, the new (counter-) creation, *is* the presence of the eschaton, and it is because of him that Christian culture is eschatological.'[14] The doctrine of the resurrection does not function primarily as a description of a past historical event (although it includes that), but rather as a way of highlighting the immediacy of God's transcendent presence to creatures. I noted in the previous chapter how Webster draws upon Barth's exposition of the *munus propheticum Christi* to speak of the way in which Christ himself bridges the gap between the historical event of the resurrection and the present of the subjective knower, making himself present and announcing his presence. This means that all human activity, including rational activity, takes place in the sphere of Christ's rule as judge and saviour.

A key point Webster wants to accentuate in the TBL is that Christ's presence is a 'disruptive presence'. He states,

> Christian faith, and therefore Christian theology, emerges out of the shock of the gospel. Christian faith, and therefore Christian theology, takes its rise in the comprehensive interruption of all things in Jesus Christ, for he, Jesus Christ, now present by the power of the Holy Spirit, is the great catastrophe of human life and history. In him, all things are faced by the one who absolutely dislocates and no less absolutely reorders. To this regenerative event, this abolition and recreation, Christian faith, and therefore Christian theology, offers perplexed and delighted testimony.[15]

---

12. Along these lines, see Ivor J. Davidson, 'Introduction', in *The Culture of Theology*, eds. Ivor J. Davidson and Alden C. McCray (Grand Rapids, MI: Baker Academic, 2019), 35–40.
13. Webster, 'Culture', 6.
14. Webster, 'Culture', 6.
15. Webster, 'Culture', 2.

Note the language used here: 'shock', 'interruption', 'catastrophe', 'abolition' and 'recreation'. God's action is highly interceptive. The tone of Webster's rhetoric is intended to communicate the fact that the culture of Christian faith, and therefore theological reason, is called into question by the very source of its existence. God cannot be objectified or made into a feature of a determinate cultural locale. This leads Webster to argue that the thinking subject is situated within a dialectical tension between 'location' and 'dislocation', a point to which I will return in my discussion of the operations of reason (in Section 5.2.3).[16] Theology is a practice in the eschatological space constituted by the presence of the risen Christ. It is not simply a set of determinate practices within a stable cultural world, but a personal encounter with the interruptive rule and speech of the Lord, who requires and generates the total remaking of the knowing subject. This leads us to Webster's account of the anthropology of the theologian.

5.2.2 Theological anthropology of the theologian

I argued earlier that Webster's critique of Enlightenment notions of rationality was directed not only towards its context-free concept of reason, but also towards the anthropological ideals which undergird the primacy placed on 'the judging function of reason'.[17] According to Webster, these ideals are inimical to Christian anthropology: 'representation', 'judgement', 'freedom' and 'originality'. They place the knowing subject in a position of control and competence in relation to its object, a position which cannot possibly do justice to the unique nature of theology's object, who is a self-revealing Subject. Once again, we see Webster's personalist account of God come to the fore. God can be known only insofar as he makes himself known, and he remains a mystery even in the event of his self-revelation, never becoming a readily available object for reason's critical scrutiny.[18] In other words, the theologian is placed in a position before God whereby his or her rational activities are not initiatory, posing questions and enacting critical judgements of its object, but rather responsive – the object (who is the primary Subject) poses critical questions to the knowing subject. Or, as Barth once put it, this person's thinking 'is conditioned and defined by his standing before God and being addressed by God'.[19]

---

16. Webster expresses this dialectic in a number of other ways: culture and anti-culture ('Culture', 4), belonging and homelessness, tangible and heavenly, and roots and astonishment ('Culture', 7).

17. Webster, 'Conversations', 5.

18. Sonderegger notes how the themes of 'freedom' and 'mystery' are central to Webster's personalist doctrine of revelation ('God-Intoxicated Theology', 35). One could also trace these themes back to Barth's dialectic of unveiling and veiling (cf. *CD* I/1, 162–86).

19. Karl Barth, *The Göttingen Dogmatics: Instruction in the Christian Religion*, vol. 1 (Grand Rapids, MI: Eerdmans, 1991), 372 (quoted in Christopher Asprey, *Eschatological Presence in Karl Barth's Göttingen Theology* (Oxford: Oxford University Press, 2010), 114).

Therefore, a theological anthropology of the theologian must develop a different set of ideals: '[H]uman life is properly a matter of answerability or of response to the disorientation brought about by a challenge, and therefore ... attention and faith are more humanly and Christianly basic than representation and judgment.'[20] The theologian is accountable to ('answerability', 'response') and oriented towards ('attention', 'faith') the actions of its object. This in turn means that the truth of theological reason and speech is not grounded primarily in the epistemic capacities of the knowing subject or in universal standards of rationality, nor in a particular social-historical tradition, but rather in an eschatological and regenerative encounter with God initiated by God.[21] Webster argues,

> [F]or Christian faith, truth is not primarily to be identified with a judgment made by us, but with our interception and remaking.... Thinking is "truthful" in so far as it is engendered by the invasion of the world, its being broken apart by the presence of that which is unconditional, an *origin* of all things which is not itself judged but which judges all things.[22]

In other words, rational objectivity is self-involving, not because the structures of the subject's mind inevitably shape its knowledge of its object, but because the knowledge of its object arises from an encounter which transforms the knowing subject. Actually, it would be more accurate to say that for Webster this eschatological encounter *establishes* the knowing subject.

The main point is this: in the TBL Webster is attempting to develop a moral psychology of the theologian in which language of divine agency and creativity is indispensable. Since his account of divine creativity is (at this point in his career) tied primarily to the resurrection of Jesus Christ, and since the presence of the risen Christ is characterized as the 'disruptive' and 'intrusive' eschatological presence of God, which completely 'abolishes' and 'recreates' human life and history, then Webster's moral psychology accords ontological priority to the eschatological, regenerate existence of the human person. His moral psychology is derived from a theology of redemption rather than a transcendental anthropology or the doctrines of creation and providence.[23] To be human is not primarily to have a set

---

20. Webster, 'Conversations', 5.

21. The line of thought here is clearly Barthian. Theological objectivity is grounded in divine rather than human subjectivity. On this, see Christoph Schwöbel, 'Theology', in *The Cambridge Companion to Karl Barth*, ed. John Webster (Cambridge: Cambridge University Press, 2000), 17–36. A similar line of reasoning can be found in Thomas F. Torrance, *Theological Science* (Oxford: Oxford University Press, 1969), 34–43.

22. Webster, 'Conversations', 5.

23. The influence of Barth on Webster's moral psychology is clear, but these themes can also be traced back to key elements of Calvin's theology. See Philip G. Ziegler, 'The Adventitious Origins of the Christian Moral Subject: John Calvin', *Militant Grace: The Apocalyptic Turn and the Future of Christian Theology* (Grand Rapids, MI: Baker Academic, 2018), 139–51.

of creaturely capacities bestowed at creation, but rather to 'subsist in the reality of Jesus Christ.'[24] And therefore, the teleology of the human person is not governed by God's original ordering of creation, but by the redemption (new creation) that is accomplished in Christ. Hence, human beings are defined primarily by what 'they *become*', and the continuity of the knowing self is rooted in God's works of grace.[25]

The upshot of this account of divine creativity is that the knowing subject has no natural capacities or creaturely resources which make him or her ready for knowledge of God prior to a personal encounter with God in his free act of self-revelation. In fact, Webster even goes so far as to say that 'the "unregenerate" state can only be seen as essentially negative, as a privation'; it contributes and anticipates nothing.[26] The purpose of making a comment like this is to accentuate the radical graciousness and newness of the divine action which grounds Christian moral psychology and therefore the existence of the theologian. For Webster, as for the early Barth, 'to be a Christian is to be remade by God into a new type of subject, and therefore not to be defined by any possessed ontology or nature, but by the eschatological relation in which this subject now exists'.[27]

The implications of this moral psychology for Webster's account of the formation of the theologian are twofold. First, the habits that form the theologian's soul and provide orientation to the activities of theological reason are 'external' rather than 'internal'. Webster rejects the notion of infused grace, worrying that the Aristotelian concepts of habit and virtue, which so often accompany accounts of infused grace, risk espousing an anthropology of immanence, in which the freedom and transcendence (and thus gratuity) of divine action are muted.[28] Instead, grace is conceived as a divine movement 'which touches the theologian's person and activity, but which does not in any straightforward way we can describe become part of his or her human make-up'.[29] Grace is a function of divine freedom and therefore conceived in punctiliar, rather than durative, terms as

---

24. Webster, 'Habits', 18. Michael Allen's interpretation of Webster's theological anthropology underestimates the extent to which Webster's anthropology in the 1980–90s is founded upon the very Christocentrism he resisted in later years (cf. 'Toward Theological Anthropology: Tracing the Anthropological Principles of John Webster'. *International Journal of Systematic Theology* 19:1 [2017]: 9–13).
25. Webster, 'Habits', 18.
26. Webster, 'Habits', 18.
27. Asprey, *Eschatological Presence*, 29.
28. The most influential work on Aristotle's account of virtue in recent decades is undoubtedly that of Alasdair MacIntyre, *After Virtue: A Study in Moral Theory* (Notre Dame, IN: University of Notre Dame Press, 1981). For a theological critique of virtue ethics based upon 'empirical reflection on the experience of human sin', see Simeon Zahl, 'Non-Competitive Agency and Luther's Experiential Argument Against Virtue', *MoTh* 35:2 (2019): 199–222.
29. Webster, 'Habits', 17.

God's ever-fresh act of giving. It is for this reason that, secondly, Webster identifies prayer as the primary act of formation for the theologian. Prayer is the theologian's acknowledgement that theological reason cannot be cultivated, but only created and received by a gracious act of God. It is the acknowledgement of human 'incapacity', 'unsuitability' and 'destitution', and therefore of utter dependence on God.[30] In other words, prayer instantiates the moral posture of humility and receptivity which is befitting to the 'eschatological existence' of the theologian, and which subverts the anthropological ideals of competence and control that are central to Enlightenment notions of rationality. For Webster, reason and piety are coinherent because reason is dependent upon an act of divine grace.

5.2.3 Operations of reason

Having established the point that for Webster, as for Barth, 'well-ordered Christian thought operates from the standpoint of the eschatological subject, that is, the new creature who is found in Christ', we turn now to a consideration of the operations of theological reason as Webster depicts them in the TBL.[31] Here it is important to remember what I said previously about the dogmatic location of reason: God's eschatological presence creates a dialectical tension between 'location' and 'dislocation'. Now we will offer an analysis of the two primary acts of theological reason to which this dialectical tension gives rise: (1) the 'positive' act of obediently following the testimony of Scripture, and (2) the 'critical' act of testing the fidelity of Christian culture to the gospel.

First, theological reason is called upon to give a responsible answer to God's self-revelation, which, because the primary human instrument of that revelation is Holy Scripture, takes the form of an obedient following and conceptual reiteration of the scriptural text. The positive act of theological reason is depicted in the language of 'obedience' and 'following' – the primary acts of faith. This language intentionally evokes the image of discipleship: theological reason is in a discipleship relation with its object. Therefore, it has a 'self-effacing' quality, meaning it does not seek to impose itself – its categories, schemes, systems and agendas – upon its object, but rather seeks to be docile and teachable before its object. Like Barth, Webster replaces Kant's ideal of 'freedom' with the ideal of 'obedience' as that which defines the thinking self, a move which frames rational activity in terms of a moral relation to God.[32] Reason is accountable, not to itself or to universal criteria of judgement, but to God's self-revelation. The divine Word posits itself by means of scriptural texts, and therefore theological reason and speech are truthful (correspond to reality) to the extent that they follow the given reality of God in Holy Scripture.

---

30. Webster, 'Habits', 19.

31. Martin Westerholm, *The Ordering of the Christian Mind: Karl Barth and Theological Rationality* (Oxford: Oxford University Press, 2015), 55.

32. For this interpretation of Barth's relation to Kant, see Westerholm, *The Ordering of the Christian Mind*, 26–8.

Thus, reason takes the form of following the movement of God's self-revelation as it is depicted in the pages of holy writ, and then obeying God's 'vocal presence' by developing a conceptual repetition of the act of reading Scripture. Webster describes the process as follows:

> Holy Scripture is the announcement of the eschatological gospel, and it is in attentive, ascetic reading of Scripture that the gospel is pressed upon the attention of the people of God. *Christian theology is the repetition in the movement of thought of this attentive, ascetic reading.* The concepts and language of Christian theology 'repeat' the act of reading Scripture; that is, they are the transposition into reflective terms of the abandonment which is the essence of attentiveness [and] hearing.[33]

In other words, theological reason is a function of the *auditus fidei*. The primary act of theological reason is exegetical, and all subsequent acts are dependent upon this primary act, because Scripture orders reason towards its object. This is why Webster found postliberal notions of theology as 'intertextuality' to be somewhat (though not completely) companionable with his early account of theological theology. The discursive habits of reading texts are modes of learning, and habits of citing and commenting upon texts are modes of rational argumentation and persuasion.[34] Attending to Scripture is a form of reasoning. Therefore, Webster argues that the 'positive' task of theology should take the form of a gloss or low-level commentary on Scripture, in which doctrines and concepts are employed to indicate 'the worlds of meaning in Scripture'.[35] Their purpose is to be light-weight and transparent to the idiom of the biblical text and thereby aid the church's faithful reading of the text.

It is for this reason that Webster even goes so far as to make the (somewhat ironic) claim that '[t]heologians should consider ceasing to write systematic treatises and confine themselves to the work of exposition of Scripture'.[36] Theology is 'exhausted in the role that it plays vis-à-vis Scripture'.[37] As we will see in the second half of this chapter, Webster moves a long way from this clarion call in his later years. Yet it is important that we do not misunderstand Webster's point here. The motivating force behind his claim is not primarily epistemological but moral and spiritual: the obedient following of God's self-revelation in Scripture is the means by which theological reason is sanctified and restored to a properly ordered relation to its object.[38] And crucially, for Webster, this 'object' is the eschatological

---

33. Webster, 'Texts', 14.
34. *CG*, 16.
35. Webster, 'Texts', 15.
36. Webster, 'Texts', 16.
37. Webster, 'Texts', 15.
38. Webster's motivation is pastoral as well. Since the primary end of theology is the edification of the church, and the primary means of this edification is the hearing of God's voice in Scripture, then the primary task of theological reason is to guide the church's reading of Scripture (cf. *HS*, 128–33).

interruption of all things in Jesus Christ, meaning the act of obediently following Scripture leads reason to a second 'critical' act.

Theological reason is called upon by its object to test the fidelity of Christian culture (preaching, liturgical practice, confessional witness, etc.) to the gospel declared in Scripture.[39] The intention of this 'critical' endeavour is not simply to check the human (and ecclesial) tendency towards closure and idolatry, but also to articulate the 'Christian difference' that lies at the heart of the gospel – namely that God is radically other and transcends all relations which he bears to creatures. Webster registers this point by appealing to the notion (borrowed from Rowan Williams) of Christ's 'catholicity'. He states, 'As the risen one who shares in God's very life, Jesus Christ is limitlessly resourceful. No one rendering of him can exhaust his potential; no single schema of tradition can issue in a "final" statement of his identity in relation to human life and history, for he is literally infinite.'[40] Human reason is limited and theological statements are provisional; they cannot possibly capture the infinite resourcefulness of Christ. The point here is that theological reason is required to test the church's fidelity and register 'Christian difference', not because of the inherently critical function of reason and its ability to transcend particular cultural locales, but because of the infinite nature of reason's object. In other words, the critical function of reason is not grounded in the transcendental nature of reason but in the transcendence of God.

God's eschatological presence opens up space for reason to engage in an act of self-criticism by revealing the 'gap' between Christian culture and its object. The event of revelation highlights the unbridgeable fissure between the gospel and the church's cultural articulations and inhabitations of it. Thus, theological reason is not only 'authorised' to reflect upon and bear witness to a 'new order of reality', but is also 'disturbed' and required to protest against the tendency of Christian culture to naturalize or routinize what is properly a 'spiritual event', an eschatological intrusion and interruption of the world (including human thought) by the presence of God.[41] By attending to this dialectic between 'authorisation' and 'disruption' in its intellectual activities, Christian theology seeks to register 'the shock of the new' and 'the sheer freedom and otherness of the gospel', and thereby bears witness to the reality of 'Christian difference'.[42] As I will argue in the next section, the desire

---

39. Along similar lines, Charles M. Wood argues that 'Christian theology may be defined as critical inquiry into the validity of Christian witness' (*Vision and Discernment: An Orientation in theological Study* (Eugene, OR: Wipf and Stock, 1985), 21), and he defines 'validity' as 'its faithfulness, its truth, its aptness to its circumstances' (24). Webster's emphasis on 'fidelity' over 'validity' signals the primacy he places on reason's responsibility to its object over its circumstances.

40. Webster, 'Traditions', 22.

41. Webster, 'Traditions', 22.

42. Webster, 'Conversations', 6; idem., 'Habits', 17.

to articulate the radical distinction between God and creatures remains a primary preoccupation of Webster's mature theology, yet the way in which he articulates this distinction changes dramatically, as does his understanding of the nature of theological reason. But first, I will offer a brief summary of my argument thus far and highlight two 'pressure points' that it revealed in Webster's account of 'theological theology' in the late 1990s.

5.3 Summary

Up to this point, our discussion has focused on Webster's account of the nature and operations of theological reason in the TBL (1998). I have argued that these lectures depict theological reason as an eschatological reality – located in an eschatological *place* (the culture of Christian faith and practice), enacted by an eschatological *subject* (the new creature in Christ), and directed to an eschatological *object* (the presence of the self-revealing, risen Christ). The movements of theological reason which correspond to this eschatological location, subject and object are modes of faith, ways of thinking and knowing that are responsive and answerable to its object: obedient following of Scripture and critical evaluation of the fidelity of Christian culture. Throughout the argument I have sought to demonstrate that there is a twofold motivation for construing matters in this way.

First, Webster wants to emphasize the ontological and epistemological priority of God (particularly his freedom and transcendence) in his account of human reason, thereby grounding theological thought and speech in divine action. This is the central tenet of Webster's account of 'theological theology':

> The distinctiveness of Christian theology lies ... in its invocation of God as agent in the intellectual practice of theology. In order to give account of its own operations, that is, Christian theology will talk of God and God's actions. Talk of God not only describes the matter into which theology enquires but also, crucially, informs its portrayal of its own processes of enquiry. In effect, theology is a contrary – eschatological – mode of intellectual life, taking its rise in God's disruption of the world, and pressing the academy to consider a quite discordant anthropology of enquiry.[43]

Reason is 'theological' not primarily because it posits God as the presupposition of its work or enquires into God as its object, but because it is set in motion by God as Subject. To speak of the activities of reason, according to Webster, one must speak about the being and activity of God. This is why Oliver Crisp's interpretation of Webster's 'theological theology' programme as being primarily about the reintegration of theology into an ecclesial and confessional context only

---

43. *CG*, 25.

gives half of the picture, missing the most crucial point.[44] As I argued above, one of Webster's chief concerns with postliberal theology was what he identified as a tendency to situate the activities of theological reason within the culture of the church in such a way that threatened to eclipse a robust account of divine action, thereby countering Enlightenment ideals of reason's transcendence by collapsing reason into cultural-linguistic immanence. Webster's response is to ground the activities of reason in the eschatological presence and activity of God in Christ. Why? To show that the activities of theological reason are not ultimately grounded in a transcendental anthropology or a settled ecclesial tradition or a set of human capacities given by God at creation, but rather in a gracious act of divine freedom whereby God makes himself present to and known by humans.

This leads us to the second major point of my argument thus far: Webster seeks to depict the activities of theological reason as modes of moral and spiritual accountability before God which require the transformation of the theologian. This reading of Webster runs counter to Michael Allen's suggestion that his account of 'theological theology' in the mid- to late 1990s was devoted primarily to polemic against modern practices of theology, and to establishing formally the priority of divine agency and of the Christian textual tradition in the theological task.[45] According to Allen, it is not until the mid-2000s that Webster begins to describe the shape of the divine economy in which the theologian is located and the Christian anthropology that arises from that location. Our discussion of the TBL has shown that Webster is already making this move in the late 1990s. The theologian is located in the eschatological presence of God, and therefore intellectual activities are events in the history of God's eschatological judgement and grace, episodes of sin and its overcoming. This is the reason why pursuing 'theological theology' is a spiritually demanding process of conversion and transformation, one which requires the unique practices of Christian culture – repentance, prayer, fear of God, teachability, deference to Scripture and freedom from self-preoccupation.[46] In this way, the intellect is made 'docile to the given' – God's eschatological presence.[47]

---

44. Crisp states, '"[T]heological theology" is a term coined by John Webster as a way of demarcating a particular approach to ST [systematic theology], one which is not merely concerned with theoretical matters, but with the life of the church' (Oliver D. Crisp, 'Analytic Theology as Systematic Theology', *Open Theology* 3:1 [2017]: 161). Darren Sarisky does a better job of capturing the core of Webster's theological theology programme: '[O]perating theologically entails that the discipline cannot frame an account of its own procedures without direct recourse to theological categories, without relating *how* its subject matter is studied to the distinctive nature of this utterly unique subject' ('Theological Theology', in *Theological Theology: Essays in Honour of John B. Webster*, eds. R. David Nelson, Darren Sarisky, and Justin Stratis (London: Bloomsbury T&T Clark, 2015), 3).

45. Allen, 'Toward Theological Theology', 220–4.

47. *CG*, 26.

46. Webster, 'Habits', 20. On the ascetic dimensions of reason in Webster's theology, see Michael Allen, 'Dogmatics as Ascetics', in *The Task of Dogmatics: Explorations in Theological Method*, eds. Oliver D. Crisp and Fred Sanders (Grand Rapids, MI: Zondervan, 2017), 195–200.

Our discussion of the TBL has also drawn attention (implicitly) to two pressure points in Webster's account of 'theological theology' in the late 1990s, which I will now make explicit. The first pressure point is methodological. One of the somewhat surprising features of Webster's early articulations of 'theological theology' is the (at times) indirect or a-theological manner of argumentation. He invests much in genealogies of modernity and ethnographic analyses of institutions and practices of learning, all in an effort to distance the practice of theology from modern convention and relocate it within the eschatological and ecclesial culture of Christian faith. Once the practice of theology is 're-regionalised', then the dynamics of theological reason are positively stated. It is somewhat ironic that his arguments rarely begin with talk of God's being and action, but rather with energetic attempts to divest himself of the traditions and intellectual habits of modernity – i.e. clearing space for 'theological theology'. The order and mode of his argumentation do not always reflect the content of that for which he is arguing.

The second pressure point has to do with the way Webster derives his anthropology of the theologian from an eschatological account of divine action and grace. His account of the nature and ends of the human person is developed exclusively from the vantage point of Christ's redemptive activity, which is depicted as a comprehensive interception and recreation of human life. This is due partly to the fact that divine creativity is identified primarily with the resurrection of Jesus Christ and partly to the fact that Christ's redemptive activity is tied closely to a theology of divine freedom. Grace is depicted as an extrinsic and interruptive act of God that is 'present only as the event of gift', but never as a creaturely effect or communication of spiritual goods.[48] As a result, the theologian is placed in a posture of prayerful waiting upon God, and the prime act of theological reason is the hearing and obedient following of God's address in Scripture. Theological reason is placed primarily in a passive and receptive posture, rather than an active one. It takes form as the *auditus fidei*, but rather little is said about the *intellectus fidei*.[49] Webster's anthropology of the theologian is intended to highlight the creativity and graciousness of divine action as well as the dependence and answerability of human reason. Yet it seems that for all his emphasis on the 'Christian difference' between God and creatures, Webster's early articulations of 'theological theology' do not always avoid a competitive understanding of the relation between God's redemptive and revelatory activity in Christ and the activities of human reason. His emphasis on divine freedom and the intrusive nature of grace results in a

---

48. Webster, 'Culture', 3.

49. On this topic, see Webster's critique of the papal encyclical *Fides et Ratio* and his subsequent dialogue with Thomas Weinandy: John Webster, 'Fides et Ratio, Articles 64–79', *NB* 81 (2000): 68–76; Thomas Weinandy, '*Fides et Ratio*: A Response to John Webster', *NB* 81 (2000): 225–35; John Webster, 'A Reply to Tom Weinandy', *NB* 81 (2000): 236–7. A key point of difference between Webster and Weinandy is the former's Reformed emphasis on the noetic effects of sin and reluctance to appeal to the capacity of 'graced reason' at this point in his career.

rather thin account of the knowing subject as the creaturely coordinate of divine revelation. As we turn to a discussion of Webster's mature theology, I will seek to show how key developments in his account of 'theological theology' help resolve both the methodological and anthropological problems identified in the TBL.

5.4 God without Measure *(2016)*

When compared with the TBL, we see both continuity and development in Webster's mature account of theological reason. Some of the formal logic remains the same: reason is located within the economy of God's revelatory and regenerative works; this dogmatic location plays a significant role in shaping a theological anthropology of the theologian; and finally, this anthropology gives rise to an account of the operations of theological reason. Yet there are significant material differences. Rather than making arguments about the socio-cultural location of reason, he develops a metaphysically ambitious account of the cognitive principles of reason. Instead of investing heavily in genealogical critiques of modern reason, he reaches for theological resources by which to build a robust account of the integrity and acts of reason. And finally, rather than accepting the limits placed upon reason by philosophical idealism, he displays more confidence in the reach of graced reason, precisely because creaturely knowledge is grounded in God's super-eminent knowledge and its ultimate telos is contemplation of God's inner life.

Much could be said about each of these material differences, yet my purpose here is to draw attention to two key theological shifts that precipitate the developments in Webster's account of 'theological theology'. First, he grounds the economy of divine revelation and the activities of human reason in the immanent perfection of God (omniscience, goodness, love), which is the material epicentre of his mature theology. Second, he situates the theologian within the wider context of the works of nature (creation and providence), which leads to a reordered account of the nature and ends of reason. Then God's works of grace are viewed in coordination with (but not as establishing) the nature and ends of created reason, so that revelation and regeneration are not viewed as interruptive divine acts, but as acts which presuppose, preserve and perfect the integrity of human intellect.[50] In the remainder of this chapter, I will seek to demonstrate the significance of these theological shifts for Webster's understanding of the nature and operations of theological reason, and will do so by offering an analysis of the cognitive principles of theology, the location and anthropology of the theologian, and the operations of reason.

---

50. Allen rightly observes that Webster's mature theology situates the economy of grace, especially its Christological elements, within the 'wider frame' of the doctrine of creation, and that this has consequences for his theology of grace, yet he does not go on to spell out the latter claim in any detail ('Toward Theological Anthropology', 16, 19–22, 24).

5.4.1 Cognitive principles of reason

In his mature theology, Webster consistently identifies two cognitive principles of theology: the objective principle is 'God's infinite knowledge' and the subjective principle is 'regenerate human intelligence'.[51] We will circle back to the concept of 'knowledge by principles' in Section 5.4.3, but for now we simply note that it is a way of knowing created realities metaphysically. One comes to know the truth about a contingent thing as one comes to know the absolute and necessary reality – the 'First Truth' – by which it exists.[52] Talk about the 'principles' of reason, therefore, is a means by which Webster seeks to resist the secularization of reason.[53] Reason is conditioned and defined not merely by its embeddedness and standpoint in time and space, but also and primarily by its divine ground and cause. We saw Webster making a similar move in the TBL by locating reason within the 'space' created by God's eschatological presence, but now Webster attempts something much more metaphysically ambitious: to show that the ultimate ground of reason is God's immanent perfection.

This is where teaching about divine omniscience comes to the fore: God knows himself and all things in a perfect, simple and single act of intuition. God's knowledge involves no process of acquisition because it is not contingent in any way, but fully actual and realized. Divine revelation is God's sharing of his own knowledge with creatures in a way that accommodates to their finite capacities – unlike divine knowledge, creaturely intelligence is limited, discursive and laborious. The purpose of drawing attention to God's super-eminent knowledge as the objective 'principle' of theology is to show that human reason and knowledge are not first of all 'causes', but rather 'effects' of God's sharing of his own knowledge: '[T]o know is to be caused by God to know something which is antecedently and fully known by him.'[54] In other words, theology is a 'subaltern' *scientia*, dependent upon a prior act of knowing which is extrinsic to the human act of knowing. Theological reason is dependent upon principles which are neither self-evident nor demonstrable, but exceed the grasp of reason and are made known *per revelationem divinam*. Thus, Aquinas argues, '[S]acred doctrine is a science because it proceeds from principles established by the light of a higher science, namely, the science of God and the blessed.'[55] Or again: 'Sacred doctrine derives its principles not from any human knowledge, but from the divine knowledge, through which, as through the highest wisdom, all our knowledge is set in order.'[56]

---

51. *GWM* I:215.
52. On the relation between contingency and necessity in Webster's thought, see Westerholm, 'Practice of Theological Theology', 57–60.
53. *DW*, viii.
54. *GWM* II:160.
55. *ST* Ia.1.2 resp.
56. *ST* Ia.1.6 ad 1. On Aquinas' understanding of theology as *scientia*, see Bauerschmidt, *Thomas Aquinas*, 51–8; Rudi te Velde, *Aquinas on God: The 'Divine Science' of the* Summa Theologiae (Aldershot: Ashgate, 2006), 23–8; 'Appendix 6: Theology as Science', in *Summa Theologiae*, vol. 1 (Cambridge: Cambridge University Press, 2006), 68–87.

Why does the mature Webster make recourse to the scholastic idiom of 'principles'?[57] First, as we have already suggested, it helps him resist the secularization of reason by drawing attention to its ontological ground in divine *scientia*. Second, it allows Webster to articulate with greater conceptual clarity a point he learned from Barth regarding the ontological and epistemological priority of God in relation to the knowing subject: the possibility and actuality of theological reason and knowledge are ultimately grounded not in human capacities but in God's self-knowledge and self-revelation.[58] Human reason rests on God's being and act as its condition of possibility and enabling source.[59] Third, the conceptuality of 'principles' enables Webster to register the radical distinction between divine and human knowledge (archetype – ectype), and therefore the limits of human knowledge, while also developing a positive account of their relation. This is something that his prior emphasis on the intrusive nature of God's revelatory action struggled to accomplish. But now, instead of speaking of God's eschatological interruption of human reason, he speaks of God's goodness and love whereby he shares his own knowledge (of himself and all things) with creatures. He states, 'God condescends to communicate to creatures a share in his knowledge and to invite them into rational fellowship.'[60] Notice the language used here: 'share' and 'fellowship', terms which seek to describe a positive relationship. Elsewhere, Webster even goes so far as to speak of a 'proportion' and 'correspondence' between divine and creaturely knowledge such that the latter can be called a 'creaturely repetition' of the former.[61] Theological reason is a form of fellowship with God; it is a finite, communicated participation in God's own knowledge.

This leads us to the subjective cognitive principle of theology, namely regenerate human intelligence. In order to understand Webster's mature thought on this matter, first we need to grasp the key developments in his account of the location and anthropology of the theologian.

5.4.2 Dogmatic location and anthropology of the theologian

Whereas Webster's argument in the TBL sought to derive the nature and ends of the theologian from God's work of redemption, thus according ontological

---

57. For a thorough discussion of the principles of theology by a Reformed Scholastic, see Franciscus Junius, *A Treatise on True Theology*, trans. David C. Noe (Grand Rapids, MI: Reformation Heritage Books, 2014).
58. *DW*, 135–41; *GWM* I:215–7.
59. This conviction is reflected in the form of Webster's mature essays. They begin with a formal specification of the object of theology – God and all things in relation to God – then foreground discussion of any given topic with teaching about God's perfect life *in se* followed by a description of God's works *ad extra*. The point of this formal structure is in part pedagogical: to teach theological reason that its movements are grounded in the being and act of God.
60. *GWM* I:216.
61. *DW*, 137–8; *GWM* II:144, 142.

priority to the eschatological subject in Christ, his argument in *God without Measure* begins with God's works of nature (creation and providence). In other words, Webster's depiction of the dogmatic location of the theologian expands – creation, providence, and redemption – in an effort to develop a richer account of the creaturely integrity and dynamics of reason. 'Divine revelation', writes Webster, 'is not magnified but restricted and made ineffectual by the absence of creaturely intellect'.[62] In what follows, I will seek to demonstrate that the doctrine of creation not only serves the purpose of construing the history in which reason is located as a divinely willed and shaped history, as Westerholm has suggested, but also supplies an identity description of the human agents whose rational acts take place in that history.[63] It provides an ontology and teleology of created intellect.

According to the mature Webster, intellect is 'essential to human creatures'.[64] It is an endowment of our created nature, a 'set of capacities bestowed and preserved by God' and exercised in relation to God, who intrinsically moves the operations of the human mind.[65] There are three aspects of the intellect to which Webster consistently draws attention: its creatureliness, its active potency and its transcendent vocation. (1) Intellect is an aspect of our creatureliness, meaning it is a gift, 'an endowment whose possession places us in relation to the one by whom we are endowed'.[66] This entails that practices of religion and prayer (rightly ordered relation to God) are intrinsic to the proper exercise of the intellect. (2) Intellect is not merely a passive or receptive potency, but also an active potency – active not in the sense of creative or poetic, but in the sense of discerning the texture of being.[67] It is the 'power of apprehension' whereby humans seek to understand created things in more than merely their phenomenal existence – i.e. in their depth and nature – thereby enabling humans to enact an intentional and deliberate relation to them.[68] In other words, the intellect funds human relationality. (3) Human intellect has a 'transcendent vocation'.[69] The ultimate telos of reason lies beyond itself 'in the apprehension of God and of all things in God'.[70] That is why Webster characterizes intellectual activity, like volitional activity, as a type of 'transcendent motion' that finds its fulfilment and perfection in the *visio Dei*.[71]

Crucial to Webster's mature anthropology of the theologian is the fact that the active bent of the intellect towards its telos is not merely a matter of external divine

---

62. *GWM* I:217–8.
63. Cf. Westerholm, 'Practice of Theological Theology', 456–60.
64. *GWM* II:145.
65. *GWM* I:218.
66. *GWM* II:145.
67. A passive potency is 'the *capacity* to receive actualization of determination', whereas an active potency is 'the *capability* to actualize or determine' (Kenneth L. Schmitz, *The Gift: Creation* (Milwaukee: Marquette University Press, 1982), 103).
68. *GWM* II:146.
69. *DW*, 134.
70. *DW*, 124.
71. *DW*, 118; *GWM* II:162.

determination, but of the intrinsic ordering of human nature by God in the act of creation. Webster states, 'In establishing another thing in being, God bestows finality, a tendency or active bent and movement towards the completion of that thing's nature. This bent and movement is an effect of God's initial donation of being, and is held and stirred by God's maintaining and governing presence to the creature.'[72] The teleological orientation of human nature (including the intellect) is an intrinsic 'effect' of God's originating and preserving action. By articulating God's creative agency through the doctrines of creation and providence, rather than Christology and eschatology, Webster seeks to develop a reordered anthropology of the theologian, one which continues to resist the concept of 'pure reason' but has the added benefit of providing space for a robust account of the integrity and activity of reason. For Webster, much hinges on this move: the ends of theology are derived from, and an expansive theology of intellectual and moral virtue is made possible by, this reordered account of human nature and ends.[73] But at this point, I want to draw attention to the fact that Webster's mature theology of revelation is coordinated with this anthropology. He argues, 'By virtue of God's work of creation and preservation, there exists a certain correspondence between the intellect of God and the intellect of creatures; there is an element in the being of the creature which is a coordinate to God's own mind. Further, it is to this creaturely element that God addresses himself.'[74] Revelation is by someone to someone, and the person addressed by God is not a mere 'privation' (as Webster claimed in the TBL), but a creature whose intellect (and being?) exists in correspondence to God. What exactly this 'correspondence' or 'element' consists of is not made clear by Webster, yet it does seem to suggest a sort of touching point for divine revelation.

And so this raises an important question about whether Webster's theology of creation and providence has opened the door for natural theology or the *analogia entis*. Bruce L. McCormack has suggested that other elements of Webster's mature theology – affinity for Thomistic metaphysics and for talk of 'an asymmetry between the immanent and the economic' Trinity – seem to require that he make a principled commitment to both.[75] There are other hints in Webster's mature theology that McCormack's suggestion may have been coming to fruition: (1) a passing mention of the fact that in the act of creation God communicates a 'likeness' of his being to creatures;[76] (2) an affirmation of a theology of participation, which provides the metaphysical underpinning for the *analogia entis*;[77] and (3) a consistent reliance on the conceptuality of the cause-effect relation, which, for Aquinas, states that

---

72. *GWM* I:111.
73. This point will be elaborated at the end of the current section and in Section 5.3.3.
74. *GWM* II:144.
75. McCormack, 'Processions and Missions', 126.
76. *GWM* I:111.
77. *GWM* I:106–7. On this topic, see Simon Oliver, *Creation: A Guide for the Perplexed* (London: Bloomsbury T&T Clark, 2017), 64–74.

created effects resemble their uncreated cause in an analogical manner.[78] And yet, he never makes an overt affirmation or principled use of natural theology or the *analogia entis* in his theology. Why? One reason may have to do with his penchant for construing the God-creature relation through descriptive and sequential accounts of divine action rather than through a coordinating concept or analogy such as 'communion' or 'relation' (I noted examples of this in Chapters 3 and 4). This, he believes, allows one to ground creaturely realities in God's being and action without eliding the radical distinction between them. But the strongest reason for Webster's lack of a principled affirmation of natural theology and the *analogia entis* seems to be his predilection for understanding the God-creature relation not only in metaphysical categories but also in moral and spiritual ones. Creaturely nature (including the intellect) *is* as it participates in a moral history of fellowship with God, a history which includes human defection and redemption.

This brings us to the topic of intellectual depravity and regeneration. According to Webster, the noetic effects of sin are grave: 'Knowledge of God and of our created nature is a casualty of the fall. After our forfeit of the state of integrity, such knowledge has become immeasurably more difficult; we understand almost nothing of God and of ourselves, and that only with great labour.'[79] Similar statements can be found (tellingly) at the beginning of essays on the doctrine of creation:

> Knowledge of the creator and of ourselves as creatures is a casualty of the fall: we will not honour the creator (Rom. 1.21), we will not acknowledge ourselves to be his creatures. Fallen intelligence tends away from God, in forgetfulness and impatience (Ps. 106.13). To know its creator, reason must be healed by repentance and the suffering of divine instruction, by which love of God is made to grow.[80]

> We might also speak of friendship with God as a condition for knowledge of him as creator and of ourselves as his creatures. In our corrupt state, such friendship is lost to us, for we despise both our creaturely condition and our creator, and need to be reconciled. Corruption inhibits knowledge.[81]

Note the presence of two crucial words in Webster's account of the intellect's depravity: 'love' and 'friendship'.[82] These words bring us to a core aspect of Webster's

---

78. Cf. Christopher R.J. Holmes, 'Revisiting the God/World Difference', *MoTh* 34:2 (2018): 159–76.
79. *GWM* II:124–5.
80. *GWM* I:84.
81. *GWM* I:102.
82. Rik Van Nieuwenhove notes how 'Thomas describes charity in terms of friendship with God (*ST* II–II, Q. 23, A. 1) who is the principle object of charity (*ST* II–II, Q. 23, A. 5, ad. 1)' ('Charity, Intellect, and Contemplation in St Thomas Aquinas: Contemporary Relevance', *Year Book of the Irish Philosophical Society* [2013]: 130 n.4).

theology of sin, namely his Augustinian emphasis on the unity of intellect (reason) and will (love).[83] For Augustine, as for Aquinas, the will (love) impels the intellect, and humanity's 'longing for God embraces the mind'.[84] Webster shares Augustine's sensitivity to the dynamics of desire which are intertwined with intellectual activities, and he is deeply aware that 'love of God' and 'knowledge about God' are inextricably bound together.[85] And so, he states: 'Intellectual life takes its rise in the appetite and the will.'[86] This claim is not intended to reduce the intellect to a mere function of desire (reason as *poiesis*) or will (reason as power), but rather to say that, as rational creatures, humans desire and love to know. 'Human creatures are by nature studious.'[87]

It is this anthropological conviction that leads Webster to conceive of the corruption of the intellect not merely as the weakening of its powers, but also as the distorted and disordered use of those powers under the auspices of vicious desire. He states, 'Intellect as a capacity or disposition remains, even though in severely impaired form; what is lacking is the intellect's purposeful and well-directed execution of itself.'[88] This loss of proper direction comes as a result of improper love and disordered desire, and ultimately leads to intellectual 'futility' (not achieving its end in knowledge of God), of which the prime example is, for Webster, the vice of 'curiosity'.[89] Curiosity is the corruption of the virtue of studiousness, a corruption which 'happens when intellectual activity is commanded by *crooked desire*'.[90] It directs the powers of the intellect to seek knowledge of improper objects

---

83. For an excellent discussion of Augustine's understanding of the intellect, see A. N. Williams, *The Divine Sense: The Intellect in Patristic Theology* (Cambridge: Cambridge University Press, 2007), 143–89.

84. A. N. Williams, 'Contemplation: *Knowledge of God in Augustine's* De Trinitate', in *Knowing the Triune God: The Work of the Spirit in the Practices of the Church*, eds. James J. Buckley and David S. Yeago (Grand Rapids, MI: Eerdmans, 2001), 131. On the interrelation of intellect and will in Aquinas, see Lydia Schumacher, *Rationality as Virtue: Towards a Theological Philosophy* (Farnham: Ashgate, 2015), 120–3; Reinhard Hütter, 'The Directedness of Reasoning and the Metaphysics of Creation', in *Reason and the Reasons of Faith*, eds. Paul J. Griffiths and Reinhard Hütter (London: T&T Clark, 2005), 173–6.

85. Cf. Williams, 'Contemplation', 129–37.

86. *GWM* II:175.

87. *GWM* I:219. This statement echoes the opening sentence of Aristotle's *Metaphysics*: 'All men by nature desire to know' (Aristotle, *Metaphysics*, trans. W. D. Ross (Oxford: Clarendon Press, 1924), I.1). Note the contrast with Webster's earlier claim that humans 'do not by nature desire to know' ('Conversations', 7). Webster's mature theology conceives of intellectual power and desire as gifts of God's original act of creation, whereas his TBL construed them as gifts of redemptive grace.

88. *GWM* II:149.

89. *DW*, 193–202; *GWM* I:222–3. On the vice of curiosity, see Paul J. Griffiths, *Intellectual Appetite: A Theological Grammar* (Washington, DC: The Catholic University of America Press, 2009), 19–22.

90. *GWM* II:150 (emphasis mine).

and for improper ends, and to do so indiscriminately. Moreover, curiosity leads the intellect to fixate on 'surfaces' without attention to their 'depth' – i.e. God who is present in all things as their cause. (I will circle back to this point in the next section when I discuss the intellectual act of *reductio*.) Much more could be said on the topic of intellectual depravity, but the main point for our purposes is this: Webster's Augustinian emphasis on the unity of intellect and will leads him to conceive of the intellect's depravity in terms of the misdirection of intellectual powers caused by disordered love and desire.[91] Therefore, the healing of reason requires not only the strengthening of natural powers which were weakened by the fall, but also the reordering of will and appetite towards fellowship with God.[92] This happens through God's work of regeneration and sanctification.

For Webster, '[t]heological science is a graced enterprise'.[93] We have argued that this is so not only because humanity is destined for an end beyond the grasp of creaturely reason, but also because the possibility of theology in a post-lapsarian world is predicated upon God's work of redemption. In other words, Webster pushes against what A. N. Williams has described as the modern tendency to discuss the reach and uses of human reason without recourse to the doctrines of reconciliation and sanctification, by showing how the drama of redemption history 'forms the persons who ponder, write, read, and interpret theology'.[94] I have already shown that this was a crucial aspect of Webster's account of 'theological theology' in the TBL, but now I will seek to demonstrate how, by coordinating his theology of grace with his account of human nature and ends established in the doctrine of creation, Webster's mature articulation of this point is able to give a richer account of the integrity and activity of reason. He does this through a theology of regeneration and of virtue.

The doctrine of regeneration describes the restorative mission of the Holy Spirit, whereby the Spirit realizes and preserves in particular human beings the new created nature that was constituted by the reconciliatory mission of the Son.[95] By the Spirit's regenerative work, 'human nature is restored and the human vocation reinstituted'.[96] Whereas the TBL described regeneration as an 'event' in which a person's identity was severed from all that was past and made completely new in Christ, thereby establishing a new eschatological subject, here Webster speaks of regeneration as the 'restoration' and 'reinstitution' of the human nature and ends

---

91. On the relation between volitional depravity and intellectual error in Augustine, see Paul J. Griffiths, 'How Reasoning Goes Wrong: A Quasi-Augustinian Account of Error and Its Implications', in *Reason and the Reasons of Faith*, eds. Paul J. Griffiths and Reinhard Hütter (London: T&T Clark, 2005), 152–8.

92. This is why, for Webster, the proper operation of theological reason requires both intellectual and moral virtues (*GWM* II:153–4).

93. *GWM* I:10.

94. A. N. Williams, *The Architecture of Theology: Structure, System, and Ratio* (Oxford: Oxford University Press, 2011), 217.

95. *GWM* II:151.

96. *GWM* II:136.

established by God at creation. Therefore, the work of regeneration corresponds to the three aspects of the intellect that we discussed above: creatureliness, active potency and transcendent vocation. (1) Regeneration restores *creatureliness*.[97] Webster argues, 'Life in the realm of regeneration conforms to the character of creaturely being, namely, that we have life and movement as we are vivified and moved by God.'[98] The activities of regenerate intellect are 'moved movements' – creaturely movements which depend on an establishing and sustaining work of God. (2) Regeneration strengthens the intellect's *active potency*, and even more, it perfects this potency by imparting a 'new principle' of action to the intellect. The light of grace supplements the light of nature.[99] (3) Regeneration reorders and guides intellectual powers towards the fulfilment of their *transcendent vocation*. The Spirit renews the appetite and will which give rise to intellectual activity and infuses habits that direct rational powers towards proper objects and ends (chiefly contemplation of God).

It is in the context of God's renewal of human nature and vocation that Webster's theology of virtue comes into its own. In this context it is made clear that the virtues which guide reason towards knowledge of God are infused by the Spirit, not acquired. Hence the emphasis is on the priority of divine grace. Yet talk of 'infused' virtues has a double function: not only does it register the prevenience of divine action, but it also clarifies the fact that God works *intrinsically* so as to honour and preserve the structure of the creaturely nature he has made. The infused virtues are the means by which the Spirit guides and directs the movement of the human intellect towards its telos. Thus, the conceptual anatomy of virtue allows Webster to develop a rich descriptive account of the integrity and dynamics of human action. Take, for example, Webster's fourfold classification of the intellectual virtues. There are virtues which dispose us (1) 'to labour to acquire intellectual goods' (love, studiousness), (2) 'to receive intellectual goods' (attentiveness, humility, modesty, docility), (3) 'to contribute to and profit from common intellectual life' (benevolence, generosity, affability, impartiality, gratitude), and (4) 'to deal with difficulty in the pursuit of intellectual goods' (magnanimity, courage, patience).[100] The explanatory power of this conceptual anatomy is profoundly appealing to Webster.

Yet, one may well ask, what has happened to Webster's earlier resistance to the Aristotelian notion of virtue? His resistance was fuelled by the conviction that this conceptuality risks displacing talk of divine action and thereby collapsing into an anthropology of immanence. Why has the mature Webster changed his mind? The answer has to do with key developments in Webster's anthropology and theology of grace, both of which are indicative of a reordered account of the God-creature relation.

---

97. On this, see Matthew Levering, 'On Humility', *IJST* 19:4 (2017): 463–8.
98. *GWM* II:152.
99. Webster, 'Editorial', 379–80.
100. *GWM* II:176.

The key anthropological development occurs as the primary doctrines from which Webster derives his account of human nature and ends shift from Christology and eschatology to creation and providence. The consequences of this shift are twofold. First, the doctrine of creation *ex nihilo* in particular allows Webster to articulate the radical distinction between God and creatures – something he was keen to do in the *Burns Lectures* through interruptive accounts of divine revelation and grace – while simultaneously establishing the basic principles of their non-competitive relation. God's difference from the world is established and revealed not by his eschatological interruption of human life, but rather by his original act of creation – an act which suggests that God is perfectly realized apart from creation and has no need to create, and therefore, that God cannot be conceived as a 'pair' with creation. Yet it is precisely this 'difference' that highlights the gratuity of God's act of creation – he gives creatures being and the power to act towards the fulfilment of their natures. God does not relate to creatures as a competitive force within the world or an intrusive force from outside the world, but as the ground and enabling source of their integrity and intrinsic worth.[101] This principle is then given conceptual expansion in the doctrine of providence through the notion of 'moved movement', which Webster employs to specify the nature of human intellectual activities. Thus, the basic features of the God-creature relation as established by the doctrine of creation now form the basic context for Webster's anthropology of the theologian. It allows him to resist the secularization of reason while also giving a more robust account of its creaturely integrity and dynamics. Second, by articulating an ontology and teleology of reason through the doctrine of creation, Webster is able to emphasize the active nature of reason in a way that he had difficulty doing in the TBL. His account of the intellect as an active and teleologically ordered potency then provides the backdrop for his understanding of the intellect's depravity and regeneration: the former describes the corruption and misdirection of intellectual powers, and the latter describes the strengthening, redirecting and perfecting of intellectual powers. Reason is construed in active terms all the way through the drama of redemption.

This lead us, finally, to a key development in Webster's theology of grace: grace is no longer identified primarily with divine freedom, and therefore construed in punctiliar terms as God's ever-fresh act of giving, but rather with divine goodness.[102] Divine goodness communicates enduring goods to creatures for their use and enjoyment. In other words, grace is durative and takes form as creaturely effects. When dovetailed with key principles from Webster's doctrine of creation – namely that 'God the Spirit moves not extrinsically, as an alien causal force, but

---

101. For an argument as to how the ontological dependence of creatures (an implication of the doctrine of creation *ex nihilo*) does not threaten but establishes creaturely integrity, see Schmitz, *The Gift*, 72–97.

102. John Webster, '"A Relation beyond All Relations": God and Creatures in Barth's Lectures on Ephesians, 1921–22', in *The Epistle to the Ephesians*, ed. R. David Nelson (Grand Rapids, MI: Baker Academic, 2017), 46–9.

intrinsically, as the mover of our movement'[103] – this new emphasis opens the theological and logical space for Webster to develop a theology of infused grace and virtue without thereby collapsing talk of divine action into an anthropology of immanence.

This reordered account of the God-creature relation, to which the developments in Webster's anthropology and the theology of grace bear witness, is the context within which to understand his mature account of the operations of theological reason. The movements of reason reflect his broader account of the relation-in-distinction between God and creatures.

5.4.3 Operations of reason

The primary operations of theological reason are twofold: First, it seeks to articulate the 'Christian distinction' between God and creation, which forms the context for all talk of their relations; and second, it seeks to discern and give a conceptual rendering of the ordered relations between God and all things.[104]

First, theological reason seeks to articulate the fact that its principle object (God) is a totally unconventional matter for human thought. Reason needs to be broken of its tendency to conceive of God as part of a larger whole or merely as the principle of the world, and therefore to think of God and creation as somehow 'paired'. Here Webster is drawing upon the insights of Robert Sokolowski, who argues that revelation (particularly the account of divine perfection which is embedded in the doctrine of creation *ex nihilo*) points reason in a different direction. Sokolowski states,

> [I]n the Christian distinction God is understood as 'being' God entirely apart from any relation of otherness to the world or to the whole. God could and would be God even if there were no world. Thus the Christian distinction is appreciated as a distinction that did not have to be, even though it in fact is. The most fundamental thing we come to in Christianity, the distinction between the world and God, is appreciated as not being the most fundamental thing after all, because one of the terms of the distinction, God, is more fundamental than the distinction itself.[105]

In other words, and this is what Webster finds particularly important, theological reason is schooled by revelation to understand that God is '*ens realissimum*' and that the distinction between God and the world is not a distinction within a whole

---

103. *GWM* II:152.
104. I have chosen to focus on the developments in Webster's understanding of the operations of dogmatic reasoning, but this is not to suggest that Webster has displaced the primacy of exegetical reasoning (cf. *DW*, 130).
105. Sokolowski, *The God of Faith and Reason*, 32–3.

but rather a distinction between that which is perfect being and that which might not have been.[106]

What is the purpose of articulating this 'Christian distinction' according to Webster? On the one hand, it orients theological reason towards the radical perfection of God, which, as we will see below, is the ultimate end of reason – adoration of God the Holy Trinity. On the other hand, it opens the logical and theological space for all other Christian mysteries.[107] Therefore, theology constantly needs to recall this distinction as the 'new context' within which we view all other doctrines.[108] This is key for Webster: the distinction between God and creatures is that which illumines the character of their relations.[109]

This leads us to the second movement of theological reason: it seeks to discern and give a conceptual rendering of the ordered relations between God and all things. This act of intellectual 'discernment' takes two forms: (1) systematic structuring and architectonic ordering, and (2) *reductio* or knowledge by principles. Webster's mature essays are replete with formal questions about the order, arrangement and proportion of doctrines in relation to one another. Added to this is careful specification of which doctrines are 'cardinal', 'distributed' and 'derivative.' Formal questions about the systematic shape and architectonic ordering of doctrine are designed to aid the mind in discerning and conforming itself to the order of being. According to Webster, theology is a 'comprehensive science' (queen of the arts and sciences), and part of its task is to articulate the metaphysical and moral 'first principles' of all created reality and thereby display its ordered unity.[110] This is made possible as theological reason comes to share (in a finite, ectypal way) in God's knowledge of himself and all things. And reason comes to share this 'divine perspective' on reality as it follows and repeats in conceptual form the movement of all things from God and to God. Architectonic ordering is about reproducing the order of being in the movement of thought.[111] Conceiving of the operation of theological reason in this way requires Webster to make a firm distinction

---

106. *GWM* I:179.

107. Sokolowski, *The God of Faith and Reason*, 37; idem., 'Creation and Christian Understanding', 179.

108. Brian J. Shanley, '*Sacra Doctrina* and the Theology of Disclosure', *The Thomist* 61:2 (1997): 170–1.

109. We noted examples of this theological rational in Chapters 2 and 3, where 'mixed' character of the God-creature relation was the foundation of its loving, gratuitous and non-competitive character.

110. *GWM* II:171–2. Note the contrast to Webster's earlier claim that theology was not 'the queen of the sciences' but rather one discipline among many ('Conversations', 6).

111. Westerholm claims that for Webster architectural questions 'provide a useful register of the degree to which theological work is conditioned by its location in the history of salvation' ('Practice of Theological Theology', 453). I am arguing that the prominence of architectural questions in his mature theology has more to do with the proper ordering of theology and economy.

between the order of being and the order of knowing. It does not matter much where theological reason begins (with consideration of God or some aspect of created reality) as long as it seeks to make manifest and conform the mind to the order of being (God then creatures, theology then economy). For Webster, the ultimate purpose of reason's structuring and ordering activities is contemplative and soteriological: 'This formal disposition of doctrines corresponds to the material order in the expository sequence, and also, by reproducing in intelligence the movement of creatures from God to perfection, participates in that same movement.'[112]

This leads us, finally, to reason's movement of *reductio*. Here Webster takes his cues from Bonaventure's *On the Reduction of the Arts to Theology*.[113] If the ordering and systematizing movement of theological reason intend to reproduce the material order of being (from Creator to creature) in the mind, then the act of 'reduction' moves in the opposite direction (from creature to Creator), seeking to make creaturely realities intelligible by tracing them back to their founding principles or causes – namely, God's immanent perfection. This metaphysical and contemplative way of knowing is reason's way of understanding all things *sub ratione Dei*.

The intellectual movement of *reductio* is grounded in a particular account of the metaphysics of creation and the anthropology of the theologian. 'Reduction' is not a poetic or imaginative act, in which causal relations are a function of the knowing subject's mind rather than embedded in the objective nature of reality.[114] Rather, 'reduction' is grounded in the metaphysics of creation, whereby created realities exist *per participationem* and therefore have a 'depth' that is not reducible to phenomenal existence. This in turn means that created realities (textual, cultural, natural) are 'signs' whose purpose is to draw the human intellect to consider not only the creaturely features of the sign but also the divine reality which is its cause and source of being. Webster states,

> By the work of divine love, finite things come to share in the universal good of being, but only in a finite manner, and only as they stand in relation to the creator God, the source of being. This relation *constitutes* creatures. Every element of creaturely being and action is what it is in 'the very dependency of the created act of being upon the principle from which it is produced'. There is, therefore, a *depth* to created things. To consider them, we have to understand not only their finite causes but the first cause, tracing them back to their source, which is God. Creatures have being as *principiata*, as effects of God their *principium*. The movement by which we understand how creatures participate in being is

---

112. *GWM* I:7.
113. *DW*, 181–92.
114. On the historical developments that led to this view, see Schmitz, *The Texture of Being*, 31–2.

this: 'we trace everything that possesses something by sharing, as to its source and cause, to what possesses that thing essentially.'[115]

Reason is situated within and seeks to apprehend a universe of created signs whose origin and end are God.

To the metaphysics of creation there corresponds the teleological orientation of human nature, 'according to which that nature is completed in knowledge of God'.[116] And so, the intellectual act of 'reduction' not only discloses the 'sign' character of created reality but also fulfils the ultimate purpose of the human person. It is a relational form of knowing whose goal is rational fellowship with and contemplation of God. Webster states, 'Contemplation – what Aquinas calls "a simple gaze" – requires the mind to move through created things to the divine reality of whose self-communication they are signs and bearers. Contemplation is rapt attention to God the cause of all things rather than to the things of which he is the cause.'[117] Contemplation is not the only end of theology; there are scientific and practical ends as well, but the former is instrumental and the latter is derivative.[118] That is why Webster could speak of contemplation of the Holy Trinity as the ultimate goal of Christology and ecclesiology alike, and why he could speak of the historical and scriptural form of revelation not as an end in itself but as that which beckons reason to consideration of the cause of revelation.[119] The ultimate object and goal of theological reason are God himself – his triune perfection.

5.5 Conclusion

My argument in this chapter has revolved around a comparative study of Webster's Thomas Burns Lectures (1998) and *God without Measure* (2016), focusing on his understanding of the relation between God and the theologian, and how this influences his characterization of the nature and operations of reason. I argued that Webster's account of 'theological theology' was driven by a consistent concern

---

115. *GWM* I:107 (quotes from Aquinas, *Summa Contra Gentiles* II.18.2 and *Compendium of Theology* I.68). This quote comes from the only occurrence of a positive evaluation of the concept of participation in Webster's corpus. Its success, argues Webster, is contingent upon theology's ability to employ the concept without threatening the distinction between uncreated and created being. On the relation between creation *ex nihilo* and participation, see Yonghua Ge, 'The One and the Many: A Revisiting of an Old Philosophical Question in the Light of Theologies of Creation and Participation', *Heythrop Journal* 57:1 (2016): 109–121.

116. *GWM* I:220.

117. *GWM* I:220.

118. On Webster's understanding of the relation between dogmatic and moral reason, see Oliver O'Donovan, 'John Webster on Dogmatics and Ethics', *IJST* 21:1 (2019): 78–92.

119. *GWM* I:6, 57–8, 193.

to register the ontological and epistemological priority of God in relation to the activities of the knowing subject. In other words, he sought to articulate how the theologian's reasoning is conditioned and defined by God's presence and action. In my discussion of Webster's early 'theological theology', I noted the way in which he sought to do this by locating reason within the eschatological culture of Christian faith and practice. Then he developed an anthropology of the theologian fitting to this eschatological location, according ontological priority to the eschatological subject in Christ. And finally, he developed an account of reason's operations from the standpoint of the eschatological existence of the theologian before the eschatological presence of God. I also identified two pressure points, one methodological and one anthropological, in Webster's early account of 'theological theology': (1) the order and mode of his argumentation did not always reflect the content of that for which he was arguing, and (2) his eschatological emphasis on divine freedom and the intrusive nature of grace resulted in a rather thin account of the knowing subject as the creaturely coordinate of divine revelation. As I turned to a discussion of Webster's mature theology, I highlighted the ways in which Webster sought to resolve these tensions: first, by grounding the act of divine revelation and the activities of human reason in God's perfect knowledge and goodness, and second, by situating the theologian within the wider context of God's works of nature (especially creation). While gaps in his mature account of theological reason still remain, particularly in relation to its social and ecclesial context and in relation to its use of philosophy and tradition, the overall intent of these developments was to offer a more robust account of the creaturely integrity and dynamics of reason.

In this way, the argument of this chapter has sought to provide further demonstration of the explanatory power of two elements of the heuristic framework given in Chapter 1. First, it has drawn attention to the significance of the overarching development of Webster's thought – from Christocentric to Theocentric – for his understanding of theological reason. This was seen in the way the ultimate ground of the activities of theological reason shifted from God's eschatological presence in Christ to God's immanent perfection. Second, it has demonstrated how the works of nature (especially the doctrine of creation) provide the context for understanding the works of grace in Webster's mature theology, including his account of intellectual regeneration and virtue. But this chapter has also brought to the surface aspects of Webster's theology of grace that were not thoroughly explored in Chapter 1. This doctrinal locus was central to his account of 'theological theology' from beginning to end, for he consistently conceived of the practice of theology as a 'graced enterprise' – an aspect of reason's regeneration and sanctification. According to Webster, theology is a work of religion, of cognitive fellowship with God.

CONCLUSION

Throughout his illustrious career, Webster had an intensive interest in questions revolving around the nature of the God-creature relation. He also had a keen ability to show how answers to these questions underwrite (often implicitly) particular doctrinal proposals, such as the nature of ecclesial mediation or biblical inspiration. His work displayed a consistent concern to articulate a *theologically grounded and ordered account of the relation-in-distinction between God and creatures*: theologically 'grounded' because he wanted to let the doctrines of the Christian faith do real intellectual work, and theologically 'ordered' because he sought to think through theological questions and topics from the standpoint of a 'material centre'. As I have tried to show throughout this book, developments in Webster's conception of the 'material centre' (and architecture) of Christian theology shaped the way he grounded, contextualized and characterized the God-creature relation.

Throughout the 1980s and most of the 1990s, Webster had a Christocentric approach to the God-creature relation. All theological claims about God, humans and their relations were derived from and grounded in the person of Christ. This is part of the reason why his early Christology sought to secure the 'unsubstitutable' identity of Jesus Christ through the use of narrative categories. Jesus' unsubstitutable identity was grounded in the details of his human history, which in turn was identified as God's own story. His account of the hypostatic union emphasized the 'indivisibility' and 'identity' of the divine and human natures in Christ. We noted a similar emphasis in his early ecclesiology, where the concepts of 'continuity' and 'coinherence' were employed to describe the relation between Christ and the church. Webster argued that the history of the atonement 'includes' the histories of those who make up the church, because the story of Jesus offers an identity description of 'not only the agent of salvation but also its recipients'.[1] Jesus' story is God's story and our story because it is the story of their relation. And finally, we saw a similar Christocentric focus in Webster's early account of theological theology in the Thomas Burns Lectures. The focus was less on the human history of Jesus Christ and more on his eschatological

---

1. Webster, 'Atonement, History and Narrative', 130–1.

presence as the risen Lord. But the point is still the same: Webster's account of divine creativity and human identity was tied primarily to the person of Christ. This led him to develop an anthropology of the theologian from the standpoint of the eschatological subject in Christ, not God's original ordering of creation. Christ provides the 'heuristic key' for understanding humanity (anthropology) as well as divinity (theology), for he is the identity of both in one person.

Around the turn of the twenty-first century, Webster adopted a Trinitarian approach to the God-creature relation. The doctrine of the Trinity replaced Christology as the cardinal Christian doctrine, the effects of which were traced in his Christology, ecclesiology and bibliology. In Christology, Webster sought to ground the unsubstitutable identity of Jesus Christ not merely in his human history but more fundamentally in the doctrine of the triune God. Language about the eternal generation of the Son and the nature of the Son as *homoousios* with the Father began to feature in his Christology (although we also noted how his account of God's being was, at this point, still closely tied to the incarnational 'becoming'). We witnessed a similar trend in his ecclesiology: Webster sought to ground the identity of the church in the doctrine of the Trinity, but to do so in such a way that accentuated the distinction between God and the church. He described the church as the fellowship of the elect (originates from the Father's free act of election) and the creature of the Word (constituted by Christ's act of reconciliation and self-revelation), whose visibility is spiritual (realized and recognized by the work of the Spirit). Evidence of this Trinitarian focus was also seen in the discussion of Webster's bibliology. He sought to develop an ontology of Scripture and anthropology of its readers that were derived from their location in the economy of grace, and crucially, the economy of grace was constituted by the revelatory missions of the Trinity: Christ's self-revealing work (depicted in ways reminiscent of Barth's account of the *munus propheticum Christi*) and the Spirit's sanctifying and inspiring works. In each of these cases, the doctrine of the Trinity was the 'material centre' that governed a key aspect (hypostatic, redemptive and communicative) of Webster's account of the God-creature relation. Yet I also noted how his Trinitarian theology was, at this stage, primarily oriented towards the works of God *ad extra*, saying very little (if anything) of God's inner life.

This began to change around the mid-2000s, when Webster adopted a Theocentric approach to theology, especially the God-creature relation. The doctrine of the Trinity still remained central, but the 'material centre' of his Trinitarian theology shifted from God *ad extra* to God *in se*. Teaching about the immanent perfection of God (*theologia*) – including both the undivided divine essence and the personal processions – preceded, grounded and governed what was said about God's works and relations to creation (*oikonomia*). Webster's early theology had focused on the God-creature relation (in Christ) as the context for understanding their distinction. His mature theology took the opposite approach: the radical distinction between God and creatures (articulated via the doctrines of divine perfection and creation) was the context for understanding the character of their relation. Yet Webster's theology of divine perfection was by no means monolithic. Early accounts employed the language of 'inclusion' to describe the relation between theology (divine processions) and economy (divine missions), thereby suggesting that God's relation to the world is somehow intrinsic to his perfection. I argued that later accounts of divine perfection dropped the language of 'inclusion'. This was due in large part to a shift in which doctrine provided the primary 'hinge' between theology and economy: from a Barth-influenced doctrine of election to a Thomas-influenced doctrine of creation. Connected to this was a shift in the primary divine perfection which accounted for the nature of God's acts and relations *ad extra*: from divine freedom to divine goodness.

The results of these shifts were numerous, but I drew attention to one in particular: the character of the Creator-creature relation, as established in God's original act of creation, became the basic context within which Webster understood all other aspects of the God-creature relation. In other words, Webster's mature theology (especially in the 2010s) situated the works of grace, including the incarnation, within the wider context of the works of nature (creation and providence). Grace presupposes, preserves and perfects created nature, so conceptualities developed in one's exposition of the latter can be employed to articulate the dynamics of the former. A unique example of this was discussed: Webster used a Thomist theory of mixed relations to describe the Word-humanity and God-church relations. Another example was the way Webster employed the logic of primary and secondary causality (often using the language of motion – 'moved movement' or 'interior movement') to develop a positive account of ecclesial and textual mediation. Yet another example was highlighted: Webster coordinated the doctrines of revelation, regeneration and illumination with teaching about the nature, powers and ends of the human intellect in an effort to develop a more robust account of the creaturely integrity and dynamics of exegetical and dogmatic reason. A final example had to do with Webster's theology of grace. Around the turn of the twentieth century, grace was identified primarily with divine freedom; it was an interruptive and ever-fresh act of divine self-giving. In the 2010s, grace was identified primarily with divine goodness; it was a durative divine action that took creaturely form and effect – i.e. infused powers and habits.

Were there time and space enough, much more could be said about Webster's account of the God-creature relation, yet this book has demonstrated a helpful way of understanding the development and contours of Webster's theology and, in this way, laid the groundwork for future studies in the young and growing field of Websterian scholarship. I conclude by suggesting a few of the topics that emerge from my book and could valuably be pursued in such future studies.

(1) Interesting work could be done on Webster's mature theology in relation to the *analogia entis*. As we noted in Chapter 5, Webster draws from aspects of Aquinas' thought (especially his doctrine of divine perfection and metaphysics of creation) that would seem to require a principled commitment to the *analogia entis*, yet what one finds is a certain Reformed (Barthian?) reserve. Exploring this topic would allow one to tease out some of the complexities of Webster's engagement with Barth and Aquinas: Did he appropriate elements of Aquinas within a Barthian framework or hold on to vestiges of Barth as he moved into a

predominantly Thomist framework?² But questions related to the *analogia entis* are of more than historical interest, for they touch on key aspects of Webster's theology – namely his account of theological reason and of divine perfection, and the way the doctrine of creation functions in both. According to Webster, God's perfection is known by the human intellect indirectly, and this occurs as reason is invited by the 'sign' character of God's works to a speculative movement, by which it comes to know the uncreated source of those works. He states,

> [P]art of the condition of finite theology is that this first material object [God *in se*] is only indirectly accessible. Systematic theological reflection *de Deo* is prompted by participation in the economy as creatures of divine goodness .... But reflective participation in the economy of God's works prompts an intellectual (in a proper sense, speculative) movement which considers God's works [in creation and salvation] not only as they present themselves in their outer face or temporal structure and effect, but also in terms of the uncreated depth of God from which they flow. There is in the outer works of God an excess which they do not exhaust .... This excess of the divine life is ineffable.³

How does human reason come to a knowledge of divine perfection? By considering the 'depth' and 'excess' in God's works of creation and redemption. But how exactly does reason consider this depth and excess? What are the dynamics of logic and language involved in this consideration, and what are the metaphysical principles that undergird them? On these topics, Webster does not give us many concrete answers. This is where a classical theology of the divine names, along with the doctrine of analogy that it presupposes, could potentially supplement Webster's theology, enabling him to give a more concrete account of how human language and logic operate in developing an account of divine perfection. For Aquinas, questions related to the analogical use of human language to name God are undergirded by questions related to the analogical nature of being in relation to God.⁴ Thus, an exploration of the *analogia entis* could serve Webster's interest in

---

2. Particularly interesting in this regard is the work of Williams and Betz, who argue that many (though not all) of Barth's theological reservations are understood and incorporated into Erich Przywara's account of the *analogia entis*. See Rowan Williams, 'Dialectic and Analogy: A Theological Legacy', in *The Impact of Idealism: The Legacy of Post-Kantian German Thought*, vol. 4, ed. Nicholas Adams (Cambridge: Cambridge University Press, 2013), 274–92; John R. Betz, 'Translator's Introduction', in *Analogia Entis*, trans. John R. Betz and David Bentley Hart (Grand Rapids, MI: Eerdmans, 2014), 83–115.

3. *DW*, 143.

4. On the interrelation of language, logic and metaphysics in Aquinas' account of the divine names, see John Milbank and Catherine Pickstock, *Truth in Aquinas* (London: Routledge, 2001), 43–51; te Velde, *Aquinas on God*, 95–122.

developing a positive material account of divine perfection while also registering the 'infinite analogical interval' between God and creatures.[5]

(2) There are ways in which my 'intra-Websterian' reading of Webster's theological development could be related back to his context and sources. One could, for example, situate Webster within the context of the recent revival in Trinitarian theology, especially as it relates to the rise of social Trinitarianism (Jürgen Moltmann, John Zizioulas, Miroslav Volf, Colin Gunton) and the reaction against it (Karen Kilby, Steve Holmes, Brian Leftow, Fred Sanders).[6] There are many issues at stake in this debate, but three are of particular interest in relation to Webster.

The first issue is the nature of divine personhood. Social Trinitarian thought stems, in part, from the conviction that traditional conceptions of the divine 'persons' as modes of subsistence are insufficiently attentive to the way relations are constitutive of persons. Carl Mosser summarizes the basic argument of social Trinitarianism as follows:

(1) Interpersonal unity is irreducibly social in nature.
(2) The members of the Trinity are persons in the full, modern sense.
(3) Therefore, the unity of the Trinity is genuinely social in nature.
(4) The divine persons interpenetrate, co-inhere and mutually indwell one another in perichoresis.[7]

The nature of divine personhood would be an interesting topic of exploration because, as I have shown, Webster's doctrine of the Trinity combines elements of traditional essentialism and modern personalism, while showing very little interest in social Trinitarianism.

Second, the Trinitarian revival of the twentieth century raised key questions about the relation between theology and economy, one of which has to do with

---

5. David Bentley Hart, *The Beauty of the Infinite: The Aesthetics of Christian Truth* (Grand Rapids, MI: Eerdmans, 2003), 242.

6. Jürgen Moltmann, *The Trinity and The Kingdom*, trans. Margaret Kohl (Minneapolis, MN: Fortress Press, 1993); John Zizioulas, *Being as Communion: Studies in Personhood and the Church* (Crestwood, NY: St. Vladimir's Seminary Press, 1985); Miroslav Volf, *After Our Likeness: The Church as the Image of the Trinity* (Grand Rapids, MI: Eerdmans, 1998); Colin E. Gunton, *The Promise of Trinitarian Theology*, 2nd ed. (London: T&T Clark, 1997); Karen Kilby, 'Perichoresis and Projection: Problems with Social Doctrines of the Trinity', *NB* 81 (2001): 432–45; Stephen R. Holmes, *The Holy Trinity: Understanding God's Life* (Milton Keynes: Paternoster, 2012); Brian Leftow, 'Anti Social Trinitarianism', in *Philosophical and Theological Essays on the Trinity*, eds. Thomas McCall and Michael C. Rea (Oxford: Oxford University Press, 2009), 52–88.

7. Carl Mosser, 'Fully Social Trinitarianism', in *Philosophical and Theological Essays on the Trinity*, eds. Thomas McCall and Michael C. Rea (Oxford: Oxford University Press, 2009), 133–4.

the way one reasons from God's acts in the economy of salvation to a doctrine of the immanent Trinity.[8] Questions related to the relation between theology and economy were never far from the surface in Webster's theology, and yet he said relatively little (as we noted above) about *how* reason moves from God *ad extra* to God *in se*. More work could be done here.

Third, divergences in recent Trinitarian theology have brought to light questions related to the nature of theology as a *ressourcement* of the tradition. Social Trinitarianism seeks to recover elements of Cappadocian theology, while respondents often look to Augustine and Aquinas, and yet others suggest there is not as much difference between East and West as one might suspect. In each case, it is assumed that dogmatic seriousness requires the theologian to be accountable to the core claims of the theological tradition and creeds, and that the tradition itself provides the resources by which to refresh and revive theology in the present, yet theological *ressourcement* takes different forms and births different results. This is where engaging Webster could be of much interest, for his own theological journey was one of an ever-deeper exploration of the Christian tradition. In a foreword to Heinrich Heppe's *Reformed Dogmatics*, Barth once noted that he found his way into the church's tradition by working backwards through it: the eighteenth century introduced him to the sixteenth century, and so on.[9] Webster's journey had a similar trajectory: Jüngel introduced him to Barth, who introduced him to the Reformed Scholastics, who introduced him to Aquinas, who introduced him to the Church Fathers. In this sense, Webster's movement through the tradition is quite different from that of many twentieth-century *ressourcement* theologians, who began with the Fathers and worked their way forward. There are issues to be explored here about the nature and role of tradition in contemporary *ressourcement* theology, of both the Catholic and Protestant varieties. But in each case, the fundamental conviction is the same: only as theology mines the riches of the past will it have something salutary and abiding to say to the present.

This conviction was at the core of Webster's theological *modus operandi* and is, in part, what makes his work so interesting and of enduring significance for the twenty-first century. As one of the richest theological voices of the late twentieth and early twenty-first century, Webster not only penned essays of extraordinary quality on a wide range of theological topics, but he also left the next generation of theologians with a robust theological vision of the nature and practice of theology. He was indeed a 'theologian's theologian'.[10] A significant aspect of his contribution

---

8. On this, see Fred Sanders, *The Image of the Immanent Trinity: Rahner's Rule and the Theological Interpretation of Scripture* (New York, NY: Peter Lang Publishing, 2005); idem., 'The Trinity', in *The Oxford Handbook of Systematic Theology*, eds. John Webster, Kathryn Tanner, and Iain Torrance (Oxford: Oxford University Press, 2007), 35–53.

9. Karl Barth, 'Forward', in *Reformed Dogmatics*, trans. G. T. Thomson (Grand Rapids, MI: Baker Book House, 1978), v–vii.

10. East, 'John Webster', 334.

to the field was his ability to remind fellow and future theologians of the nature of their common vocation. Webster's theology invites theologians into an act of concentrated contemplation of God and all things in relation to God, an act which is moral and spiritual as well as intellectual. This book is one attempt to understand some of the ways Webster himself sought to fulfil this noble vocation, with the hope of paving the way for others to do the same.

BIBLIOGRAPHY

Primary Literature

Webster, John. '"A Relation beyond All Relations": God and Creatures in Barth's Lectures on Ephesians, 1921-22'. *The Epistle to the Ephesians*. Edited by R. David Nelson. Grand Rapids, MI: Baker Academic, 2017, pp.31–50.
Webster, John. 'A Reply to Tom Weinandy'. *New Blackfriars* 81 (2000): 236–7.
Webster, John. 'Atonement, History and Narrative'. *Theologische Zeitschrift* 42 (1986): 115–31.
Webster, John. 'Attributes, Divine'. *The Cambridge Dictionary of Christian Theology*. Edited by Ian A. McFarland, David A. S. Fergusson, Karen Kilby, and Iain R. Torrance. Cambridge: Cambridge University Press, 2011, pp.45–8.
Webster, John. 'Being Constructive: An Interview with John Webster'. *Christian Century* 125 (2008): 32–4.
Webster, John. *Barth*. London: Continuum, 2000.
Webster, John. *Barth's Earlier Theology: Four Studies*. London: T&T Clark, 2005.
Webster, John. *Barth's Ethics of Reconciliation*. Cambridge: Cambridge University Press, 1995.
Webster, John. *Barth's Moral Theology: Human Action in Barth's Thought*. Edinburgh: T&T Clark, 1998.
Webster, John. 'Chalcedonian Christology after Berdyaev in Barth and Jungel'. *Fifty Year Commemoration to the Life of Nicolai Berdyaev (1877-1948)*. Edited by George O. Mazur. New York, NY: Semenenko Foundation, 1999, pp.45–58.
Webster, John. 'Christology, Imitability and Ethics'. *Scottish Journal of Theology* 39 (1986): 309–26.
Webster, John. *Confessing God: Essays in Christian Dogmatics II*. London: Bloomsbury T&T Clark, 2005.
Webster, John. 'Conversations: Engaging Difference'. *Stimulus* 7:1 (1999): 2–8.
Webster, John. 'Criticism: Revelation and Disturbance'. *Stimulus* 7:1 (1999): 9–14.
Webster, John. 'Culture: The Shape of Theological Practice'. *Stimulus* 6:4 (1998): 2–9.
Webster, John. 'Discovering Dogmatics'. *Shaping a Theological Mind: Theological Context and Methodology*. Edited by Darren C. Marks. Aldershot: Ashgate, 2002, pp.129–36.
Webster, John. *Eberhard Jüngel: An Introduction to his Theology*. Cambridge: Cambridge University Press, 1986.
Webster, John. 'Eberhard Jungel'. *The Modern Theologians: An Introduction to Christian Theology in the Twentieth Century*. Volume 1. Edited by David F. Ford. Oxford: Blackwell Publishers, 1989, pp.92–106.
Webster, John. 'Editorial'. *International Journal of Systematic Theology* 14:4 (2012): 379–80.
Webster, John. 'Eschatology, Ontology and Human Action'. *Toronto Journal of Theology* 7:1 (1991): 4–18.
Webster, John. 'Fides et Ratio, Articles 64–79'. *New Blackfriars* 81 (2000): 68–76.
Webster, John. 'Foreword'. *Trinitarian Theology after Barth*. Edited by Myk Habets and Phillip W. Tolliday. Eugene, OR: Pickwick, 2011, pp.xi–xii.

Webster, John. *God Is Here: Believing in the Incarnation Today*. Hampshire: Marshall Morgan & Scott, 1983.
Webster, John. *God without Measure: Working Papers in Christian Theology*. 2 Volumes. London: Bloomsbury T&T Clark, 2016.
Webster, John. 'God's Perfect Life'. *God's Life in Trinity*. Edited by Miroslav Volf and Michael Welker. Minneapolis, MN: Fortress Press, 2006, pp.143–52.
Webster, John. 'Habits: Cultivating the Theologian's Soul'. *Stimulus* 7:1 (1999): 15–20.
Webster, John. *Holiness*. London: SCM Press, 2003.
Webster, John. 'Holy Scripture'. *Between the Lectern and the Pulpit: Essays in Honour of Victor A. Shepherd*. Edited by Rob Clements and Dennis Ngien. Vancouver, BC: Regent College Publishing, 2014, pp.173–81.
Webster, John. *Holy Scripture: A Dogmatic Sketch*. Cambridge: Cambridge University Press, 2003.
Webster, John. 'Immanuel'. Lecture 4. Kantzer Lectures in Revealed Theology from Carl F.H. Henry Center. Deerfield, IL: 17 September 2007.
Webster, John. 'Introduction'. *God's Being Is in Becoming: The Trinitarian Being of God in the Theology of Karl Barth – A Paraphrase*. Translated by John Webster. Grand Rapids, MI: Eerdmans, 2001, pp.ix–xxiii.
Webster, John. '"It Was the Will of the Lord to Bruise Him": Soteriology and the Doctrine of God'. *God of Salvation: Soteriology in Theological Perspective*. Edited by Ivor J. Davidson and Murray A. Rae. Burlington, VT: Ashgate, 2011, pp.15–34.
Webster, John. 'Jesus Christ'. *The Cambridge Companion to Evangelical Theology*. Edited by Timothy Larsen and Daniel J. Treier. Cambridge: Cambridge University Press, 2007, pp.51–63.
Webster, John. 'Jesus – God for Us'. *Anglican Essentials: Reclaiming Faith within the Anglican Church of Canada*. Edited by George Egerton. Toronto: Anglican Book Centre, 1995, pp.89–97.
Webster, John. 'Jesus' Speech, God's Word: An Introduction to Eberhard Jüngel'. *Christian Century* 112 (1995): 1174–8.
Webster, John. 'Locality and Catholicity: Reflections on Theology and the Church'. *Scottish Journal of Theology* 45 (1992): 1–17.
Webster, John. 'Perfection and Participation'. *The Analogy of Being: Invention of the Antichrist or the Wisdom of God*. Edited by Thomas Joseph White. Grand Rapids, MI: Eerdmans, 2011, pp.379–94.
Webster, John. 'Reading Scripture Eschatologically (I)'. *Reading Texts, Seeking Wisdom: Scripture and Theology*. Edited by David F. Ford and Graham Stanton. London: SCM Press, 2003, pp.245–56.
Webster, John. 'Response to George Hunsinger'. *Modern Theology* 8:2 (1992): 129–32.
Webster, John. 'Ressourcement Theology and Protestantism'. *Ressourcement: A Movement for Renewal and in Twentieth-Century Catholic Theology*. Edited by Gabriel Flynn and Paul D. Murray. Oxford: Oxford University Press, 2012, pp.482–94.
Webster, John. 'Review Article: Canon and Criterion: Some Reflections on a Recent Proposal'. *Scottish Journal of Theology* 54 (2001): 221–37.
Webster, John. 'Review Article: Webster's Response to Alyssa Lyra Pitstick, *Light in Darkness*'. *Scottish Journal of Theology* 62:2 (2009): 202–10.
Webster, John. 'Rowan Williams on Scripture'. *Scripture's Doctrine and Theology's Bible: How the New Testament Shapes Christian Dogmatics*. Edited by Markus Bockmuehl and Alan J. Torrance. Grand Rapids, MI: Baker Academic, 2008, pp.105–24.

Webster, John. *Rudolph Bultmann: An Introductory Interpretation*. Leicester: Religious and Theological Studies Fellowship, 1980.

Webster, John. 'Texts: Scripture, Reading and the Rhetoric of Theology'. *Stimulus* 6:4 (1998): 10–16.

Webster, John. 'The Church as Theological Community'. *Anglican Theological Review* 75 (1993): 102–15.

Webster, John. 'The Church as Witnessing Community'. *Scottish Bulletin of Evangelical Theology* 21 (2003): 21–33.

Webster, John. *The Culture of Theology*. Edited by Ivor J. Davidson and Alden C. McCray. Grand Rapids, MI: Baker Academic, 2019.

Webster, John. *The Domain of the Word: Scripture and Theological Reason*. London: Bloomsbury T&T Clark, 2012.

Webster, John. 'The Human Person'. *The Cambridge Companion to Postmodern Theology*. Edited by Kevin J. Vanhoozer. Cambridge: Cambridge University Press, 2003, pp.219–34.

Webster, John. 'The Identity of the Holy Spirit: A Problem in Trinitarian Theology'. *Themelios* 9:1 (1983): 4–7.

Webster, John. 'The Imitation of Christ'. *Tyndale Bulletin* 37 (1986): 95–120.

Webster, John. 'Traditions: Theology and the Public Covenant'. *Stimulus* 6:4 (1998): 17–23.

Webster, John. 'ὑπὸ πνεύματος ἁγίου φερόμενοι ἐλάλησαν ἀπὸ θεοῦ ἄνθρωποι: On the Inspiration of Holy Scripture'. *Conception, Reception, and the Spirit: Essay in Honor of Andrews T. Lincoln*. Edited by J. Gordon Mcconville and Lloyd K. Pietersen. Eugene, OR: Cascade Books, 2105, pp.236–50.

Webster, John. *Word and Church: Essays in Christian Dogmatics*. London: Bloomsbury T&T Clark, 2001.

Secondary Literature

Allen, Michael. 'Toward Theological Theology: Tracing the Methodological Principles of John Webster'. *Themelios* 41:2 (2016): 217–37.

Allen, Michael. 'Dogmatics as Ascetics'. *The Task of Dogmatics: Explorations in Theological Method*. Edited by Oliver D. Crisp and Fred Sanders. Grand Rapids, MI: Zondervan, 2017, pp.189–209.

Allen, Michael. 'Toward Theological Anthropology: Tracing the Anthropological Principles of John Webster'. *International Journal of Systematic Theology* 19:1 (2017): 6–29.

Allen, Michael. 'Reading John Webster: An Introduction'. *T&T Clark Reader in John Webster*. Edited by Michael Allen. London: T&T Clark, 2020, pp.1–19.

Aquinas, Thomas. *Summa Theologiae*. 61 Volumes. Cambridge: Cambridge University Press, 2006.

Aquinas, Thomas. *Summa Theologiae*. Latin/English Edition of the Works of St. Thomas Aquinas. Volumes 13–20. Translated by Fr. Laurence Shapcote, O. P. Edited by John Mortensen and Enrique Alarcón. Lander, WY: The Aquinas Institute for the Study of Sacred Doctrine, 2012.

Aristotle. *Metaphysics*. Translated by W. D. Ross. 2 Volumes. Oxford: Clarendon Press, 1924.

Ashford, Bruce R. 'Wittgenstein's Theologians? A Survey of Ludwig Wittgenstein's Impact on Theology'. *Journal of the Evangelical Theological Society* 50:2 (2007): 357–75.

Augustine. *De Trinitate*. Translated as *The Trinity: Works of Saint Augustine*. Volume I/5. Translated by Edmund Hill. Hyde Park, NY: New City Press, 1991.

Augustine. *De Doctrina Christiana*. Translated as *On Christian Teaching*. Translated by R. P. H. Green. Oxford: Oxford University Press, 1997.

Ayres, Lewis. '"There's Fire in That Rain": On Reading the Letter and Reading Allegorically'. *Modern Theology* 28:4 (2012): 616–34.

Ayres, Lewis. 'The Word Answering the Word: Opening the Space of Catholic Biblical Interpretation'. *Theological Theology: Essays in Honour of John B. Webster*. Edited by R. David Nelson, Darren Sarisky, and Justin Stratis. London: Bloomsbury T&T Clark, 2015, pp.37–53.

Ayres, Lewis and Stephen E. Fowl. '(Mis)Reading the Face of God in *Interpretation of the Bible in the Church*'. *Theological Studies* 60:3 (1999): 513–28.

Barth, Karl. *Church Dogmatics*. 14 Volumes. Translated by G. W. Bromiley. Edinburgh: T&T Clark, 1936ff.

Barth, Karl. 'Forward'. *Reformed Dogmatics*. Translated by G. T. Thomson. Grand Rapids, MI: Baker Book House, 1978, pp.v–vii.

Barth, Karl. *The Göttingen Dogmatics: Instruction in the Christian Religion*. Volume 1. Grand Rapids, MI: Eerdmans, 1991.

Bauerschmidt, Frederick Christian. *Thomas Aquinas: Faith, Reason, and Following Christ*. Oxford: Oxford University Press, 2013.

Baylor, T. Robert. '"He Humbled Himself": Trinity, Covenant, and the Gracious Condescension of the Son in John Owen'. *Trinity without Hierarchy: Reclaiming Nicene Orthodoxy in Evangelical Theology*. Edited by Michael F. Bird and Scott Harrower. Grand Rapids, MI: Kregel Academic, 2019, pp.165–94.

Betz, John R. 'Translator's Introduction'. *Analogia Entis*. Translated by John R. Betz and David Bentley Hart. Grand Rapids, MI: Eerdmans, 2014, pp.1–115.

Boersma, Hans. 'The Eucharist Makes the Church'. *CRUX* 44:4 (2008): 2–11.

Boersma, Hans. *Nouvelle Theologie and Sacramental Ontology: A Return to Mystery*. Oxford: Oxford University Press, 2009.

Boersma, Hans. *Heavenly Participation: The Weaving of a Sacramental Tapestry*. Grand Rapids, MI: Eerdmans, 2011.

Boersma, Hans. *Scripture as Real Presence: Sacramental Exegesis in the Early Church*. Grand Rapids, MI: Baker Academic, 2017.

Bourdieu, Pierre. *Outlines of a Theory of Practice*. Translated by Richard Nice. Cambridge: Cambridge University Press, 1977.

Brittain, Christopher Craig. 'Why Ecclesiology Cannot Live by Doctrine Alone: A Reply to John Webster's "In the Society of God"'. *Ecclesial Practices* 1 (2014): 5–30.

Case, Brendan. 'Relations in Creation and Christology: A Response to Porter'. *New Blackfriars* 99 (2018): 1–20.

Carson, D. A. 'Three More Books on the Bible: A Critical Review'. *Collected Writings on Scripture*. Wheaton, IL: Crossway, 2010.

Clarke, W. Norris. *Explorations in Metaphysics: Being-God-Person*. Notre Dame, IN: University of Notre Dame Press, 1994.

Cleveland, Christopher. *Thomism in John Owen*. New York, NY: Routledge, 2016.

Crisp, Oliver. 'Analytic Theology as Systematic Theology'. *Open Theology* 3:1 (2017): 156–66.

Davidson, Ivor J. 'In Memoriam: John Webster (1955–2016)'. *International Journal of Systematic Theology* 18:4 (2016): 360–75.

Davidson, Ivor J. 'John'. *Theological Theology: Essays in Honour of John Webster*. Edited by R. David Nelson, Darren Sarisky, and Justin Stratis. London: T&T Clark, 2015, pp.17–36.

Davidson, Ivor J. 'Introduction'. *The Culture of Theology*. Edited by Ivor J. Davidson and Alden C. McCray. Grand Rapids, MI: Baker Academic, 2019, pp.1–42.

D'Costa, Gavin. 'Revelation, Scripture and Tradition: Some Comments on John Webster's Conception of "Holy Scripture"'. *International Journal of Systematic Theology* 6:4 (2004): 337–50.

de Lubac, Henri. *Catholicism: Christ and the Common Destiny of Man*. Translated by Lancelot C. Sheppard. London: Burns & Oates, 1950.

de Lubac, Henri. *The Splendour of the Church*. Translated by Michael Mason. Glen Rock, NJ: Paulist Press, 1963.

de Lubac, Henri. *Corpus Mysticum: The Eucharist and the Church in the Middle Ages: A Historical Survey*. Translated by Gemma Simmonds CJ, Richard Price, and Christopher Stephens. Notre Dame, IN: University of Notre Dame Press, 2007.

De Nys, Martin J. 'God, Creatures, and Relations: Revisiting Classical Theism'. *The Journal of Religion* 81:4 (2001): 595–614.

Dekker, Willem Maarten. 'John Webster's Retrieval of Classical Theology'. *Journal of Reformed Theology* 12:1 (2018): 59–63.

Del Colle, Ralph. 'The Church'. *The Oxford Handbook of Systematic Theology*. Edited by John Webster, Kathryn Tanner, and Iain Torrance. Oxford: Oxford University Press, 2007, pp.249–66.

Dolezal, James E. *God without Parts: Divine Simplicity and the Metaphysics of God's Absoluteness*. Eugene, OR: Pickwick, 2011.

Duby, Steven J. *Divine Simplicity: A Dogmatic Account*. London: T&T Clark, 2016.

Duby, Steven J. 'Trinity and Economy in Thomas Aquinas'. *Southern Baptist Journal of Theology* 21:2 (2017): 29–51.

Dupré, Louis. *Passage to Modernity: An Essay in the Hermeneutics of Nature and Culture*. Yale, CN: Yale University Press, 1995.

East, Bradley Raymond. 'John Webster, Theologian Proper'. *Anglican Theological Review* 99:2 (2017): 333–51.

East, Bradley Raymond. *The Church's Book: Theology of Scripture in Ecclesial Context in the Work of John Howard Yoder, Robert Jenson, and John Webster*. PhD dissertation. Yale University, 2017.

Emery, Gilles. *The Trinitarian Theology of Saint Thomas Aquinas*. Translated by Francesca Aran Murphy. Oxford: Oxford University Press, 2007.

Emery, Gilles. 'Essentialism or Personalism in the Treatise on God in St. Thomas Aquinas'. *Trinity in Aquinas*. 2nd Edition. Washington, DC: Catholic University of America Press, 2008, pp.165–208.

Enns, Peter. *Inspiration and Incarnation: Evangelicals and the Problem of the Old Testament*. Grand Rapids, MI: Baker Academic, 2005.

Fowl, Stephen E. *Engaging Scripture*. Oxford: Blackwell Publishers, 1998.

Frei, Hans W. *The Identity of Jesus Christ: The Hermeneutical Bases of Dogmatic Theology*. Philadelphia, PA: Fortress Press, 1967.

Frei, Hans W. *Types of Christian Theology*. Edited by George Hunsinger and William C. Placher. New Haven, CT: Yale University Press, 1992.

Frei, Hans W. 'Scripture'. *The Oxford Handbook of Systematic Theology*. Edited by John Webster, Kathryn Tanner, and Iain Torrance. Oxford: Oxford University Press, 2007, pp.345–61.

Ge, Yonghua. 'The One and the Many: A Revisiting of an Old Philosophical Question in the Light of Theologies of Creation and Participation'. *Heythrop Journal* 57:1 (2016): 109–21.

Gorman, Michael. 'Christ as Composite According to Aquinas'. *Traditio* 55 (2000): 143–57.
Gorman, Michael. *Aquinas on the Metaphysics of the Hypostatic Union*. Cambridge: Cambridge University Press, 2017.
Greggs, Tom. 'Proportion and Topography in Ecclesiology: A Working Paper on the Dogmatic Location of the Doctrine of the Church'. *Theological Theology: Essay in Honour of John B. Webster*. Edited by R. David Nelson, Darren Sarisky, and Justin Stratis. London: Bloomsbury T&T Clark, 2015, pp.89–106.
Greggs, Tom. 'The Call to Focus on God: A Review of Webster's *God without Measure*'. *Modern Theology* 34:4 (2018): 657–63.
Griffiths, Paul J. 'How Reasoning Goes Wrong: A Quasi-Augustinian Account of Error and Its Implications'. *Reason and the Reasons of Faith*. Edited by Paul J. Griffiths and Reinhard Hütter. London: T&T Clark, 2005, pp.145–59.
Griffiths, Paul J. *Intellectual Appetite: A Theological Grammar*. Washington, DC: The Catholic University of America Press, 2009.
Gunton, Colin E. 'The Church on Earth: The Roots of Community'. *On Being the Church: Essays on the Christian Community*. Edited by Colin E. Gunton and Daniel W. Hardy. Edinburgh: T&T Clark, 1989, pp.48–80.
Gunton, Colin E. *A Brief Theology of Revelation*. Edinburgh: T&T Clark, 1995.
Gunton, Colin E. *The Promise of Trinitarian Theology*. 2nd Edition. London: T&T Clark, 1997.
Gunton, Colin E. *The Triune Creator: A Historical and Systematic Study*. Grand Rapids, MI: Eerdmans, 1998.
Gunton, Colin E. *The Christian Faith: An Introduction to Christian Doctrine*. Oxford: Blackwell, 2002.
Hart, David Bentley. 'No Shadow of Turning: On Divine Impassibility'. *Pro Ecclesia* 11:2 (2002): 184–206.
Hart, David Bentley. *The Beauty of the Infinite: The Aesthetics of Christian Truth*. Grand Rapids, MI: Eerdmans, 2003.
Hart, Trevor. 'Revelation'. *The Cambridge Companion to Karl Barth*. Cambridge: Cambridge University Press, 2000.
Hauerwas, Stanley. *The Peaceable Kingdom: A Prier in Christian Ethics*. London: SCM Press, 1984.
Healy, Nicholas M. 'Ecclesiology and Communion'. *Perspectives in Religious Studies* 31:3 (2004): 273–90.
Healy, Nicholas M. 'The Logic of Karl Barth's Ecclesiology: Analysis, Assessment and Proposed Modifications'. *Modern Theology* 10:3 (1994): 253–70.
Healy, Nicholas M. 'Practices and the New Ecclesiology: Misplaced Concreteness?'. *International Journal of Systematic Theology* 5:3 (2003): 287–308.
Healy, Nicholas M. *Hauerwas: A (Very) Critical Introduction*. Grand Rapids, MI: Eerdmans, 2014.
Henninger, Mark Gerald. 'Aquinas on the Ontological Status of Relations'. *Journal of the History of Philosophy* 25:4 (1987): 491–515.
Higton, Mike. 'Frei's Christology and Lindbeck's Cultural-Linguistic Theory'. *Scottish Journal of Theology* 50:1 (1997): 83–95.
Higton, Mike. 'Reconstructing *The Nature of Doctrine*'. *Modern Theology* 30:1 (2014): 1–31.
Higton, Mike. 'George Lindbeck and the Christological Nature of Doctrine'. *Criswell Theological Review* 13:1 (2015): 47–61.
Holcomb, Justin S. 'Being Bound to God: Participation and Covenant Revisited'. *Radical Orthodoxy and the Reformed Tradition: Creation, Covenant, and Participation*. Edited

by James K. A. Smith and James H. Olthuis. Grand Rapids, MI: Baker Academic, 2005, pp.243–62.
Holmes, Christopher R. J. 'The Church and the Presence of Christ: Defending Actualist Ecclesiology'. *Pro Ecclesia* 21:3 (2012): 268–80.
Holmes, Christopher R. J. 'Revisiting the God/World Difference'. *Modern Theology* 34:2 (2018): 159–76.
Holmes, Stephen R. *The Holy Trinity: Understanding God's Life*. Milton Keynes: Paternoster, 2012.
Holmes, Stephen R. 'Scripture in Liturgy and Theology'. *Theologians on Scripture*. Edited by Angus Paddison. London: Bloomsbury T&T Clark, 2016, pp.105–18.
Horton, Michael S. 'Participation and Covenant'. *Radical Orthodoxy and the Reformed Tradition: Creation, Covenant, and Participation*. Edited by James K. A. Smith and James H. Olthuis. Grand Rapids, MI: Baker Academic, 2005, pp.107–32.
Horton, Michael S. *Covenant and Salvation: Union with Christ*. Louisville, KT: Westminster John Knox Press, 2007.
Hunsinger, George. 'Hans Frei as Theologian: The Quest for a Generous Orthodoxy'. *Modern Theology* 8:2 (1992): 103–28.
Hunsinger, George. 'Election and the Trinity: Twenty-Five Theses on the Theology of Karl Barth'. *Modern Theology* 24:2 (2008): 179–98.
Hütter, Reinhard. 'The Directedness of Reasoning and the Metaphysics of Creation'. *Reason and the Reasons of Faith*. Edited by Paul J. Griffiths and Reinhard Hütter. London: T&T Clark, 2005, pp.160–93.
Jenson, Robert W. 'The Church as *Communio*'. *The Catholicity of the Reformation*. Edited by Carl E. Braaten and Robert W. Jenson. Grand Rapids, MI: Eerdmans, 1996, pp.1–12.
Jenson, Robert W. *Systematic Theology*. 2 Volumes. Oxford: Oxford University Press, 1997ff.
Jenson, Robert W. 'Once More the *Logos Asarkos*'. *International Journal of Systematic Theology* 13:2 (2011): 130–3.
Jenson, Robert W. *Theology as Revisionary Metaphysics: Essays on God and Creation*. Edited by Stephen John Wright. Eugene, OR: Cascade Books, 2014.
Jüngel, Eberhard. *God as the Mystery of the World: On the Foundation of the Theology of the Crucified One in the Dispute between Theism and Atheism*. Translated by Darrell L. Guder. Edinburgh: T&T Clark, 1983.
Jüngel, Eberhard. *Theological Essays*. Translated by J. B. Webster. Edinburgh: T&T Clark, 1989.
Jüngel, Eberhard. *God's Being Is in Becoming: The Trinitarian Being of God in the Theology of Karl Barth – A Paraphrase*. Translated by John Webster. Grand Rapids, MI: Eerdmans, 2001.
Junius, Franciscus. *A Treatise on True Theology*. Translated by David C. Noe. Grand Rapids, MI: Reformation Heritage Books, 2014.
Kelsey, David H. *The Uses of Scripture in Recent Theology*. London: SCM Press, 1975.
Kerr, Fergus. 'John Webster and Catholic Theology'. *New Blackfriars* 98 (2017): 457–81.
Kilby, Karen. 'Perichoresis and Projection: Problems with Social Doctrines of the Trinity'. *New Blackfriars* 81 (2001): 432–45.
Kretzmann, Norman. *The Metaphysics of Theism: Aquinas' Natural Theology in Summa Contra Gentiles I*. Oxford: Clarendon, 1997.
Kretzmann, Norman. *The Metaphysics of Creation: Aquinas' Natural Theology in Summa Contra Gentiles II*. Oxford: Clarendon, 1999.

LaCugna, Catherine Mowry. *God for Us: The Trinity and Christian Life*. San Francisco, CA: Harper San Francisco, 1991.
Leftow, Brian. 'Anti Social Trinitarianism'. *Philosophical and Theological Essays on the Trinity*. Edited by Thomas McCall and Michael C. Rea. Oxford: Oxford University Press, 2009, pp.52–88.
Levering, Matthew. *Participatory Biblical Exegesis: A Theology of Biblical Interpretation*. Notre Dame, IN: University of Notre Dame Press, 2008.
Levering, Matthew. *Engaging the Doctrine of Revelation: The Mediation of the Gospel through Church and Scripture*. Grand Rapids, MI: Baker Academic, 2014.
Levering, Matthew. 'On Humility'. *International Journal of Systematic Theology* 19:4 (2017): 462–90.
Lindbeck, George A. *The Nature of Doctrine: Religion and Theology in a Postliberal Age*. London: SPCK, 1984.
Long, D. Stephen. *The Perfectly Simple Triune God: Aquinas and His Legacy*. Minneapolis, MN: Fortress Press, 2016.
MacIntyre, Alasdair. *After Virtue: A Study in Moral Theory*. Notre Dame, IN: University of Notre Dame Press, 1981.
Marshall, Bruce D. 'The Dereliction of Christ and the Impassibility of God'. *Divine Impassibility and the Mystery of Human Suffering*. Edited by James F. Keating and Thomas Joseph White. Grand Rapids, MI: Eerdmans, 2009, pp.246–98.
Marshall, Bruce D. 'The Unity of the Triune God: Reviving an Ancient Question'. *The Thomist* 74 (2010): 1–32.
McCormack, Bruce. 'What's at Stake in Current Debates over Justification? The Crisis of Protestantism in the West'. *Justification: What's at Stake in the Current Debates*. Edited by Mark Husbands and Daniel J. Treier. Downers Grove, IL: InterVarsity, 2004, pp.81–117.
McCormack, Bruce. 'Grace and Being: The Role of God's Gracious Election in Karl Barth's Theological Ontology'. *The Cambridge Companion to Karl Barth*. Edited by John Webster. Cambridge: Cambridge University Press, 2000, pp.92–110.
McCormack, Bruce. 'Election and the Trinity: Theses in Response to George Hunsinger'. *Scottish Journal of Theology* 63:2 (2010): 203–24.
McCormack, Bruce. 'Processions and Missions: A Point of Convergence between Thomas Aquinas and Karl Barth'. *Thomas Aquinas and Karl Barth: An Unofficial Catholic-Protestant Dialogue*. Edited by Bruce L. McCormack and Thomas Joseph White. Grand Rapids, MI: Eerdmans, 2013, pp.99–126.
McFarland, Ian A. 'Present in Love: Rethinking Barth on the Divine Perfections'. *Modern Theology* 33:2 (2017): 243–58.
McFarland, Ian A. 'The Gift of the *Non aliud*: Creation from Nothing as a Metaphysics of Abundance'. *International Journal of Systematic Theology* 21:1 (2019): 44–58.
McPartlan, Paul. *Sacrament of Salvation: An Introduction to Eucharistic Ecclesiology*. Edinburgh: T&T Clark, 1995.
McWhorter, Matthew R. 'Aquinas on God's Relation to the World'. *New Blackfriars* 94 (2013): 3–18.
Michelson, Jared. 'Covenantal History and Participatory Metaphysics: Formulating a Reformed Response to the Charge of Legal Fiction'. *Scottish Journal of Theology* 71:4 (2018): 391–410.
Michelson, Jared. 'Reformed and Radically Orthodox?: Participatory Metaphysics, Reformed Scholasticism and Radical Orthodoxy's Critique of Modernity'. *International Journal of Systematic Theology* 20:1 (2018): 104–28.

Milbank, John. *The Word Made Strange: Theology, Language, Culture*. Oxford: Blackwell, 1997.
Milbank, John. 'Alternative Protestantism: Radical Orthodoxy and the Reformed Tradition'. *Radical Orthodoxy and the Reformed Tradition: Creation, Covenant, and Participation*. Edited by James K. A. Smith and James H. Olthuis. Grand Rapids, MI: Baker Academic, 2005, pp.25–41.
Milbank, John and Catherine Pickstock. *Truth in Aquinas*. London: Routledge, 2001.
Moberly, R. W. L. 'The Nature of the Church in Theological Interpretation: Culture, Volk, and Mission'. *Journal of Theological Interpretation* 11:1 (2017): 101–17.
Molnar, Paul D. *Divine Freedom and the Doctrine of the Immanent Trinity: In Dialogue with Karl Barth and Contemporary Theology*. London: T&T Clark, 2002.
Moltmann, Jürgen. *The Trinity and the Kingdom*. Translated by Margaret Kohl. Minneapolis, MN: Fortress Press, 1993.
Mosser, Carl. 'Fully Social Trinitarianism'. *Philosophical and Theological Essays on the Trinity*. Edited by Thomas McCall and Michael C. Rea. Oxford: Oxford University Press, 2009, pp.131–50.
Muller, Earl. 'Real Relations and the Divine: Issues in Thomas's Understanding of God's Relation to the World'. *Theological Studies* 56 (1995): 673–95.
Mullins, R. T. 'Simply Impossible: A Case against Divine Simplicity'. *Journal of Reformed Theology* 7 (2013): 181–203.
Murphy, Francesca Aran. *God Is Not a Story: Realism Revisited*. Oxford: Oxford University Press, 2007.
Nelson, R. David. 'Webster and Ebeling on Christian Texts: A Placeholder for a Theological Theology of Language'. *Theological Theology: Essays in Honour of John B. Webster*. Edited by R. David Nelson, Darren Sarisky, and Justin Stratis. London: Bloomsbury T&T Clark, 2015, pp.203–18.
Oakes, Kenneth. 'Theology, Economy and Christology in John Webster's *God without Measure* and Some Earlier Works'. *International Journal of Systematic Theology* 19:4 (2017): 491–504.
O'Donovan, Oliver. 'John Webster on Dogmatics and Ethics'. *International Journal of Systematic Theology* 21:1 (2019): 78–92.
Oliver, Simon. *Philosophy, God and Motion*. London: Routledge, 2005.
Oliver, Simon. 'Introducing Radical Orthodoxy: From Participation to Late Modernity'. *The Radical Orthodoxy Reader*. Edited by John Milbank and Simon Oliver. London: Routledge, 2009, pp.3–27.
Oliver, Simon. 'Trinity, Motion and Creation *Ex Nihilo*'. *Creation and the God of Abraham*. Edited by David B. Burrell, Carlo Cogliati, Janet M. Soskice, and William R. Stoeger. Cambridge: Cambridge University Press, 2010, pp.133–51.
Oliver, Simon. 'Aquinas and Aristotle's Teleology'. *Nova et Vetera* 11:3 (2013): 849–70.
Oliver, Simon. *Creation: A Guide for the Perplexed*. London: Bloomsbury T&T Clark, 2017.
Owen, John. *The Works of John Owen*. 24 Volumes. Edited by William H. Goold. Edinburgh: T&T Clark, 1850–5.
Paddison, Angus. *Scripture: A Very Theological Proposal*. London: T&T Clark, 2009.
Pannenberg, Wolfhart. *Basic Questions in Theology*. Translated by George H. Kehm. Philadelphia, PA: Fortress Press, 1970, pp.137–210.
Pannenberg, Wolfhart. *Systematic Theology*. Volume 1. Translated by Geoffrey W. Bromiley. Grand Rapids, MI: Eerdmans, 1991.

Plantinga, Alvin. *Does God Have a Nature?* Milwaukee, WI: Marquette University Press, 1980.
Rempel, Brent A. '"A Field of Divine Activity": Divine Aseity and Holy Scripture in Dialogue with John Webster and Karl Barth'. *Scottish Journal of Theology* 73:3 (2020): 203–15.
Rennie, Charles J. 'Analogy and the Doctrine of Divine Impassibility'. *Confessing the Impassible God: The Biblical, Classical, & Confessional Doctrine of Divine Impassibility*. Edited by Ronald S Baines, Richard C. Barcellos, James P. Butler, Stefan T. Lindbald, and James M. Renihan. Palmdale, CA: RBAP, 2015, pp.47–80.
Rogers, Katherin A. *Perfect Being Theology*. Edinburgh: Edinburgh University Press, 2000.
Sanders, Fred. 'Holy Scripture under the Auspices of the Holy Trinity: On John Webster's Trinitarian Doctrine of Scripture'. *International Journal of Systematic Theology* 21:1 (2019): 4–23.
Sanders, Fred. *The Image of the Immanent Trinity: Rahner's Rule and the Theological Interpretation of Scripture*. New York, NY: Peter Lang Publishing, 2005.
Sanders, Fred. 'The Trinity'. *The Oxford Handbook of Systematic Theology*. Edited by John Webster, Kathryn Tanner, and Iain Torrance. Oxford: Oxford University Press, 2007, pp.35–53.
Sarisky, Darren. 'A Prolegomenon to an Account of Theological Interpretation of Scripture'. *Theological Theology: Essay in Honour of John B. Webster*. Edited by R. David Nelson, Darren Sarisky, and Justin Stratis. London: Bloomsbury T&T Clark, 2015, pp.247–66.
Sarisky, Darren. 'Theological Theology'. *Theological Theology: Essays in Honour of John B. Webster*. Edited by R. David Nelson, Darren Sarisky, and Justin Stratis. London: Bloomsbury T&T Clark, 2015, pp.1–15.
Sarisky, Darren. 'The Ontology of Scripture and the Ethics of Interpretation in the Theology of John Webster'. *International Journal of Systematic Theology* 21:1 (2019): 59–77.
Schillebeeckx, Edward. *Jesus: An Experiment in Christology*. London: Collins, 1979.
Schmitz, Kenneth L. *The Gift: Creation*. Milwaukee: Marquette University Press, 1982.
Schmitz, Kenneth L. *The Texture of Being: Essays in First Philosophy*. Edited by Paul O'Herron. Washington, DC: The Catholic University of America Press, 2007.
Schner, George. *Education for Ministry: Reform and Renewal in Theological Education*. Kansas City: Sheed & Ward, 1993.
Schumacher, Lydia. *Rationality as Virtue: Towards a Theological Philosophy*. Farnham: Ashgate, 2015.
Schwöbel, Christoph. 'The Creature of the Word: Recovering the Ecclesiology of the Reformers'. *On Being the Church: Essays on the Christian Community*. Edited by Colin E. Gunton and Daniel W. Hardy. Edinburgh: T&T Clark, 1989, pp.110–55.
Schwöbel, Christoph. 'Theology'. *The Cambridge Companion to Karl Barth*. Edited by John Webster. Cambridge: Cambridge University Press, 2000, pp.17–36.
Schwöbel, Christoph and Colin E. Gunton (eds.). *Persons, Divine and Human: King's College Essays in Theological Anthropology*. Edinburgh: T&T Clark, 1991.
Shanley, Brian J. '*Sacra Doctrina* and the Theology of Disclosure'. *The Thomist* 61:2 (1997): 163–87.
Shanley, Brian J. 'Divine Causation and Human Freedom in Aquinas'. *American Catholic Philosophical Quarterly* 72:1 (1998): 99–122.
Shults, F. LeRon. *Reforming Theological Anthropology: After the Philosophical Turn to Relationality*. Grand Rapids, MI: Eerdmans, 2003.

Smith, James K. A. *Introducing Radical Orthodoxy: Mapping a Post-secular Theology*. Grand Rapids, MI: Baker Academic, 2004.
Sokolowski, Robert. 'Creation and Christian Understanding'. *God and Creation: An Ecumenical Symposium*. Notre Dame, IN: Notre Dame University Press, 1990.
Sokolowski, Robert. *The God of Faith and Reason: Foundations of Christian Theology*. Washington, DC: The Catholic University of America Press, 1982.
Sonderegger, Katherine. *Systematic Theology*. Volume 1: The Doctrine of God. Minneapolis, MN: Fortress Press, 2015.
Sonderegger, Katherine. 'The God-Intoxicated Theology of a Modern Theologian'. *International Journal of Systematic Theology* 21:1 (2019): 24–43.
Sumner, Darren. 'Christocentrism and the Immanent Trinity: Identifying Theology's Pattern and Norm'. *The Task of Dogmatics: Explorations in Theological Method*. Edited by Oliver D. Crisp and Fred Sanders. Grand Rapids, MI: Zondervan, 2017, pp.144–61.
Taylor, Derek W. *Reading Scripture in the Wake of Christ: The Church as a Hermeneutical Space*. PhD Dissertation. Duke University, 2017.
Te Velde, Rudi. *Aquinas on God: The 'Divine Science' of the* Summa Theologiae. Aldershot: Ashgate, 2006.
Tillard, J.-M.-R. *Church of Churches: An Ecclesiology of Communion*. Translated by R. C. De Peaux. Collegeville, MN: The Liturgical Press, 1992.
Tillard, J.-M.-R. *Flesh of the Church, Flesh of Christ: At the Source of the Ecclesiology of Communion*. Translated by Madeleine Beaumont. Collegeville, MN: The Liturgical Press, 2001.
Titus, Eric J. 'The Perfections of God in the Theology of Karl Barth: A Consideration of the Formal Structure'. *Kairos: Evangelical Journal of* Theology 4:2 (2010): 203–22.
Thompson, John B. *The Ecclesiology of Stanley Hauerwas: A Christian Theology of Liberation*. New York, NY: Routledge, 2016.
Torrance, Thomas F. *Theological Science*. Oxford: Oxford University Press, 1969.
Vanhoozer, Kevin J. *Is There a Meaning in This Text?: The Bible, the Reader, and the Morality of Literary Knowledge*. Grand Rapids, MI: Zondervan, 1998.
Vanhoozer, Kevin J. *Remythologizing Theology: Divine Action, Passion, and Authorship*. Cambridge: Cambridge University Press, 2010.
Vanhoozer, Kevin J. *Biblical Authority after Babel: Retrieving the* Solas *in the Spirit of Mere Protestant Christianity*. Grand Rapids, MI: Brazos Press, 2016.
Vanhoozer, Kevin J. 'Love without Measure? John Webster's Unfinished Dogmatic Account of the Love of God, in Dialogue with Thomas Jay Oord's Interdisciplinary Theological Account'. *International Journal of Systematic Theology* 19:4 (2017): 505–26.
Van Nieuwenhove, Rik. 'Charity, Intellect, and Contemplation in St Thomas Aquinas: Contemporary Relevance', *Year Book of the Irish Philosophical Society* (2013): 129–50.
Volf, Miroslav. *After Our Likeness: The Church as the Image of the Trinity*. Grand Rapids, MI: Eerdmans, 1998.
Watson, Francis. 'Does Historical Criticism Exist? A Contribution to Debate on the Theological Interpretation of Scripture'. *Theological Theology: Essays in Honour of John B. Webster*. Edited by R. David Nelson, Darren Sarisky, and Justin Stratis. London: Bloomsbury T&T Clark, 2015, pp.307–18.
Weinandy, Thomas. 'Aquinas and the Incarnational Act: "Become" as a Mixed Relation'. *Doctor Communis* 32 (1979): 15–31.
Weinandy, Thomas. '*Fides et Ratio*: A Response to John Webster'. *New Blackfriars* 81 (2000): 225–35.

Westerholm, Martin. *The Ordering of the Christian Mind: Karl Barth and Theological Rationality*. Oxford: Oxford University Press, 2015.

Westerholm, Martin. 'On Webster's *God without Measure* and the Practice of Theological Theology'. *International Journal of Systematic Theology* 19:4 (2017): 444–61.

White, Thomas Joseph. 'The Crucified Lord: Thomistic Reflections on the Communication of Idioms and the Theology of the Cross'. *Thomas Aquinas and Karl Barth: An Unofficial Catholic-Protestant Dialogue*. Edited by Bruce L. McCormack and Thomas Joseph White. Grand Rapids, MI: Eerdmans, 2013, pp.157–89.

White, Thomas Joseph. *The Incarnate Lord: A Thomistic Study in Christology*. Washington, DC: The Catholic University of America Press, 2017.

Wippel, John F. *The Metaphysical Thought of Thomas Aquinas: From Finite Being to Uncreated Being*. Washington, DC: The Catholic University of America Press, 2000.

Wood, Charles M. *Vision and Discernment: An Orientation in Theological Study*. Eugene, OR: Wipf and Stock, 1985.

Williams, A. N. 'Contemplation: *Knowledge of God in Augustine's* De Trinitate'. *Knowing the Triune God: The Work of the Spirit in the Practices of the Church*. Edited by James J. Buckley and David S. Yeago. Grand Rapids, MI: Eerdmans, 2001, pp.121–46.

Williams, A. N. *The Divine Sense: The Intellect in Patristic Theology*. Cambridge: Cambridge University Press, 2007.

Williams, A. N. *The Architecture of Theology: Structure, System, and Ratio*. Oxford: Oxford University Press, 2011.

Williams, Rowan. 'Dialectic and Analogy: A Theological Legacy'. *The Impact of Idealism: The Legacy of Post-Kantian German Thought*. Volume 4. Edited by Nicholas Adams. Cambridge: Cambridge University Press, 2013, pp.274–92.

Wittman, Tyler R. 'Facticity and Faithfulness: Divine Simplicity in Barth's Christology'. *Pro Ecclesia* 26:2 (2017): 415–34.

Wittman, Tyler R. 'On the Unity of the Trinity's External Works: Archaeology and Grammar'. *International Journal of Systematic Theology* 20:3 (2018): 359–80.

Wittman, Tyler R. *God and Creation in the Theology of Thomas Aquinas and Karl Barth*. Cambridge: Cambridge University Press, 2019.

Wittman, Tyler R. 'John Webster on the Task of a Properly Theological *Theologia*'. *Scottish Journal of Theology* 73:2 (2020): 97–111.

Wolterstorff, Nicholas. 'Suffering Love'. *Philosophy and the Christian Faith*. Edited by Thomas V. Morris. Notre Dame, IN: University of Notre Dame Press, 1988, pp.196–237.

Wolterstorff, Nicholas. 'The Travail of Theology in the Modern Academy'. *The Future of Theology: Essays in Honor of Jürgen Moltmann*. Edited by Miroslav Volf, Carmen Krieg, and Thomas Kucharz. Grand Rapids, MI: Eerdmans, 1996, pp.35–46.

Zahl, Simeon. 'Non-Competitive Agency and Luther's Experiential Argument against Virtue'. *Modern Theology* 35:2 (2019): 199–222.

Ziegler, Philip G. 'The Adventitious Origins of the Christian Moral Subject: John Calvin'. *Militant Grace: The Apocalyptic Turn and the Future of Christian Theology*. Grand Rapids, MI: Baker Academic, 2018, pp.139–151.

Zimmermann, Jens. *Recovering Theological Hermeneutics: An Incarnational-Trinitarian Theory of Interpretation*. Grand Rapids, MI: Baker Academic, 2004.

Zizioulas, John. *Being as Communion: Studies in Personhood and the Church*. Crestwood, NY: St. Vladimir's Seminary Press, 1985.

INDEX OF NAMES

Allen, Michael 6 n.8, 115, 157 n.24, 162, 164 n.50
Aquinas, Thomas 23 n.49, 25, 28 n.71, 29, 31–4, 39–41, 62–3, 65, 71–3, 110–2, 140–1, 145, 165, 177, 181–2
Aristotle 31–2, 33 n.94, 157, 170 n.87
Augustine 71–2, 141, 170–1

Barth, Karl 11 n.8, 12, 16–7, 16 n.23, 27 n.68, 37, 57–8, 95, 100–1, 119–20, 124–5, 129–30, 141, 145, 153–9, 166, 181, 184
Bauerschmidt, Frederick Christian 65 n.78
Baylor, T. Robert 74 n.125
Betz, John R. 182 n.2
Bonaventure 176
Bonhoeffer, Dietrich 130
Brittain, Christopher Craig 107

Calvin, John 130, 156 n.23
Carson, D. A. 124
Case, Brendan 66 n.81
Clarke, W. Norris 35, 35 n.102
Congdon, David W. 127 n.51
Crisp, Oliver D. 161–2

De Lubac, Henri 90 n.27, 99
Del Colle, Ralph 93 n.39

East, Brad 6, 13 n.15, 79–80
Emery, Gilles 28 n.71

Frei, Hans W. 49–50, 53–4

Gorman, Michael 62, 65
Gunton, Colin E. 88–9, 122 n.28

Healy, Nicholas M. 113 n.116
Hegel, George Georg Wilhelm Friedrich 31–32, 47 n.7, 77
Henninger, Mark Gerald 34 n.97

Holcomb, Justin S. 98 n.49
Holmes, Stephen R. 143 n.132
Hunsinger, George 53

Jenson, Robert W. 22, 27, 76–8, 88–9
Jüngel, Eberhard 10–2, 10 n.4, 12 n.13, 46–48, 51 n.21, 53, 150 n.1

Kant, Immanuel 21 n.39, 31–32, 158
Kretzmann, Norman 34 n.100

Levering, Matthew 137, 143 n.132

Marshall, Bruce D. 70 n.101
McCormack, Bruce L. 168
Michelson, Jared 98 n.49, 103 n.73
Milbank, John 98 n.49
Moberly, R. W. L. 127 n.51
Mosser, Carl 183
Murphy, Francesca Aran 76–7 n.136

Oliver, Simon 40–1, 108 n.93, 112 n.111
Owen, John 110, 144

Paddison, Angus 133
Pannenberg, Wolfhart 31–2

Rennie, Charles J. 29 n.77
Rogers, Katherin A. 26

Sarisky, Darren 139
Schmitz, Kenneth L. 40 n.119, 173 n.101
Shanley, Brian J. 39
Shults, F. LeRon 31–2
Sokolowski, Robert 24, 39, 174–5
Sonderegger, Katherine 7, 10 n.1, 28, 69–70, 120, 155 n.18
Sumner, Darren 54 n.36

Taylor, Derek W. 111 n.107, 129–30, 139
Tillard, Jean-Marie 88–9

Vanhoozer, Kevin J. 32 n.90

Westerholm, Martin 6, 153, 167, 175 n.111
White, Thomas Joseph 80 n.149
Williams, A. N. 171

Williams, Rowan 160, 182 n.2
Wittman, Tyler R. 7, 17 n.25, 33
Wolterstorff, Nicholas 35
Wood, Charles M. 160 n.39

Zizioulas, John 88–9

INDEX OF SUBJECTS

baptism 110–1

causality 36–42, 110, 140
   cause-effect 63, 70–1
   intrinsic-extrinsic 40–1, 112
   motion 100, 105–8, 139
      interior motion 139–41
      moved movement 106–12, 172–3
   primary-secondary 36–40, 140–1
Christology
   Christocentrism 10–3, 46
   Christomorphism 10–3
   communicatio idiomatum 47, 52–3
   divine identity of Jesus 46–8
   and divine aseity 56–7, 135–6
   and divine infinity 160
   eternal generation 68, 73–4, 77
   extra Calvinisticum 61 n.64
   as heuristic key 12, 46
   homoousios 55–6
   human history of Jesus 10–2, 73–5
   hypostatic union 61–7, 138
   and metaphysics 55–6, 76–80
   munus propheticum Christi 12, 129, 135, 154
   and narrative description 76–80
   narrative identity of Jesus 48–53
   person-nature distinction 63–5
   and Trinity 54, 56, 60, 77, 81
   unsubstitutable identity of Jesus 46, 49–51, 53–4, 61, 179–80
Creation
   act of pure generosity 27, 58, 67, 105
   analogia entis 103, 168–9, 181–3
   cardinal doctrine 23–5
   and covenant 103–4
   ex nihilo 104–5, 173
   non-necessity 34 n.100, 104
   as sign 176–7
creatures
   correspondence to God 166, 168

creatureliness 104, 108–9, 121 n.24, 122–4, 167, 172
   integrity 112, 115, 124, 139–40, 144–5, 164, 167, 171, 173
   intellect 167, 172
   intrinsic worth 173
   moral psychology 156–7
   nature 145, 167
   participation 97–8 n.49, 168, 176–7
   teleological orientation 167–8, 177
   will 39, 170–1
curiosity 170–1

ecclesiology
   and Christology 84–5
   communio 88–9, 91, 99, 106
   creatura verbi divini 90–1, 126
   and election 87, 89, 100–3
   and ethnography 113
   mediation 93, 109–12
   and participation 87–9, 97, 99, 103 n.72
   passivity 92–4, 126–8
   social-historical phenomenon 109–10
   spiritual visibility 91, 127
   and Trinity 87–94
eschatology 125, 150–6

faith 90, 126–7, 132

God
   abstraction 11, 15
   aseity 57, 59, 78–9, 135–6
   becoming 11, 47, 57
   essence 20, 23 n.49, 28–9, 33, 59, 68, 77–9, 180
   freedom 19, 56–7, 89, 91, 124
   goodness 144–5, 150, 173, 181–2
   immutability and impassibility 29, 62–3, 64 n.75
   omniscience 165

Index of Subjects

perfection 7, 20, 26–30, 34, 59, 63, 96–102
   and election 100–3
   inclusive vs exclusive 3 n.4, 7, 96–102
   neo-Hegelian 27
   non-comparative 28–30, 38, 98
   perfect being 26–7
   self-sufficient 20, 67
personalism 120, 124, 129, 155
relation to creatures
   benevolent 25, 105, 144
   communicative 116, 118, 126, 136, 144
   gratuitous 15, 30, 36
   loving 22, 33, 35–6, 75 n.127, 100, 105
   non-competitive 3, 7, 25, 30, 33, 36–42, 66, 99, 104–6, 111, 113, 115, 118, 123–4, 138, 138–42
   non-constitutive 20, 30, 33 n.93, 35, 62, 105
   non-necessary 20, 30, 33 n.93, 35
   real (*realis*) vs non-real (*rationis*) 30–6, 62–7, 100, 104–5
self-determination 47, 57, 101–2
self-identification 48
self-revelation 120, 124–5, 129–30, 155
simplicity 16–7, 28–30
will 87, 89, 102–3
grace 41, 95, 149–50, 157–8, 163–4
   durative 173, 181
   economy of salvation 17–8, 128–9, 133–4
   eschatological 95, 124
   ex nihilo 95, 123
   extrinsic 163
   infused 41, 110, 145, 157, 174
   intrinsic 172–4
   mediated 25, 109–12
   and nature 25, 140–1, 145, 164, 181
   punctiliar 157, 173

Holy Spirit 85–6, 92, 122–4, 144–5, 171–2

postliberal theology 151, 153, 162
providence 39–41, 108, 112 n.111, 138–41

regeneration 110, 131, 171–3
revelation
   as event 131–2, 145
   form and content 47, 59, 61, 66–7
   and reconciliation 120–1, 128–9
   textual mediation 140–2
   and Trinity 119–22, 124–5, 136

sanctification
   and scripture 121–2, 138
   and human reason 128–9, 133, 171, 178
Scripture
   and church 126–8, 143–4
   clarity 131–2
   ontology 118–25, 137–42
   and participation 137
   and reader
      hermeneutics 80 n.49, 125, 129 n.64, 131
      historical critical methods 51 n.21, 117, 132
      illumination 144–5
      spiritual and moral posture 128–30, 132–3
      theological ethics of reading 130–3, 144–6
   and resurrection 135–6
   as sign 141–2, 145–6
   textual properties 140–1
   and tradition 127, 143–4
   and Trinity 116–7, 136
   verbal inspiration 123–5, 140–3
sin 107, 130–1, 169–71

Trinity 13–21
   cardinal doctrine 10, 13–4, 19–20, 60, 116, 180
   immanent and economic 16–7, 20, 23 n.49, 77, 113 n.116, 168
   processions and missions 20, 23 n.47, 68–73
   social trinitarianism 183–4
theology
   cognitive principles 165–6
   dogmatic location 6, 18–9, 116–8, 134–5, 150, 166–7
   and economy 7, 21–4, 59–61, 81, 112, 180–1, 183–4

as *ressourcement* 184
as *scientia* 165-6
theological theology 161-4, 177-8
theological reason
  auditus fidei 159, 163
  contemplation 81, 113, 164, 172, 177
  critical act 160
  as cultural practice 151-3, 162
  deduction 113
  eschatological 153-4, 156, 161
  as exegetical reason 158-60
  knowledge by causes or principles 73, 165
  metaphysical 76-80, 175
  moral 156-9, 162
  order of knowing vs order of being 113, 175-6
  participation in divine knowledge 166, 175
  positive act 158-60
  reductio 105-6, 113, 135, 176-7
  responsive 155-6
  telos 167-8, 171, 175

virtue(s) 41, 157, 172-4
  infused 172
  of receptivity 131
visio Dei 167

www.ingramcontent.com/pod-product-compliance
Lightning Source LLC
Chambersburg PA
CBHW061828300426
44115CB00013B/2287